NOT MUCH OF AN ENGINEER

Forty years on; Sir Stanley Hooker and Sir Frank Whittle.

Not much of an Engineer

an autobiography

Sir Stanley Hooker

assisted by
Bill Gunston

Airlife
England

This edition published in 2002 by
Airlife Publishing, an imprint of
The Crowood Press Ltd
Ramsbury, Marlborough
Wiltshire SN8 2HR

www.crowood.com

This impression 2023

British Library Cataloguing-in-Publication Data
A catalogue record for this book is available from the British Library.

ISBN 978 1 85310 285 1

Printed & bound in India by Parksons Graphics Pvt. Ltd.

Contents

This is a love story between aircraft
engines and two people.
Kate Hooker

Foreword
by The Lord Keith of Castleacre

Most laymen regard higher mathematics as a dull subject and consequently suspect that those who practise it must be somewhat sombre and live in a rarefied atmosphere.

Stanley Hooker's life story and the way he has written it clearly disprove this view.

Stanley first came into my life when in October, 1972, I went to Rolls-Royce as Chairman of a company recently rescued from bankruptcy, but still proudly possessing one of the greatest of names. He rapidly became my guide, philosopher and friend. He held my hand, technically, throughout the seven years I was with the company and I shall always be deeply grateful to him.

This brilliant mathematician, who won almost every available scholarship and academic prize, is possessed of a warm and loveable character. He has a capacity for making enduring friendships with all types, kinds and nationalities. A truly modest man, he is generous to a degree. He was the first to give credit to others when things went right; equally the first to assume the blame when things went wrong. As the reader will discover, he also has a ready wit and an excellent sense of humour.

Almost by accident, he became one of the world's most brilliant engineers. His clear and precise mind was combined with the engineering equivalent of green fingers when it came to solving abstruse problems, as he so clearly demonstrated when he led the technical rescue work on the RB211, thereby saving it for the nation following the Rolls-Royce bankruptcy.

If asked to pinpoint his greatest contribution to the nation, I suppose one would start with his work as a supersonic airflow expert, analysing superchargers, thereby giving them improved and more predictable performance. This resulted in the Merlin engine keeping ahead of the Germans, with inestimable benefit to the R.A.F., throughout the war.

Stanley changed the face of the aero-engine business when he introduced Lord Hives to Sir Frank Whittle and persuaded the former that he should take the gas turbine seriously. He then went on to father the design of the Nene engine which was to become the forerunner of the modern gas turbine and which was licensed to the Americans and, foolishly, sold by the Government of the day, to the Russians. Incidentally, Meteors — powered by the Rolls-Royce Welland engine built at Barnoldswick under Stanley's guidance — were first used in action to chase and destroy flying bombs in August 1944.

He was also a supporter and promoter of vectored thrust and played a major part in the development of the Pegasus engine. This enabled Sydney Camm to design the Harrier which demonstrated its outstanding capabilities in the Falklands war.

Stanley has that rare and invaluable facility of making complicated technical matters understandable to the layman. He is the master of the blackboard and chalk and is able to give even people like myself a reasonably clear idea of how the engine works.

This book records how he left Derby to go to Bristol in 1948; how he returned temporarily in 1967; and how he finally became director of engineering at Rolls-Royce in 1971.

I have often wondered how different the course of Rolls-Royce and indeed British high technology engineering might have been if those two outstanding but determined men — Lord Hives and Stanley Hooker — had been a little more flexible and a little less precipitate in September 1948 and had Stanley not left Derby to go to Bristol.

I hope that everyone who reads this book will enjoy it as much as I have done.

Keith of Castleacre
March 1984

Chapter 1
The Professional Student

It was a damp, cold day in January 1938 when I garaged my car at the junction with the Osmaston Road and began to walk up Nightingale Road towards the great Rolls-Royce works in Derby.

The dreariness of the street, with its terrace of redbrick workers' houses on the left, interspersed with the odd conversion to a general grocer's or tobacconist, and on the right a small open lot used as a works car park, matched the foreboding in my mind. Not a soul was in sight, nor was there any noise, because the workshops were set back from the road behind the front façade of offices.

With each step I took, my heart sank further. Why had I left my comfortable and interesting job in the Scientific Research Department of the Admiralty? And what was I going to do in the formidable Rolls-Royce company, which represented the very pinnacle of engineering excellence?

I was no engineer. I had been trained in Applied Mathematics, so how could I hope to compete with, or even to help, the semi-Godlike engineers with which, I was convinced, Rolls-Royce must be stocked — doubtless trained by the legendary Sir Henry Royce himself?

The apprehension grew as I approached the main entrance on my right. It stood back a few yards from the pavement, with an oval drive in and out in front. At the door stood a very smart uniformed commissionaire. I approached him with caution.

'Yes, sir, you will find Mr Elliott's office in the next block. Take the next gate on the right, and then the entrance to the Engineering Offices is on your left'.

I found my way easily enough, and stumbled along the corridor until I reached the office marked A. G. ELLIOTT, Chief Engineer. I knocked and was told to enter. It was not a large office, and very sparsely furnished. Mr Elliott sat at his desk, back to the windows and facing the door. In the further corner sat his personal assistant, A. Livesey.

Elliott clearly had not the foggiest idea who I was, and had forgotten that he was to interview me. He spoke very quietly and enquired about my business. I explained that I was the new man joining the firm, by name Hooker. He smiled as the memory came back and said, 'Of course, welcome to Rolls-Royce. We have prepared an office for you, and Mr Livesey will show you to it'.

The interview was over that quickly, and it was not at all what I had expected. Livesey led me around the corridor, and at a junction he opened a door, and said 'This is your office, cheerio'. The walls were painted metal for the first four feet from the floor, and frosted glass above. It was about eight feet square and contained a desk, a chair, an empty bookcase and a telephone, and nothing more. I sank bewildered into the hard chair and gazed at the nothingness of the wall.

All around me there was a hive of industry. I could hear telephones ringing, the clacking of typewriters, and the hum of conversation. Mostly the offices were much larger open spaces with similar dividing walls, but housing groups of men working with intense concentration. A very large area was clearly devoted to design, and full of towering drawing-boards.

Later I learned that rumour and curiosity was rife about the new so-called 'mathematical whizz kid' who had been granted the rare privilege of a private office. At the time I was just ignored, completely.

And so the day wore slowly on. I had anticipated that I would have been put into the charge of some awe-inspiring engineer, who would have allocated me some simple tasks while instructing me in the mysteries of the super aero engines that Rolls-Royce was designing and producing. But it was not so. I, who had never seen an aero engine at close range, and who only had a schoolboy's knowledge of its inside, did not even know the names of the engines Rolls-Royce was producing.

At 5.00 pm there was a general exodus, and I departed with the rest, thoroughly dispirited at the emptiness of my first day. However, after my evening meal, I cheered up a bit when it occurred to me that the only possible explanation must be that the powers that be were still debating my ultimate fate, and had not yet reached any conclusion about the job I was to do.

On the next day I arrived promptly at 8.30 am with the rest of the staff, but I had with me *The Times,* and my pipe and tobacco. In those days I only smoked occasionally in the evenings, but I felt the need of a comforter. Never was *The Times* read more completely and carefully, as the second day proved to be a replica of the first. Nobody came near me.

Things being thus, I had plenty of time to cogitate on the curious chain of events which had led me, at the age of 31 years, to be seated in an office in the Engineering Department of the great Rolls-Royce company doing nothing — especially as I had had no previous aspirations to be an engineer.

I was born on 30 September 1907, at Sheerness, Kent. After various vicissitudes through World War I, I was sent to Borden Grammar School, near Sittingbourne, in 1919.

For the first four years, I had an uninspiring career, because I soon found that I could maintain an 'invisible' position, about mid-form, with the minimum of effort on my part. I was, however, quite interested in physics and mathematics, and in the examinations at the end of each year usually managed to acquire the prize awarded jointly for these subjects.

At the end of the fourth year, in June 1923, I knew that I, with the rest of the fifth form, was required to take the Matriculation Examination for London University. Since there was no escape, I decided to try a little harder, and unnoticed I put in a couple of terms' good work. To the immense surprise of masters, boys and myself, I did very well indeed in the examination; so well, in fact, that the school was granted a half-day's holiday in celebration.

This was a turning point, because it was then decided that I must try for London University by way of three more years at school, and by taking a Royal Scholarship in Physics. There were six such scholarships given annually, and they had to be won in open competition. They were tenable for three years at Imperial College, London, and were worth £150 per annum, of which the college took £62.10s (£62.50) for fees.

In 1926 I won such a scholarship, and also, in the Entrance Examination for Imperial College, I was awarded a free place, so that the whole of the £150 was mine. This was a princely sum for a young student in those days.

When I went up to Imperial in 1926 I elected to take the course in Honours Mathematics. The Professor of Mathematics was Sydney Chapman, whose main interest was geophysics. I found him a very cold and distant man, and I had no interest in his subject. Much more to my liking was his Assistant Professor, who was a volatile jew, Hyman Levy. His interest was hydrodynamics, and so I elected to specialise in that subject.

It was Levy who introduced me to the Kármán Vortex Street, which is the series of eddies which are shed alternately from each side of a body moving through a fluid such as air or water. These eddies produce the drag of the body, and are spaced in a particular manner which was first evaluated by Professor von Kármán at Göttingen.

Under Levy's guidance, I produced two papers — one published by the *Philosophical Magazine* and the other by the Royal Society — slightly extending von Kármán's theory. In this manner I came to know, and become friends with, the great man himself. Years later this was to prove an enormous advantage to me and of great benefit to the British aero industry.

At the end of my third year at Imperial College, I was awarded the Governors' Prize for Mathematics (£5 worth of books!), and I began vaguely to think of an academic career as a lecturer and, hopefully, later as a professor. But in September 1928 I was awarded The Busk Studentship in Aeronautics. This had been instituted by the Busk family in memory of Edward Busk who was killed as a pioneer aviator. I still remember with gratitude and affection the personal letters which came from either his mother or his widow at the beginning of each term, with a cheque for £50.

The Aeronautics Department was situated in the basement of the Huxley Building in Exhibition Road, South Kensington. This also housed the Mathematics Department, so I did not move far, but fell under the tuition of Professor Leonard Bairstow, W. S. Farren, and H. Roxbee Cox (now Lord Kings Norton), who respectively initiated me into the mysteries of the lift and drag of wings, the design of aircraft structures, and the design of airships. I suppose this was my first tentative step in the direction of engineering, but, because of Levy's influence in directing me towards hydrodynamics (the flow of fluids), I found that the most interesting part of the Aeronautics course was the aerodynamic flow of air around the wings of aircraft, thus producing the lift and the drag.

The department had a small wind tunnel, and I was able to make experiments on the flow of air and found, somewhat to my surprise, how much I enjoyed such work. In fact, the appreciation, liking and knowledge of aerodynamics which I gained at that time have been a great strength to me throughout my career, especially when I was moved into the field of gas turbines.

In 1929 an income of £150 per year was an enviable one, particularly as I was living quite cheaply with my sister and her husband in a flat in Battersea. The economy of the country was very depressed, and jobs were hard to come by, and so it seemed quite reasonable to carry on as a student while I could get such funds to support me. In fact the student life, with its long vacations during which I did no work but had a pleasant time with my friends in Kent, suited me very well.

But fate intervened, and in December 1929, I suffered a broken leg in a football match against University College Hospital. I was taken to Ealing Hospital and spent two wearisome months in Plaster of Paris. I went home to Kent in March 1930 but on Good Friday I had a motor-cycling accident, breaking my leg again, and this time my right arm for good measure. This time I was taken to a little country Cottage Hospital in the small and delightful market town of Faversham. I knew the town well; all my friends were within 10 or 20 miles, and visited me frequently.

Most of the time I was the only male patient in the hospital, and had the undivided attention of all the young nurses and sisters. While my right arm was no problem, merely requiring to be pulled straight and bandaged, my right leg was in a sorry mess. The country doctor who dealt with it was a tough middle-aged ex-rugger player, but was superb to me. It took him three goes at setting the leg, extending over a week, and when he was finally finished, he showed me the X-ray, and there it was with all the jagged bones fitted together like a jig-saw puzzle. He said to me 'I am satisfied that those bones will join together and be stronger than before, but you will have to watch the circulation and take care of that leg'. And so it proved. I had two further operations on the leg during the 1950s, and on the last occasion my friend Gordon Paul, the great Bristol surgeon, said to me 'I have done all that science can do for that leg. From now on you must watch it'.

At the time when I was taken to the Faversham Cottage Hospital it was the custom for people injured in road accidents to be treated and boarded free of charge. So here I was in hospital with £3 a week coming in and no outgoings at all. In fact, from my earlier incarceration I had capital in hand.

The total staff at the hospital consisted of three young probationer nurses — pros as they called themselves — a day and a night sister, and what seemed to be a very severe matron. Apart from one farmer, who came in to have a hernia fixed, I was the only male patient for the several months I was there. The farmer was in the next room, and when he came in I could hear my doctor quizzing him:

'Do you smoke?'

'Yes, I like my pipe.'

'Well, you will have to lay off it for some time after this operation, because after the anaesthetic smoking will make you cough, and coughing will be very painful.'

The farmer agreed that there would be no problem.

After the operation, I could hear him coming to from the anaesthetic, muttering and moaning in the usual way. A few minutes later I heard him cough, and then give a sharp cry of pain. Again this was repeated, and then the smell of the tobacco smoke wafted into my room. He had lit up immediately, and, although the nurses rushed in, all he would say was 'Don't tell the doctor, please.'

These young nurses, nubile young ladies of about eighteen, looking lovely in their fresh blue uniforms and white cuffs and caps, fastened on to me as their prize exhibit, and never was anyone 'nursed' like it. They were full of high spirits and fun, and, once the initial pain of the break had subsided, they took particular pleasure in giving me 'blanket baths' in bed. Never was any patient kept so well washed! They were like several cats with one kitten.

On their afternoons off, I persuaded them to go into town and buy such delicacies as lobster, oysters (Whitstable was the neighbouring town), foie gras, Stilton cheese and the like, with a bottle of wine. In the evening, when their duty was finished, with the connivance of the night sister (and the matron, I found out later), they would come to my room and we would all have supper together, with me having to be fed until I learned to use my left hand effectively. I taught them to play whist and we sang together. They made the dreariness of being bed-ridden into an experience which I can now look back to with enormous pleasure and gratitude. I can never forget them, and wonder where they are today.

The first broken leg was on 29 December 1929, and the second on Good Friday, 1930. Thus it was that for ten months to October 1930 I did no studying or academic work of any kind. I had written to Mrs Busk telling her of the happenings and offering to forgo the money, but, generously, she would not hear of it, and so I continued to get the £50 per term.

I gave no thought to what should happen next, until one day at Faversham a letter arrived from Professor Bairstow saying that he had recommended me as a candidate for the Armourers and Braziers Research Fellowship in Aeronautics. I was bidden to appear at the Guild of Armourers and Braziers in London. Having delayed as long as I could, I appeared on crutches and that won the day! I now had £250 per annum to continue my studies and research in the Aeronautics Department of Imperial College. Fate had intervened again, and I was committed to at least two further years of academic life.

I do not wish to give the impression that this Fellowship was handed to me on a plate. Professor Bairstow had an all-consuming obsession, and that was to solve the equations of motion of a viscous fluid. All fluids have the property of viscosity, though in the case of air it is less obvious than with oil or treacle. It is this property which gives an aircraft its drag, and wings their lift. Without the property of viscosity, neither birds nor aeroplanes could fly, and winds would blow around the world undiminished for ever. In the real world in which we live air's viscosity gradually dissipates, like friction, all air motion into heat. Unfortunately the equations, which are well established, are very intractable. Bairstow decided to try to solve them by numerical methods, and employed two ladies to operate with numbers, just as present-day computers do, although the ladies were a few million times slower.

For my part, I had taken a modified and much simpler form of the equations, called Oseen's Equations, after their creator, and had managed to solve these for the case of low-speed flow past a circular cylinder. Bairstow was interested, and it was for this reason he recommended me for the Armourers and Braziers Fellowship.

But when I returned to Imperial in October 1930 I became much more interested in the flow of air at very high speeds, where another of its properties, compressibility, becomes very important. At speeds up to about 300 mph air can be regarded as incompressible, like water. In other words, the pressure differences caused by the air velocities are small compared with the pressure of the atmosphere, and so the air behaves as if its density remained constant.

For example, at 200 mph the maximum pressure that air can

exert is only 5 per cent of the atmospheric pressure, which has a negligible effect on the air density and the flow. But at 400 mph the pressure increases to 21 per cent and at 600 mph to 51 per cent. These pressure increases have a significant effect upon the density of the air, and, hence, upon its flow pattern and the forces that the air exerts.

Since the speed of even the fastest fighters was only about 200 mph at that time, mathematical and experimental studies of airflow around wings and other aircraft parts had ignored the compressibility effects on the flow. But in 1930 Professor G. I. Taylor (later Sir Geoffrey Taylor of Trinity College, Cambridge) began to send his theoretical work on the flow of air as a compressible gas to the Aeronautical Research Committee, who duly published it in their *Reports & Memoranda.*

Of the many great applied mathematicians in the field of aerodynamics or fluid motion whom I have had the good fortune to know, G. I. Taylor ranks at the very top — before Prandtl of Göttingen, von Kármán of Aachen or Southwell of Oxford. The breadth of G. I.'s theoretical work was vast, and it always had a practical slant. He was adept at devising experiments to verify his theories, many of them of fascinating simplicity.

At this time, in the early 1930s, there were few people in the world studying the effects of compressibility on the flow of air. There was Büsemann in Germany, who went to the USA after World War II, Ackeret in Zurich, who evolved the first simple theory of the effect on the lift and drag of a wing, and there was G. I. Taylor in England. Years earlier Lord Rayleigh, Rankine and Stokes — all British — had shown how significant this property of the compressibility of air could become, especially when the velocity exceeded the speed of sound.

Taylor's papers interested me greatly, and I began to dabble myself. I evolved what I thought to be a brilliant mathematical solution to the flow around a circular cylinder at speeds approaching the velocity of sound, and sent it to the Aeronautical Research Committee, of which G. I. was a member. Alas, the theory contained a subtle flaw, and Taylor slaughtered it in devastating fashion. I was stunned, almost to the point of physical sickness. How could a man of his eminence be so savage to a young man of my insignificance?

But I did not then know G. I. Shortly afterwards I received a note asking me to meet him in the rooms of the Royal Aeronautical Society, which were then in Arlington Street, off Piccadilly.

With great trepidation, I turned up at the appointed time, to meet for the first time this great man. I was charmed immediately. He said that my theory was a brave effort, and that he was sorry that he had had to be so critical. He then went on to give me a personal tutorial on the subject, and encouraged me to pursue this type of study. He said, 'Send your work to me first, and I will do all I can to help.' And thus began a friendship which was to affect profoundly the whole course of my future.

I did not appreciate at the time — and very few other people did either — that the understanding of the aerodynamic flow of compressible air was to lead on to supersonic flight once an engine of sufficient power was available. Nor did I know that a young Royal Air Force officer called Frank Whittle was at the University of Cambridge designing the first jet engine which would ultimately give this power. Whittle had a superb grasp of the relationship between supersonic airflow and the thermodynamics of the gas turbine. He was one of the first men to weld together and formulate the science of Gas Dynamics, which is now a normal course for engineers at the beginning of their studies.

Fate decreed that I was to follow a course of study, first at Imperial College and afterwards at Oxford University, which by chance specifically trained me for the tasks which, years later, were to be allocated to me by Rolls-Royce. Now, on reflection, I would not wish to change a day of it. I sometimes think that perhaps I could have worked harder, but 'unconscious of their fate, the little children play.'

Back at Imperial College, I continued to study G. I. Taylor's work, and, to his evident satisfaction, even extended the scope of some of his publications.

It was well known, of course, that there was an exact similarity between the flow of a 'perfect' gas (one without viscosity) and the flow of an electric current through an electrolyte, such as a solution of copper sulphate. Taylor evolved a method of making the flow of the electric current simulate the flow of a compressible fluid. He took a shallow square tank which he filled to a depth of about one inch (25mm) with copper sulphate solution. Two opposite walls of the tank were made of copper strips, and a current was passed between them. Such an arrangement produced a uniform flow of electricity from one wall to the other, and if a non-conducting obstacle was placed in the centre of the tank, then the flow lines of the electric current would pass around it, exactly as air would if the obstacle was in a uniform stream of air. This was straightforward stuff, but Taylor made the base of the tank in paraffin wax, and used a circular cylinder embedded in the wax as the obstacle. By carving the wax away or adding more at the appropriate places, the depth of the electrolyte around the obstacle could be varied, and Taylor showed that this depth was exactly analogous to the density of compressible air as it flowed around the cylinder. Where the air velocity was high, the depth of the electrolyte had to be reduced; when the air velocity was low, the depth had to be increased. By this relatively simple experimental technique, Taylor was able to evaluate the effects of compressibility on the flow, and obtained the answer to a problem which was quite intractable by mathematical methods.

Although I was better with pen and paper than as an experimenter, I wrote to G. I. to ask him if I could use the tank at Imperial College. He replied that he had given it to Professor R. V. Southwell, who was head of the Engineering Science School at Oxford, but that he would write to Southwell and tell him of my interest. I had never met Southwell, but knew him from his reputation as an applied mathematician in the fields of Fluid Dynamics and the Elasticity of Materials.

A little later, I was delighted to get a letter from Southwell, inviting me to meet him for tea at London's Athenaeum Club, a venue which I regarded with great 'awe'. The upshot was that Southwell invited me to go to Oxford to work with the tank; moreover since he was a Fellow of Brasenose College (BNC), he undertook to persuade the Principal of that College to accept me as a member of it for post-graduate study.

Secretly, I had always wanted to go to Oxford, but had thought that I would have difficulty in getting a college to accept me, and that I could not afford it. But now, with £250 per year from the Armourers and Braziers Fellowship, I had ample funds, and so jumped at this God-sent opportunity. In those days, one could buy a made-to-measure suit for £5, and a reasonable secondhand motor car for £20, so that £250 was equivalent to several thousand pounds today.

I realised that I was in danger of becoming a 'professional student', but jobs were very difficult to get, and pay was low. I was doing at least as well on my emolument as I would have done in a job, even if I could have got one! So, with all the other young men fresh from the great public schools, I went up to Oxford in October 1932, and became a commoner of Brasenose *"in statu pupillari"*.

I must confess that I had always been jealous and envious of public school boys. Coming from my humble origins, I expected to get the cold shoulder, and was prepared to be cold and distant myself. After all, was I not already 24 years old with a Bachelor's Degree in mathematics, so why should I bother about these snobbish young puppies, who had been born with a silver spoon in their mouths?

But I had got it all wrong; and they soon showed me what a fool I had been. I was immediately accepted by all, and spent four of the happiest years of my life enjoying the great camaraderie that existed in BNC. There is no doubt that the public schools give to their product an indefinable something which is of inestimable value to Britain. Those jealous and bigoted people who seek to destroy them — in the name of anti-class privilege or for vote-catching — are misguided, small-minded fools. We should have more public schools, and not fewer; thus could we increase the output of leaders for all walks of life, with their unparalleled record of excellence.

Alas, the young men I lived with in BNC for those unforgettable four years were ripe for slaughter in World War II. It is so terribly sad to read their many names on the Roll of Honour at the entrance to the College Chapel. Yet I always remember them as generous, happy, high-spirited young men, who promised to have the world at their feet.

The School of Engineering Science was situated at the junction of Parks Road and the Banbury Road. It was a small two-storeyed building, with a tiny library up an iron staircase in the attic. The staff was small. Under Professor Southwell were E. B. Moullin, a fellow of Magdalen, as the Reader in Electricity, and A. M. Binnie, a don of New College, specialising in Hydraulics. There was a small workshop in the basement, where a very skilful man made the apparatus necessary for the experimental work.

At this period, engineering was hardly the 'in-thing' at Oxford. The annual intake of students was about a dozen, several of whom were Rhodes Scholars from the Empire. For these reasons, Southwell concentrated on the mathematical and theoretical background to Engineering Design, and how wise he was. My later experience in Rolls-Royce showed me that no university course could possibly compare with the knowledge gained by rubbing shoulders with experienced, practising engineers actually doing the job in a factory. On the other hand, once one's student days are over, and one is gaining practical experience by doing a job, it is extremely difficult again to pick up the mathematical and theoretical background so vital to anyone who aspires to lead in engineering.

Although I had no examinations to sit, I was in the end aiming to write a thesis for a doctorate in Philosophy, so I attended many of Southwell's lectures, particularly those on the Strength of Materials. I supplemented these by attending A. E. H. Love's course on Elasticity held in the Clarendon Laboratory.

Love was an old man with a white walrus moustache, who lectured straight from the enormous tome he had written — the classic work on the subject. It was a purely mathematical treatise of great erudition, and the old boy could reproduce page after page of it on the blackboard without a note or reference. I watched him with awe and admiration. Although I never specialised in this subject, the grounding I got from him and from Southwell has served me in great stead. Many times it prevented me from being "blinded by science", when the real test of the strength of materials came in the gas turbine engine.

When I first arrived at the Engineering Laboratory, Southwell was away on sabbatical leave as a visiting professor at the Massachusetts Institute of Technology. So I was left to my own devices for a couple of terms. I had been allocated a small office overlooking The Parks, and in this seclusion I again turned to G. I. Taylor for inspiration.

It was well known that if air was compressed to, say 100 lb per square inch, and then released to the atmosphere through a nozzle which first contracted to a throat and thereafter expanded in a divergence, the velocity of the escaping air would exceed the velocity of sound. In the case just quoted the jet would reach approximately twice the speed of sound.

At the National Physical Laboratory, Stanton had made such a jet of air, and in it had measured the lift and drag of wing sections. Because of the large power required to compress the air initially, the experiments had to be conducted on a small scale; Stanton's jet was just 2 in (50mm) in diameter. Nonetheless, the measured results were the first that had ever been made. They provided the first tentative information necessary for the dream of supersonic flight, which 20 years later was to become a reality for fighter aircraft, and 40 years later a routine occurrence for old ladies in the Concorde.

When an aircraft accelerates through the speed of sound, it generates waves or pressure pulses in the air. At the speed of sound the pressure waves are small, like sound waves. As the speed increases, a bow wave is set up at the nose and at the leading edge of the wings like the wave at the prow of a ship. This has a large amplitude, and can no longer be regarded as a simple sound wave. This shock-wave is responsible for the supersonic 'bang' of the Concorde and other supersonic aircraft.

Professor Ackeret at Zurich had already evolved a theory of the lift and drag of a wing at supersonic speeds, on the basis that the waves generated were small, like sound waves. His theory, therefore, applied to speeds near the velocity of sound. Despite this, Taylor applied Ackeret's theory to Stanton's experiments, and compared the measured results with the theoretical calculations. The agreement was reasonably good, even though the experiments had been made at Mach 1.8 (1.8 times the velocity of sound). I decided to extend Taylor's calculations, using real shock-waves, such as would be generated at Mach 1.8. The results, as expected, were even closer to Stanton's experimental measurements. Both theory and experiment showed that, as the speed increased from below to above that of sound, the centre of lift of the wing moved rearwards from about one-quarter of the chord (distance across the wing) at subsonic speeds to one-half of the chord at supersonic speeds. Thus, an aircraft flying through the speed of sound would rather suddenly become nose-heavy, since the centre of lift would move rearwards from the centre of gravity. This effect was to confuse pilots when, in the early 1950s, they first ventured through the speed of sound in conventional fighters.

In 1932-33 this work was only an interesting hobby. I had no conception whatever that it would prove basic to my first job in Rolls-Royce, and that the knowledge I was acquiring would ultimately give me such a head-start in that great firm.

In another part of the Laboratory, young Frederick Llewellyn Smith was experimenting with the only internal-combustion engine the Lab possessed. It was a single-cylinder petrol engine, and Llewellyn Smith was interested in the combustion process that went on during the power stroke. He had designed a high-speed valve which opened very briefly during the power stroke; out would puff a little of the combustion gases into a collector. The gases were then analysed chemically, and he could vary at will the point in the power stroke when he took his sample.

I asked him, 'What are you going to do when you leave Oxford?'.

'I am going to get a job with Rolls-Royce at Derby', he replied.
'Have you fixed it?'.

'No', he said, 'but I am sure they will take me on'.

I admired his confidence, and was envious of his engineering degree and the practical work he was doing on piston engines. He, on the other hand, was very intrigued by my theoretical work, and regarded it with the same awe that I lavished on his engine.

We became good friends, but our ways parted in 1934 when he went off, sure enough, to join Rolls-Royce. Three years later he wrote to me to ask if I would like a job at Derby with Rolls-Royce, and it was through Llewellyn Smith, who eventually became a Director of Rolls-Royce and ran the Motor Car Division at Crewe, that I was first introduced to the company that was to change my whole life.

When I arrived at Oxford a post-graduate student from the Laboratory was just finishing, and offered me his rooms in the Woodstock Road. In those days every member of the University was required to live either in College or in registered and approved lodgings where the landlady could keep an eye on one — which most did, very unwilling to risk the danger of losing their licences. Having taken these rooms, which were exceedingly comfortable — and, thereby, having acquired a landlady who was a splendid cook — I found to my consternation that for the first two years a freshman had the option of rooms in College. Thus, of the entrants in my year, I was the only one not to live in College.

It was also a College rule that everyone had to attend a minimum of 24 chapels per term. This meant that, on three evenings of every week, I had to attend the evening Chapel Service in College from 7.00 to 7.30 pm. These very simple and short services gave me great pleasure and comfort, for in the early days I felt as lonely as a stranger in a foreign land. This chapel rule was revoked during my time at BNC. Like many others, I seldom went again, mainly because time did not seem to permit. The half-hour before dinner was thrown away in idle chatter or other inconsequential things, and the custom of going to chapel before dinner — which had been going on for centuries, and gave so much ease to my mind at least — was thrown away, as I now know many other customs at BNC have been, all for nothing more than the so-called 'march of progress'.

Dinner was at 7.30 pm, and since the Hall was not large enough to seat everybody, the 'freshers' had to dine in one of the lecture theatres. Thus, all the new boys were thrown together, and this proved to be a great boon to me, for it was at dinner that I began to make new friends. Soon I was being invited to their rooms for coffee after dinner, to play cards, or even just to talk. Bridge was one of the passions of my life, and I shall never forget the many winter evenings spent playing with such pleasant companions. The mellowed rooms, panelled with ancient oak and warmed by a blazing coal fire, gave a feeling of immunity from the world at large, and conjured up a sense of belonging to a family which was directly descended from those who had lived and studied in these peaceful and graceful surroundings for centuries before.

After the impersonal life of Imperial College, where one attended lectures or studied from 9.30 am until 5.00 pm, after which everyone went their separate ways, I found the communal life at BNC very much more to my taste. I never cease to be thrilled when I walk through the massive doors at the lodge into the old quad, and into another world.

My contemporaries lived in College for the first two years, during which I enjoyed their hospitality. In the third year I opted to live in College, while they were in digs, and so returned their hospitality. My rooms became a focal point for many people and 'open house' for them all — so much so, that I never attempted to do any work in my rooms, but always went back to my little office in the laboratory.

Life at Oxford was governed by many rules and regulations, none of which I found irksome, and none that prevented us all from enjoying ourselves. It was permitted to lunch or dine in the town, but not to visit any of the pubs or go to any of the local dances. We were required to wear a cap and gown after dark in the town, although this rule was not strictly enforced, and one never bothered with a mortar-board and used to use one's gown as a muffler. One was not permitted to have ladies in BNC before 1.00 pm, and they were required to leave by 7.00 pm — not a great hardship.

The lodge gate was closed at 9.00 pm but one could demand admittance free until 10.00 pm, after which the fine was one shilling (5p) until midnight. Admittance after midnight was reported to the Proctors, who dealt with the matter by a fine of £1, provided one had an adequate excuse.

Despite the restrictions outside College, inside parties and celebrations could go on ad-lib. If they were too noisy the Dons would telephone the Porter and ask him to call on the offending party to request less noise. Thus, the restrictions on the town's facilities were more than made up for by the freedom inside College — except, of course for female company.

Excursions to London were allowed at week-ends, although one always had to be back in College or digs before midnight. This entailed catching the 'Flying Fornicator' from Paddington, which arrived at Oxford about 11.40 pm, and left barely enough time to get to College before midnight.

Today, all is changed, and it is sad for me to go back and see men dressed in any old clothes, lounging around in mixed company at all hours. This so-called freedom is at the expense of that happy though mildly disciplined life which had been going on for centuries, and was, to me, a part of Oxford's great contribution to the moulding of character.

Brasenose was primarily a Law College. The Vice-Principal was W. T. S. Stallybrass, an authority on law of world renown. He was 'Sonners' to us all, and combined with law, a love of cricket and athletics. As a consequence, BNC was replete with 'blues' in cricket, athletics, rowing, rugger and so-forth — some of international fame, such as Mitchell Innes who played cricket for England; Sean Wade, the Irish international rugger player; Bob Cherry, the Olympic oarsman, and Alex Obolensky, whose rugger will never be forgotten, and who was killed early in the War while training to be an RAF pilot.

BNC was not short of stars. Two of my best friends were John and Paul Bradbury, whose sister I married in 1937. Unhappily, this marriage was to end in divorce after the war. On the scholastic side, there was Leslie Scarman, now Lord Justice Scarman; John Freeman, who became Ambassador to the USA; John Profumo, so likeable and charming; Val Duncan, destined to be Chairman of Rio Tinto-Zinc; John Gorton, who turned up as Prime Minister of Australia; and, interwoven with the story that follows, Reginald Verdon Smith, who had the great distinction of winning the Vinerian Prize for Law.

Part of the ritual of life was that every afternoon should be spent playing games or taking exercise to keep fit or to sublimate other desires by sheer physical tiredness. With the memories of broken limbs still fresh, this was not to my liking, so that in the afternoon, I would go to my little office in the Lab to work. Thus, my evenings would be free for the 'flicks', bridge, or any other form of entertainment that happened to be going.

The cinema was very popular. I remember the occasion when *Sanders of the River* was showing, and the scene came of the natives paddling Sanders ferociously down-river. Suddenly a voice in the audience rang out, 'Well rowed, Balliol', and pandemonium followed. Balliol had the reputation, probably unfairly, of having more coloured students, as well as budding prime ministers, than any other college.

The servants, known as 'scouts', were all male, and each had a staircase to look after with about six or so rooms and occupants. They arrived early in the morning, lit the fires and generally tidied up before producing hot water for shaving and washing. They stayed on duty until after lunch and then returned again in the evening to serve dinner in Hall. A very friendly relationship existed between us, and I never knew a surly one.

The cost of rooms varied from £10 to £20 per term, according to size and position. Dinner in Hall cost 3/6d (17½p) and one was required to dine in Hall at least three times per week or be charged accordingly. Drink in Hall was confined to beer served in splendid silver mugs, but there were two varieties: one of normal strength, and the other, called Audit Ale, which was very potent indeed. It was dark with a peculiar flavour, and was brewed specially for the College. He was a tough man, indeed, who could drink more than two pints (just over one litre).

There were certain subjects that were taboo at table. If anyone transgressed, an application could be made to the High Table, at which the Dons dined in style, always in black ties, for permission to "sconce" the offender. If granted, a magnificent two-handled, heavily embossed silver mug would be brought in by the scouts, and filled with at least two pints of Audit Ale. The accused then had to rise and empty the mug in one drink. If he failed he had to buy ale for all, but I never saw anyone fail; struggle hard perhaps, but fail — never.

If one lived in College, then three breakfasts per week had to be eaten in Hall. This was to get the slackers out of bed, and not only was one charged for the breakfasts, but fined to boot if one failed to appear the necessary number of times. My friend Dick Wilkins could never face breakfast, and only made it on one occasion five minutes before service ended. His astonished scout took his order of bacon and eggs and came back a few minutes later saying there was no more bacon, only sausages. Dick said he would have those and away went Albert, the scout, only to return to say that they also were gone now. Dick said he didn't care, he would have anything, so away went Albert, and never came back at all, because a practice fire alarm was staged, and he was in the Brigade. Dick never tried again, but just paid his fines.

Lunch was taken in one's rooms, and one ordered in advance either rolls and butter, still called 'commons', or a bowl of soup for a few pence, or chop and chips at one shilling (5p). Guests could be entertained for lunch, and a special menu ordered from the chef. Each room was equipped with a reasonably sized table, and chairs would be conjured up by the scouts. Sherry decanters, cigarette boxes, flowers, and so forth, would appear like magic, borrowed by the scouts from other rooms on the staircase, such was the communal life. For a small fee the College silver could be hired to decorate the table, and there was no end to the sophistication that could be lavished on the entertainment of guests of standing from outside the College.

A speciality of the chef was Hare Pie. This was hare in aspic, and it sat on its dish looking like a yellow translucent half rugger ball filled with gravel. I do not remember anybody ever eating it, but as it was the *pièce de résistance* of the chef, it had to be ordered as one of the courses. The other speciality of the College was hot mulled claret which was exceptionally good, both in winter and summer. For special occasions it would be served in silver carafes, but normally it came in the jugs that were in the bedrooms for hot water, since mulled-claret parties were apt to get a trifle rumbustious.

On one occasion Cecil Borland, who aspired to be an athletics blue, borrowed my room to give lunch to the President and Secretary of the University Athletic Club. He ordered a splendid lunch and returned to College just before 1.00 p.m. to find that other of my friends had arrived earlier and had, uninvited, set to on the lunch. The smiles left their faces when they heard the gravity of the situation, but the scouts rose magnificently to the task, and the debris was swept away with a new lunch arriving at high speed. The great men were intercepted at the Lodge and taken to other rooms for sherry, and never knew how close to a débâcle the occasion had been.

One summer, my friend Douglas Swan invited me to his father's box for a day at Ascot. This meant hiring full morning dress from Moss Bros. Rather self-conscious, I left my rooms in the corner of the Old Quad, resplendent in a grey topper, to run the gauntlet to the Lodge. Alas, I did not pass inspection. Pat Swire ran to his rooms to return with a red carnation for my buttonhole, and another produced a pair of racing binoculars, complete with a bunch of tags from Tattersalls. With cheers of encouragement and a number of betting commissions, we set forth. Pat Swire gave me £1 and a list of horses on which to bet the proceeds of each race. To my amazement, he picked the winners of the first four races, and the pound had then become more than £100. I was instructed to bet the whole lot on the fifth race, but caution prevailed and I only put one-half on it. The horse lost, but I was still able to bring back over £50 to the grateful Pat.

I was not much of a betting man, since it was against all my mathematical training to gamble on such unreliable data. Dick Wilkins and John Body were always keen on a flutter, and used to place their bets with the local bookmaker, an honest man called West. Because I was a post-graduate student, I was allowed to have a car at Oxford and was, therefore, in demand to take them to sundry race meetings. On one occasion they both wanted to go to Warwick races but, unfortunately, I was going to Southampton for some reason. They tried to persuade me to go to Warwick, but I refused and, finally John said 'All right, Stanley, you go South and we will go North'. 'And your money will go West', I replied.

Body and Wilkins were particular friends of mine. They both came from wealthy backgrounds, and both were reading Law, John seriously and Dick reluctantly; Dick left after two years to become a very successful jobber on the Stock Exchange. John Body's ambition was to own a Derby winner, but, alas, he was killed in the RAF in the early days of the War. He was an atrocious car driver, and I have no doubt an equally atrocious pilot. I tried hard to persuade him to transfer to the Army or the Navy where he would not have to depend so much on individual, co-ordinated mechanical skill, and where his undoubted gifts of leadership could be used to equal advantage. When I heard of his death I cabled his father, 'It could just as likely have been the V.C. . . .'.

The activities of the Oxford Union Debating Society were never very popular in BNC. No one seemed to aspire to be a politician. I attended a few of the debates, and was present when the famous motion — 'That this House would not fight for its King and Country' was carried. This anachronistic result was due entirely to the façile philosophical verbiage with which Professor C. E. M. Joad, the proposer of the motion, hypnotised the young audience. I remember him telling the story of Lytton Strachey, who was a Conscientious Objector in World War I, being cross-examined by the committee for such affairs. Colonel Blimp said, 'Well now, tell me what would you do, Strachey, if you came home to find a German Officer raping your sister?'. (A German Officer, mark you, there was nothing peculiar about our Colonel!) Strachey replied, in his squeaky voice, quoth Joad, 'Well, I suppose I would try to get between them'. But this House *did* fight for its King and Country most heroically and generously in the hour of need of the whole world.

So far as my work was concerned, nobody in BNC had the slightest idea what I did. I had a moral tutor, who was supposed to look after my behaviour, but I never saw him, and I went my own way unrestricted. This suited me well, because I had reached a stage in my studies and research where I was quite independent. I concentrated more and more on the effects of compressibility on airflow, and published several reports on this subject. One, in particular, on oscillations in the airflow in a conical nozzle, attracted G. I. Taylor's attention, who wrote that I had discovered a new solution, which he regarded as a considerable feat.

I mention this because in the same letter he asked me if I had considered applying for an 1851 Exhibition, of which he was an elector. These Exhibitions, as they were called, had been funded following the Great Exhibition of 1851, and were the most valuable in the country. They were worth £450 per annum with an extra £50 to cover books, fees and other expenses. I had never dreamed of getting one, but, nonetheless, I applied and was duly awarded this great distinction, with its financial advantages.

I thus became quite a wealthy student. Most people, in those days, could exist very comfortably, either in college or out, on about £250 for the three academic terms. My 'battels', as the College charges were called, amounted to £70 to £90 per term, despite the entertaining I did and the rather expensive rooms I had. This included all fees, food, drink and accommodation. I drank little in those days, only the occasional pint of Audit Ale, and I did not smoke. I kept sherry and some spirits in my rooms for visitors, but otherwise led an economical life, apart from the small hospitality extended to the many visitors who used my rooms. Most of them were friends who were in digs in the town and needed a focal point inside College.

I used to work in my office at the Lab on most mornings and afternoons. I have always been disposed to work in fits and starts, and I suppose this is only natural when one is doing theoretical work, because one can only move forward when the inspiration comes along. One cannot solve a mathematical problem by just sheer hard application. There has to be a spark of insight, which can, however, be cultivated by simply mulling continuously over the problem. On most occasions the means of moving forward comes almost unconsciously, like a flash of light as one's brain continuously sifts the facts that have been fed into it. Once the light has dawned, a quite valuable paper can be written in a week; that is, one worthy of publication in the *Proceedings* of the Royal Society, the *Philosophical Magazine* or the *Reports & Memoranda* of the Aeronautical Research Committee. It was upon one's output to these journals that one was judged.

In my subject, the experimental information was very sparse. Wind tunnels, where models could be tested in a stream of air simulating motion through the atmosphere, were well-known and available, but their speeds were limited to about 100 mph (160 km/h). For speeds up to 1,000 mph, in which I was interested, the power required to drive such tunnels was enormous and very expensive, and no laboratory in the world had such facilities. If the density of the air was reduced, then the power required to drive it at high speeds would be reduced in proportion, and I wrote a report on the design of such a tunnel.

I did not know it at the time, but this report was picked up by a man called Wood, at the Royal Aircraft Establishment. Such a tunnel was made, and used for examining the shockwaves at the nose and tail of shells when fired from guns. This had an important effect upon my career.

In 1935 my period at Oxford was coming to an end. I had obtained a DPhil degree (Doctor of Philosophy) by putting my reports together in a thesis entitled *Some Problems in Supersonic Air Flow and Elasticity,* and now the problem was getting a job.

I went up to Oxford a callow, gauche young man, rather shy and somewhat lacking in self-confidence, although with a solid background of mathematical training. I left with a much more mature and rounded personality. For the priceless gift of *savoir faire* I owe a great debt to Oxford, Brasenose College and the many accomplished and splendid young men who, in the friendliest possible way, enlarged my world.

The carefree, yet ordered, batchelor life at BNC provided exactly the right atmosphere for me to work well at the Lab during the day and to enjoy myself in the evenings. The years I spent at Oxford were very happy ones, but in June 1935 I left to face the hard world alone for the first time.

My original idea of an academic career had long since faded, because, in those days, jobs as university lecturers were few and far between. Nor, after the gracious living at Oxford, was I attracted by a job in a non-residential university, just commuting to and fro at 9.00 am and 5.00 pm.

There was, however, one advertisement in *The Times* that attracted me. It was a new Professorship in Aeronautics at the Pei Yang Technical College at TienTsien in China. It offered £1,000 a year, plus a house and servants, and the thought of a glamorous life in the Far East attracted me greatly. I applied and was interviewed at the Chinese Legation, which was up some back stairs in Soho. All went well at the interview, and I was then summoned to the Foreign Office in Whitehall to be vetted for my suitability to represent the British Raj in the Orient. Again all went well, and I was told that I had been selected. However, the operations of the Japanese in Manchukuo delayed the appointment, which in the end the war brought to nothing.

When in 1972 I at last visited China, I stood on the platform of the railway station at TienTsien, and my mind went back to that near miss of nearly 40 years earlier. I must say, I was more than relieved that things had happened in the way they did. Even stranger, the wheel of fate turned a full circle and, in 1974, I was invited by Li Chang, the Minister for Foreign Trade, to become an Honorary Professor of the Peking Aeronautical Institute, a distinction which I prize highly.

In 1935 it was clear to me that Hitler was heading for war, so I decided that I must go into the Navy, in which Service I had more than the necessary qualifications to join as a Lieutenant-Commander. However, I was diverted into the Scientific and Research Department of the Admiralty. I started work in September 1935 at the Admiralty Laboratories at Teddington as a Scientific Officer at £450 a year. I had hardly settled in the place when I was suddenly summoned to Whitehall to see the Director of Scientific Research, Charles (later Sir Charles) Wright. He was a tall, rugged Canadian who had been the physicist on Scott's fatal expedition to the South Pole. Later, when I knew him better, I tried to get him to tell me about it, but he said that it was too awful to discuss.

When I saw him on this occasion he told me that I had been seconded to the Director of Ballistic Research and was to report to him at Woolwich Arsenal forthwith. Ballistics was concerned with the range and flight of shells and rockets. The Director, Alwyn (later Sir Alwyn) Crowe, told me that I would have been offered a job with him earlier, but his budget would not permit, so he had hijacked me from the Admiralty. This was the unexpected direct result of the report I had written on the supersonic tunnel while at Oxford.

My first job was to work on the underlying mathematics behind the anti-aircraft (AA) rocket, which in World War II was used in vast numbers in Z-batteries. A great argument was being waged about AA guns versus AA rockets. It went thus. The great difficulty in predicting the height, speed and course of an aircraft made the chance of a lethal shot with the standard 3·7 or 4·5 inch anti-aircraft gun about 1 in 20,000. In fact, in the War they did better; if I remember correctly they scored about 1 in 10,000. To defend Britain against German aircraft attack, thousands of very expensive guns would be required, whose barrels would need frequent replacement.

Cordite rockets were cheap, so why not fire a cloud of these at an aircraft? No expensive gun to wear out — just a bunch of simple rails to launch the rockets. But there were problems with the rocket. Nobody had ever extruded cordite to the required size of 3 in (76·2 mm) in diameter. Even once this had been done, the rockets had a tendency to burst on the launcher, and sometimes were seen sailing off in a direction at right-angles to the direction of projection.

So the argument went on, and when war started we had not made the guns and shells, and the rockets were not ready either. When the war ended we had both in ample supply!

Woolwich Arsenal was a remarkable place. At the main gates, there were large workshops. Once past these, large tracts of 'country' opened up, sloping gradually down to the river. Green fields, paths and edges were everywhere, joining the steam-heated underground bunkers where cordite was stored.

At the end of one of these paths was a small collection of single-storey wooden huts, where the Directorate of Ballistic Research was housed. Nearby were two test houses where the rockets could be tested while clamped down, and the thrust and burning time determined. The rockets were fired by a 'quick match' which itself was ignited electrically. We had one nasty accident when a rocket apparently failed to ignite, and the men who went into the test bed to investigate were killed by the delayed ignition.

I remember that the first real trials of the rocket in free flight were made at Orford Ness, Essex, and I was invited by Alwyn Crowe to be present. There was a considerable gathering of top brass to see these trials, and all appeared to go well. But the photographs showed that at least one of the rockets travelled approximately 90° in the wrong direction, so evidently the stability was marginal.

One other job I was given in 1937 by Crowe, and that was to calculate the weight and size of a rocket which could hit Berlin. The propellants were specified as either liquid oxygen and kerosene or nitric acid and kerosene. The former was the better combination since all the constituents were combustible, whereas with nitric acid, the nitrogen therein was virtually dead weight.

The conclusion was that it could be done, but the rockets would be enormously large by previous standards, weighing many tons. The report was discussed by the Secret 'M' Committee of the Admiralty, chaired by an Admiral, and with many important members. I attended the meetings in awe, but nothing came of it because we were just not ready to visualise such huge rockets as a practical proposition. A few years later, the German V.2s landed on London, and my calculations came back to me vividly — particularly the conclusion that the range of a single rocket was strictly limited to about 350 miles (560km) which placed much of England out of range.

It is odd that the best scientific advice offered to the Prime Minister in 1942-44 was that such a rocket was quite impossible. Great efforts were made to stop any serious consideration of such a weapon, even after they began falling on London!

Of course, today multi-stage rockets are used, and the launch weight is an order of magnitude greater than that of the V.2, but, back in 1937, we limited ourselves to a small rocket weighing only a few pounds. In retrospect, I think this was correct. The enormous effort that the Germans put into the V.2 never did pay off. If, instead, it had been invested in more and better aircraft, who knows what might have been the outcome?

While at Woolwich, I worked with W. R. (now Sir William) Cook. When I met him, I was very surprised to find that he had kept well abreast of the work on supersonic airflow, which up until now I had thought was mainly of academic interest. I did not know that Woolwich had for years been photographing bullets and shells in flight, and could easily see the air shock-waves and flow in the pictures.

Cook was a great smoker. On his desk, he had a row of seven pipes which he smoked alternately. There was also a block of opaque yellow stuff about 4 in (10 cm) cube, which sat on the desk next to the ashtray. I asked what it was.

'Oh, that', replied Cook, 'that's a lump of cordite'.

'Good God', I said, 'Isn't it very risky?'.

'Not at all, it's only dangerous when burning in a confined space'.

Thus I learned that cordite could be extruded, carved or machined like any other plastic material. The tubes of cordite used in the rocket were about 24 in long, 3 in diameter, and had a star-shaped hole up the middle. The shape of this hole was important, because it controlled the area of the burning surface and prevented the rocket from bursting prematurely.

Though I was very interested in all this work, I had my suspicions about its direct relevance to the war which seemed imminent. When, therefore, in the autumn of 1937 I had a letter from my friend Llewellyn Smith, asking me if I was interested in a job in the Engineering Department of Rolls-Royce, I was intrigued, and shortly afterwards I went to Derby for an interview with Colonel T. B. Barrington, who was then Chief Designer, Aero Engines. I waited in his office, from which I could see the serried rows of drawing boards and the impressive-looking men working at them.

The door of the office opened and in came a man, slightly older than myself, with a very large and high forehead and an air of quiet confidence and authority. He shook my hand rather diffidently.

'My name is Rubbra, I am the Assistant Chief Designer'.

God knows, I did not doubt it, as I spoke for the first time with a real live Rolls-Royce engineer. Rubbra and I were destined to work together in great harmony, and with great success for many years to come, but then there seemed no way I would ever be able to equal him. I remember being shocked by his comparative youth. I expected Rolls-Royce engineers to be grizzled men with beards and at least 50 years old. Perhaps I had imprinted on my mind unconsciously the picture of Sir Henry Royce. Rubbra had the air of a quiet, deep-thinking man, which indeed he was.

Barrington came in, and we had a short conversation about my career to date, and he talked rather vaguely about the necessity for stressing more accurately the components in an engine. This depressed me somewhat, because although I had studied the general theory of the forces produced by the elasticity of materials, it was by no means my main subject. Then he took me to lunch at the Midland Hotel at Derby Station, with its frightful exterior and very comfortable interior, and after lunch we parted on the general line, 'don't call us, we'll call you'.

I was not surprised that the interview had been unsatisfactory. I still could not figure how I could get into that great engineering organisation, so I returned to the Admiralty Research Laboratory, and forgot about Rolls-Royce. This was made easier by my being promoted, at this time, to Senior Scientific Officer at £850 p.a. To reach such heights in a little over two years was very unusual, so I was not dissatisfied with prospects for the future.

Two months later, like a bolt from the blue, came a letter from the Works Manager of Rolls-Royce, Ernest W. Hives. As I found later, he was always referred to as Hs, and he was the King of the Derby works. The letter requested my presence at Derby for an interview with Hs.

Naturally I went, and was ushered into his office which was over the front entrance to the works. The office was half panelled in oak, had a blazing fire on one side, and Hs sat at his desk across one corner. Today that desk is one of my treasured possessions, for from it, Hs inspired, directed and led the great contribution to the war effort which Rolls-Royce was destined to make under his colossal and dominating leadership.

I was instantly impressed by the aura of good humour yet relentless energy that seemed to surround him. I saw that he had copies of my published works on his desk. After seating me, he thumbed them through casually and asked,

'What's a Kármán Vortex Street?'

I explained as best I could, and then he said, leaning forward 'You're not much of an engineer are you?'

I had to agree and he replied:

'Never mind, this place is full of the best engineers in the world and we will teach you if you have it in you. They tell me you are a mathematician of ability. Tell me about your career'.

Which I did. He then suddenly came to life, and leaning forward said, 'When can you start?'

Now, I had only regarded my trips to Derby as exploratory and, in fact, I had not mentioned to my Chief in the Admiralty that I was seeing Rolls-Royce. I told Hs that I wanted to know what I should be expected to do, and for how much.

Hs ignored this and said, 'Whom do you work for now?' I told him the Director of Scientific Research in the Admiralty, whereupon he picked up the telephone and said, 'Get me Mr Charles Wright at the Admiralty in Whitehall'.

My heart sank, because I knew now that I should be faced with an instant decision.

The 'phone rang, and Hs said, 'I have a man called Hooker here, who says that he works for you, and who wants a job with us'.

I could not hear the reply, of course, and do not remember how the conversation went from there. Finally, Hs put the 'phone down and said, 'He says that you are a dirty dog to leave him after he has just promoted you, but he recommends you and says that we can have you'. I said, 'Now you have shopped me completely, and you have put me at a great disadvantage'.

'I see', he said, 'I did not mean to do that'.

He had a twinkle in his eye, and said:

'How much do you say you are worth?'

With great trepidation I said that it would not have been worth my while leaving the Admiralty for less than £1,000 p.a., but now I was in his hands.

He laughed and said, 'I'll tell you what I will do. I will give you £1,000 for the first year, £1,100 for the second, and £1,250 for the third', and then he added mischievously, 'if you last that long'.

And then he began to talk to me about the knowledge of mechanical design the company had built up, due to Henry Royce's insistence on as near to mechanical perfection as one could get; of its great manufacturing skills; and of the loyal workforce which had a father-to-son tradition.

'This door is always open to our men', he said. 'Only the other day a fitter came in and said, "Our Bill is leaving school on Friday". So I said to him, "You had better send him round to see us on Monday, and we will see what we can do with him".'

He went on, 'I am no mathematician or scientist, but I have a feeling that we are going to need such people in the future. We need a more technical and analytical approach to some of our engineering problems, and I am going to look to men like you to give us that lead'.

I left his office elated. His giant strength of character, warm sense of humour, and generous approach had completely captivated me. We were destined to become great friends, 'like father and son' he said to me on one occasion, and he was to give me great power in Rolls-Royce in the next few years. But neither of us foresaw that. And yet, eleven years later, I was to quarrel bitterly with him, and I left Rolls-Royce to join the Engine Division of Rolls-Royce's chief rival, the Bristol Aeroplane Company. When two people so close quarrel, the rift can be very deep, and thus it was; but, happily, some ten years later still, we were reconciled by an act of superb generosity on his part.

Oxford 1933. S.G.H. fourth from left second row. Llewellyn Smith (later a Director of Rolls-Royce) is third from left second row. Eric Warlow-Davies is third from left back row.

The 1934 International Congress of Fluid Dynamics at Cambridge included the following, all seated in the second row: Melville Jones (at the end on left), Leonard Bairstow (second from left), G. J. Taylor (fourth), Ludwig Prandtl (fifth), S. Timoshenko (eighth) and T. von Kármán (ninth). S. G. H. is in the group but out of the picture.

Hs.
The Lord Hives, C.H., M.B.E. of Duffield.

Chapter 2
The Merlin

And so, in January 1938, here I was seated in my Spartan little office in Nightingale Road, Derby. After a few days, I resolved that I must end my isolation and go forth to explore the surroundings. I discovered that just across the corridor was a door marked 'Library', so in I went and found the Librarian very friendly and helpful. He explained the surrounding geography, and who was who.

The overall Chief Engineer was A. G. Elliott, who was primarily a design engineer, and had been Royce's right-hand man for many years. Under him were Barrington as Chief Designer, and Jimmy Ellor as Chief Experimental Engineer. All people who designed and made drawings were responsible to Barrington, and all people who tested engines and components or did other experimental work were responsible to Ellor. The information that Ellor's department produced was fed to the Design department, who incorporated it into modified designs to improve the engines.

Since I knew nothing of design, it was clear that I must direct my attention to the work being done in the Experimental Department. So, one afternoon after lunch, I took my courage in both hands, and wandered diffidently into the next office, which I knew housed the engineers responsible for testing the single-cylinder research engines. In it were about half-a-dozen highly efficient-looking young men, all busy at reports or examining blueprints. Over in the corner sat a quiet grey-haired man gazing into space, and since he looked the most innocuous, I went over and asked him what he did. He replied, 'I am in charge of testing superchargers'.

'What does that mean?', I asked.

'Well, we have a rig back there in the test area, driven by two electric motors each of 250 horsepower, on which we can drive a test supercharger, and measure its performance independently of the engine. In fact, this is a typical set of curves that we get'.

He picked up a bunch of sheets from his desk, and showed them to me. Plotted on them was the amount of air that the supercharger pumped, the pressure it produced, and the temperature rise of the air due to its compression.

I asked, 'Could I borrow one of these curves?' 'Certainly', he replied, 'take a complete set'.

I bore them back in triumph to my office. By the grace of God I had stumbled on the one man whose job it was to produce test results which were right up my street, namely, the flow and compression of air.

I was not to know that Hs, under advice from Llewellyn Smith, had given instructions that I was to be left to soak in the atmosphere of Rolls-Royce for the time being, in the hope that I would find my own feet in an area to which I could contribute. His attitude was that I was not to be deviated into any routine task until I had had a chance to settle down, and get some idea of what went on. And, although I felt neglected, it happened in just the way he had hoped.

I had never even seen a supercharger, and had no idea how it managed to compress air by centrifugal action. I rushed to the Library and borrowed two books, *The Internal Combustion Engine*, by D. R. Pye and Stodola's great work on *Steam Turbines*. Both contained chapters on the elementary theory of centrifugal compression, and I was soon able to compare the theory with the experimental results which Frank Allen had given me. There were wide disagreements.

In both Stodola and Pye the theory was very sketchy, and I was soon able to extend it to include the separate efficiencies of the rotor and the diffuser. Briefly, a centrifugal supercharger consists of a rotor carrying a number of equally spaced radial vanes. In the case of the Merlin supercharger, which I was examining, the rotor was 10.25 in (260 mm) in diameter and had 16 vanes. It was driven by the engine through a step-up gear, and revolved at 28,000 rpm. The air entered at the centre of the rotor, moved out radially under the centrifugal force, and was flung off the rim into a stationary 12-vaned diffuser, the object of which was to convert the velocity of the air into the pressure which forced greater masses of air into the cylinders of the engine.

If one thinks of the cylinders and pistons of an engine as the heart which converts the force of the burning air and petrol mixture into mechanical power by the downward motion of the piston, then the supercharger is the lungs of the engine, and by its efficiency controls the power output.

Clearly, the efficiency of the supercharger depends upon the efficiency of its component parts — the rotor and the diffuser — and to get the best results the maximum efficiency of the rotor must be made to coincide with the maximum efficiency of the diffuser. I found, by mathematical analysis and much to my surprise, that this happy coincidence did not occur on the Merlin supercharger, and that changes to both the rotor and diffuser were necessary. I even computed that the efficiency of the supercharger would improve from the existing 65 per cent to a new level of 75 per cent by such changes, but could it be true? How could the great Rolls-Royce firm have missed this?

I checked and rechecked my calculations over the following weeks, and became very fluent in the aerodynamics of the supercharger. I could find no flaw in my deductions. So I took my courage in both hands and persuaded A. G. Elliott's secretary to type the report for me. With great diffidence I appeared in Elliott's office and handed it to him. He casually glanced through it, and said,

'This looks very interesting, I must send a copy to Mr Ellor'.

I learned later that Ellor's speciality was superchargers, and that he had come to Rolls-Royce from the Royal Aircraft Establishment at Farnborough, some ten years previously. He had been responsible for the giant supercharger on the famous 'R' engines which won the Schneider Trophy in Mitchell's Supermarine S.6 and S.6B seaplanes.

I returned to my office wondering what would happen next. Interminable days went by. Then suddenly, one evening just as I was leaving my office, the door burst open and in came the great Ellor himself. He had in his hand my report, and my heart came to my mouth.

'Did you write this?', he asked abruptly. I admitted to being the culprit, and then smiling broadly he said,

'Well done, jolly good stuff. From now on you are in charge of supercharger development', and he shook me warmly by the hand and departed!

The bleak depression of the preceeding weeks lifted like magic, and I drove home elated. I had no idea what it all meant, but doubtless in good time all would be revealed to me. The casual way Ellor had informed me could only be a preliminary before a proper ceremony of appointment at which my duties would be explained to me, and amidst the applause of the assembled company, I would descend to take up my office — or so I imagined!

But not a bit of it. Life went on unchanged. Then a couple of days later a fine upstanding young man with red hair called on me and said,

'My name is Doug Nelson. I hear that you are my new boss'.

I smiled at him warily, and replied,

'That must have been as big a surprise to you as it is to me'.

'Not really', he said, 'you see I have just read your report and I wish that I could have written it'.

There wasn't a trace of jealousy, rancour or disdain in him as we warmly shook hands. I invited him to sit on my empty desk and describe the set-up to me. I remember thinking of W. S. Gilbert's attractive line, 'Tell me, pretty maiden, are there any more at home like you'? He said there were a few, including 'Prof' Allen who sat in the office next door, and who had given me the original set of curves.

Frank Allen was really an electrical expert, and had been chosen because the governing arrangement on the electric motors which drove the supercharger test rig was the Ward-Leonard system, which only he understood. It was his duty, also, to compare successive tests to see if, by chance, any improvement in performance had been effected. But Doug Nelson told me that the supercharger for the Merlin III, which was the current production engine for the Hurricane and Spitfire fighters, had not been changed since its original design in 1934.

Let me hasten to add that the Merlin III supercharger was easily the best in the world at that time, as I was to discover later when I became more knowledgeable about the performance of contemporary superchargers in Germany and the USA.

The other members of the team, Nelson went on, were Frank Barnes and Frank Nicholls who operated the test rig and produced the experimental data. Any modification to the supercharger was designed by 'Flap' Fletcher's section, but they belonged to the Main Engine Design Department, and it was Nelson's responsibility to act as the link between the Design Office and the Experimental Workshop to ensure that the superchargers were built to the specified test standard.

At this stage I had to admit to Nelson that I had never seen a supercharger in the flesh. He immediately offered to take me on a tour of inspection, a suggestion I welcomed with open arms. We left the office block by the back door which led along a short corridor into the Experimental Workshop, which was the kingdom of one Horace Percival Smith, or HPS. He was a complete autocrat. He allowed no one into his shop except on a 'need to be there' basis. We made a courtesy call on him, and found him seated at a table covered with blueprints. By his side was the longest array of pushbuttons I had ever seen.

He looked up. 'Yes, yes, yes, what do you want, what do you want?', he barked abruptly in his repetitive style. Nelson explained that I was the new man in charge of supercharger development, whereupon he pressed a couple of buttons, and almost instantaneously two men in overalls burst into the office. 'This is Roy Speed, who is in charge of the supercharger assembly, and his assistant'. He then turned to them and said 'You now take your instructions from this man, and he is to be allowed into the Shop at all times'. Then he smiled and we all shook hands.

The informality of the whole thing astounded me. I had yet to learn of the tremendous esprit-de-corps that existed between the engineers and the Experimental Workshop, and the single-minded purpose of all to work together with energy and harmony to improve Rolls-Royce engines. It was enough for them to know that I had been appointed for me to be accepted.

HPS was an impressive character. He was well dressed, with his hair parted exactly in the middle and well smoothed with hair-cream. He wore thick horn-rimmed glasses and oozed authority and efficiency. The whole workshop stood in 'awesome' respect for him, and men were prepared to work day and night at his command. Little did I know that the time was to come when HPS on passing my office would open the door, put his head in and bark rapidly,

'What do you want me to make. What do you want me to make?', and leave.

The greatest privilege that one could enjoy in Rolls-Royce was the right — which had to be earned — of entry direct to HPS with a request for something to be made. Woe betide you if you wasted the great man's time on something trivial.

The four of us backed rapidly out of his office, like schoolboys leaving the Headmaster's study after clemency. Roy Speed laughed and said,

'Thank God it was only to meet you. I thought I must have put my foot in it somewhere. What do you want, anyway'.

I threw caution to the winds and said could I please see a supercharger.

'Which supercharger', he replied, 'I've got half-a-dozen over there that I'm building'.

I said, 'Any one will do, because I've never seen one before'.

The two shop-men gazed at one another in amazement. They then led the way into the largest workshop that I had ever been in. On the right were the machine tools in rows upon rows, each with its busy operator. On the left was a fenced-off area equipped with large benches on which were laid out components of stripped down aero engines, each bench labelled with its engine number, while inspectors equipped with micrometers, clock-gauges and magnifying glasses pored over the component parts looking for cracks and measuring wear or other deficiences arising from the last test of the engine. The whole place hummed with activity.

We passed through the shop to the further end where the engines were built for experimental test. Roy Speed went up to one and laid a hand on it. 'This here', he said 'is a Merlin engine. This is the front end where the propeller is bolted on, and this contraption on the back end is the supercharger with the gears that drive it'.

My mind boggled as I looked at my end, with, as I could read, its SU carburettor, and rods and levers operating the throttles. I felt I ought to say something intelligent, and stuttered,

'What is the power of the Merlin'?

He lapsed automatically into the lilt of *Eskimo Nell:*

'It has the driving force of a thousand horse ... and it's your job to make it do better. Nobody has managed to do that yet, so the best of British luck to you'.

We both laughed, he confidently and I nervously.

An apprehensive Nelson said, 'Come on, don't let's hang about here or Horace will jump down our necks for holding up the work. I am going to take you now to see the test rig'.

We left by the side doors and turned left down the wide driveway between two rows of workshops. I suppose it was about a quarter of a mile before we turned right and came to the experimental test beds, where engines were roaring away, belching flames and fumes from their short exhaust pipes.

The test beds were of the simplest and crudest form, open at each end, with a small cubby-hole for the driver and his instruments. The noise was absolutely tremendous and everything seemed to vibrate — even one's chest. And yet testers were leaning over each engine while it was running at full power, making sundry adjustments with no protection other than small ear plugs. I watched one take a short piece of steel between his teeth and put the other end on the cylinder block of an engine running at full throttle. In this way he could detect the onset of 'detonation' in the cylinders. A detonating engine could be self-destructive by literally hammering small holes in the cylinder head and pistons.

The main object of experimental testing was to run the engine to the point of destruction, and thus determine the weakest and most vulnerable components, which would then, subsequently, be strengthened by design action. Testers were so skilled that they could detect the slightest change in an engine's note - even when dozing in the tester's cabin. In this way they would save many engines from 'blowing up', and thus preserve valuable evidence from being destroyed. Their simple philosophy was 'We will test the engine as soon as you give it to us, be it morning, noon or night, weekends or holidays'. They were the tough-guys of the factory.

That morning we passed them by, and entered a small building where, in its polished pristine glory, was the Supercharger Test Rig. It consisted of two electric motors in line, each of 250 horsepower. Between the two motors was the control panel, which enabled each to be run at any desired speed, or the motors could be coupled together as one unit of 500 horsepower. The extreme ends of the two motors were arranged to accommodate a supercharger, so that two tests could be made simultaneously if desired. All around were the manometers and pressure gauges for recording the performance.

I was received with great respect by the Chief Tester, Frank Barnes, and his assistant, Frank Nicholls, who had already heard of my appointment. I felt at home immediately in these surroundings. This was not a factory but a laboratory, and I could recognise the measuring apparatus and soon grasped the set-up. My spirits rose, and with them my confidence. This was *my* laboratory, and although I knew nothing as yet of the mechanical arrangement of the supercharger, I could easily understand the test apparatus. The data it produced in terms of airflow, air pressure and temperature were something I could handle with ease.

I returned to my office well satisfied, and indeed thrilled, by the morning's tour. I was very happy at the co-operation I had received all round.

Doug Nelson said, 'Do you want me to get you some drawings of the Merlin blower?'

I took the plunge, 'Certainly, which can I have?'

He returned with a cross-sectional general arrangement, and drawings of the rotor, diffuser and other components. I spread them out on my desk, and found to my surprise that I had little difficulty in interpreting them. I put this down to Professor Levy's insistence that the mathematical students at Imperial College should take a course in projective geometry, and thereby learn the elements of drawing and of projecting sections.

And thus it was, as a Junior Section Leader, that I put my foot on the first rung of the engineering ladder in Rolls-Royce. This step was to take me some 30 years later, through many vicissitudes and trials, to the 'plum' job in Engineering, that of being the Chief Engineer and Technical Director.

When I had travelled to Derby for the interview with Hs, I had gone by car. On the return journey, about 10 miles south of Derby I noticed a sign off to the right which said 'Donington Hall Residential Hotel'. I was committed to Rolls-Royce, so decided to make a detour and explore this place. Donington Hall proved to be a magnificent country mansion situated just outside the attractive village of Castle Donington, by today's East Midlands Airport. The Hall had a large park around it, which included the famous Castle Donington motor-racing circuit, and one could walk for miles through the splendid grounds of this country estate. There was even a nine-hole golf course which I enjoyed very much. The Hall itself was only sparsely furnished, and the space available to the few residents was enormous. The bedrooms were very large, and one had been converted to four or five bathrooms.

Since the weekly charge covering bed, breakfast and dinner was only £3, it seemed an ideal place, particularly as the works was on the south side of Derby, and so I booked in as from January 1938. I discovered that there were three other members from Rolls-Royce in residence; Cyril Lovesey, who was a small dapper man about 40 years old; Christopher Ainsworth-Davis; and Francis Tudor Wayne, who was an efficiency consultant seconded to Rolls-Royce at the time. There were three other residents, an Army captain who was in charge of the Army Depot nearby, the local bank manager, and an ex-Naval commander.

Altogether, they made an interesting and amusing bunch.

For some time I had no idea what Lovesey and Ainsworth-Davis did in Rolls-Royce, but eventually I discovered that Lovesey was a real king-pin: Deputy Chief Experimental Engineer under Ellor. He had been in the RAF at the end of World War I, had taken a degree in Engineering at Bristol University, and then joined Rolls-Royce. He had been the man in charge of the 'R' engines which won the Schneider Trophy in 1929 and 1931, and then held the world air speed record at 408 mph (657 km/h). He was a man of great experience in mechanical engineeering, and was affectionately known in the firm as Lov.

Ainsworth-Davis was a junior engine designer at the time, and was being trained in Rubbra's office to the special standards required by Rolls-Royce, and which had been inherited from the natural genius of Royce himself, who seemed to have known instinctively what constituted good sound design. Sir Henry Royce had died in 1933, but his methods and principles lived on through his protégés Elliott and Rubbra.

The friendship and partnership between the Hon Charles S. Rolls and the self-made engineer Henry Royce which began at the beginning of the century was, indeed, an event of great portent.

Rolls, the young sporting aristocrat, hailed from Monmouth, and was educated at Eton and Cambridge where, in 1898, he took a degree in Mechanics and Applied Sciences. All things mechanical interested him, and he was certainly the first undergraduate at Cambridge to own a motor car, at that time a French Peugeot. On leaving Cambridge, he spent some time learning to be a mechanic at the LNWR locomotive works at Crewe in order to be able to cope with the various failures and breakdowns that the unreliable motor cars of the day were susceptible to. Of his motor journeys he said:

'In those days, your passage through the districts was recorded in every local newspaper, and if ever you dared to stop in a town for a moment to take in benzoline or anything, you had to fight your way back to the car. Out in the country, on the other hand, every other man climbed up a tree or telegraph pole to get out of your way; every woman ran away across the fields; every horse jumped over the garden wall as a matter of course; and the horse in every butcher's cart that was left at the side of the road with the tailboard open, bolted scattering various spare parts of animals about the road'.

He was fascinated by motor cars, always searching for the best car, and taking a leading part in the sporting-car events of the day. Thus he gravitated to Manchester, where Royce had made his first few cars. It is recorded that Rolls made a prophetic statement that it was his ambition that there should be a car made which would be connected with his name and would become as well known as a Broadwood or Steinway grand piano.

Thus, Rolls and Royce met at Manchester, and Rolls had his first run in a car designed and made by Royce. The two men took to each other immediately, and both recognised the mutual benefits of a partnership. For Royce here was the very man, with his great motoring record, who could introduce his car to London Society. Rolls knew he had found the greatest car designer in the world.

The third element of administration and organisation was supplied by Rolls' friend Claude Johnson, Secretary of the Automobile Club. He became Secretary of the new Rolls-Royce firm, in which post he stayed until he died.

Henry Royce's background could scarcely have been more different from those of his two partners. He wrote of his early days:

'Owing to the want of success (through unsteadiness) and early death of my clever father, who was of a well-known milling family, my mother was left unprovided for, and I became a newspaper boy from ten to eleven years of age. Then one more year at school, from eleven to twelve years of age, and then a telegraph boy from thirteen to fourteen, when I went as an apprentice on locomotive engine work under the Great Northern Railway from fourteen to seventeen years of age when I acquired some skill as a mechanic but lacked technical, commercial and clerical experience'.

He was born in 1863 at Alwalton near Peterborough, where his father was a flour miller, and was only nine when his father died. His apprenticeship at the GNR was paid for by his aunt, but the little money she had ran out before he completed his indentures, and he had to leave at the age of 17 to find other work. He found it in Leeds with a firm of toolmakers, where he worked long hours each week, from 6.00 am to 10.00 pm and all Friday night, for the princely sum of eleven shillings (55p) a week.

Recalling this period of his life he wrote: 'I was offered employment at the newly formed Electric Light and Power Generating Company at Bankside, London, at 22 shillings a week, which I accepted, and for maximum economy lived in a 'third floor back' in the Old Kent Road'.

He was transferred to Liverpool, and then the company failed. However, in association with A. E. Claremont, they decided to set up business together, Claremont having a capital of £50 and Royce £20. Thus in 1884, the firm of F. H. Royce and Co was born in Cooke Street, Manchester, where they manufactured first bell sets and later lampholders and dynamos. By 1899, things had progressed sufficiently for them to raise £30,000 to build a new works, and to extend their scope to cranes. These were much superior to the imported ones, but more expensive because of Royce's insistence on quality and reliability.

In 1903, against the wishes of his partner, Royce began to indulge in his great desire — to build a motor car, and to repair and modify the various makes of cars belonging to his friends. From this small beginning came the great firm of Rolls-Royce, which was to stand throughout the world as the pre-eminent engineering company.

Royce had added to his practical training by attending night classes at technical schools, but, above all things, he was one of those rare people who are natural-born engineers and designers. He had an instinct for excellence of design, and would spend great time and patience in the consideration of engineering drawings before allowing the parts to be manufactured. On the other hand, he constantly appealed to experiment, and would examine with great care every part after it had been run. No wear, frettage or indication of malfunctioning was too trivial for him to notice, and make efforts to correct.

After Rolls was killed flying at Bournemouth in 1910, and Royce had his severe illness in the years following, the firm was kept together by Claude Johnson. He regarded Royce as his precious jewel, and insisted that he lived in milder climes than grey Derby. Accordingly, Royce spent the winters in the south of France at Le Canadel and, later, the summers at West Wittering in Sussex. In both places, he had his senior designers with him. When I joined Rolls-Royce, official drawings still bore the nomenclature LeC., while most of those made at Derby were kept from Royce and known as D.E.S. (Derby Experimental Schemes).

From what one reads, Royce appears as a cold, austere martinet who would not tolerate any opposition. His early marriage had failed, and for the last 20 years of his life he was cared for by Nurse Aubyn who never left his side, and appeared to exert authority over him. Whether she was more than a nurse we shall never know but, if so, good for Henry for it would be one of the few humane attributes in his character.

Before World War I, Royce's great passion had been the design and manufacture of motor cars. He was a perfectionist, and with his natural skill and capacity to gather around and to lead firmly men of similar objectives, the Rolls-Royce car soon became the finest in the world. Perhaps it was because of Rolls' death as a pilot that Royce took no interest in aviation prior to World War I, but when the cataclysm broke on the world, it was clear that the great factory at Derby would have to give up luxury motor cars and devote its skill and capacity to the war effort.

Just prior to the outbreak of war in 1914, Royce was approached by the War Office, who wished him to make an aero engine of French design. He took one look at it and refused point-blank. However, the Admiralty encouraged him to design his own engine, and in August/September 1914, he began the design of the 200 hp engine, as it was then known, and which subsequently became the famous Eagle, later developed to 375 hp.

At the time, for reasons of health, Royce was living at Ramsgate in Kent, and had with him his usual bureau of designers. After the outbreak of war, he never once visited the factory at Derby, and this was regarded as a blessing in disguise by the inhabitants thereof. Royce's presence in the shops was very obstructive, since he would stop work and sack people on the instant if they were not doing the job exactly as he thought it ought to be done. I was told that they left by the front door, and were immediately re-engaged at the back door.

And so, from 200 miles away, he controlled the design and manufacture of the 200 hp engine, and nothing was allowed to be done unless it had his thumbprint upon it. A constant stream of drawings and instructions flowed from Ramsgate to Derby, and in December 1915, these were bound into a volume of a limited edition of 100, entitled *The First Aero Engines made by Rolls-Royce Ltd.* The preface to this volume states 'In the opinion of the Board of Directors, the Memoranda and letters written by Mr F. H. Royce, the Engineer-in-Chief, in connection with the design, testing and manufacture of these engines are so admirable as evidence of extreme care, foresight, and analytical thought, that the Directors decided to have them printed and bound in order that copies may be available for study and as an example to all grades of Rolls-Royce Engineers, present and future'.

The book is headed 'Confidential, not to be shown to anyone without the authority of the Directors'. I am happy to say that Copy No 72 is in my possession today, almost 70 years later.

The first note on the 200 hp engine is dated 26 August 1914, and states 'We are working at the new 200 hp engine to find out the space required. We propose to fit it with wrought steel cylinders and steel jackets. Each cylinder is to be separate'. Royce had already made up his mind that the engine should have 12 cylinders in two banks of six, inclined to each other in a 60° Vee format. This became the standard arrangement for Rolls-Royce aero-engines for the next 30 years.

A typical note was the one dated 24 October 1914 to Wormald, who was then Works Manager at Derby. Royce stated 'I am very surprised to hear there was any difficulty about finding machines to work on the aero-engine cylinders. I am afraid the position is that we must find machines. We have worried the RFC and the Admiralty. We have also worried and worked continually on the design of this, and there must be no delays put in the way of the progress of the engine, because we must either do the work promptly or abandon the idea of doing it altogether. We cannot possibly have it hanging about, otherwise it will be only a disgrace to us'.

His admonition was heeded and by February 1915 the engine was running on the test bed. A note from Royce dated 4 March 1915 records his satisfaction at the engine having given 225 hp at 1,600 rpm — already more than its design power. Thus in six months Royce had designed and the Derby Works had made the most powerful aero-engine in the world. Weighing 700 lb, it was destined to play a great part in the war effort, and Royce would allow no other firm to make it.

One sees references to E. W. Hives as being in charge of the testing programme. Hives had joined Rolls-Royce at the beginning of the century as a car mechanic for Rolls, and had graduated to being the chief rally driver. He it was who drove a 40/50 Silver Ghost on the famous trip from London to Edinburgh and back, in top gear all the way, in 1911. Hives retained his enthusiasm all his life for driving Rolls-Royce cars, which he did with great élan.

I remember driving to London with him in 1946 in the first straight-eight Rolls-Royce. This car had been ready just as war broke out, and had been shipped to Canada for safety during the war. It was very fast indeed, with a top speed in the order of 120 mph. We were en route to London, long before motorways, and were doing a steady 100 mph (161 km/h) when he started to feel for his cigarette case. He tried all his pockets, changing hands on the steering wheel meanwhile. He then extracted a cigarette and went through the same process finding his lighter. Meanwhile we were streaking past other traffic on what today would be regarded as a second-class road. My hair stood on end, but I dared not say a word.

He very occasionally hit things. On one occasion, while travelling with his colleague Bill Lappin, they ran into a car full of bookmakers and racing touts. Hs stopped and Lappin went back. The victims were very belligerent and were threatening to knock the block off the lunatic who had hit them. Lappin said 'You mustn't do that. Do you know he is the Manager of Rolls-Royce'.

'The Manager of Rolls-Royce, eh', was the reply. 'In that case we won't hit him, we'll sue him?'

The excitement of testing the Eagle engine and its successors in World War I changed Hives' allegiance from cars to aero engines. The Eagle was the powerplant for the Handley Page and Vickers heavy bombers, and a scaled-down version called the Falcon became the main engine fitted to the Bristol Fighter, which ended the war as the supreme two-seater fighter.

It was Hs' experience, gained in World War I, which fitted him so admirably to lead Rolls-Royce in World War II. He alone amongst us knew the power of the aeroplane in warfare, and the enormous efforts that would be required from Rolls-Royce to satisfy the demands for the engines. We in Britain have cause to be thankful that this strong, sagacious man, at the height of his powers, was in the right place at the right time to co-ordinate the effort that was necessary to bring our country to victory in the air.

After World War I, Hives became Chief Experimental Engineer, covering both cars and aero engines, and three young graduates from Bristol — A. C. Lovesey, R. N. Dorey and A. A. Rubbra — joined the firm. All three were destined for top positions — Lovesey in Engineering, Rubbra in Design, and Dorey in Management.

Lovesey was a keen amateur aviator and owned his own Gipsy Moth, which he flew all over Europe in his spare time. At the time when I met him at Donington Hall, he was still a batchelor and worked very long hours, seldom leaving the factory before 7.00 pm, just in time for dinner.

Being Deputy Chief Experimental Engineer, he had a large

staff because all engine test, performance and build came under his command. The pattern for developing an engine had been set by Royce himself. We find him writing on 22 March 1915: 'Re. 200 hp Aero Engine — Short Duration Tests, etc. We presume that you are continuing the test at high compression and increased speed, first finding out how fast you can run for one or two hour spells with the lubrication as in the 20 hour test, and then whether the big-end will bear an increase of speed with (1) "Castrol", (2) cooler oil, or (3) higher pressure'.

In other words, Royce laid down the principle of gradually increasing the speed and power of the engine in steps in order to find the weakest link. Thereafter, the engine would be pulled back slightly, and long-endurance runs made to demonstrate the mechanical integrity. All this philosophy, and much more, is now embodied in the Type Test which all engines must undergo before going into full production.

It was Lovesey's main task to get the Merlin through its Type Test, and to join with Rubbra in the design of modified parts to overcome any mechanical failure that occurred during testing. He had great powers of concentration, and it was his custom to deal with the many problems individually, one at a time, and not spread himself over the whole gamut of difficulties facing him.

He would arrive in his office, and gather around him the appropriate specialists, and together they would begin to examine the evidence of a particular failure. Day after day the same people would gather with him, and gradually they would piece together the mechanism of the failure, and decide upon the appropriate action. He never made a snap decision, and when his investigation was complete he would give a masterly summary and exposition of the problem. Hives described him as the finest development engineer in the world.

Although his methods were first-class for solving problems, they were no way to run a large department, because the rest of his staff did not exist while he was concentrating with the few. This was temporarily very frustrating for many of his engineers who felt they were not getting their fair share of his attention.

It came to pass that I shared an office with him as his assistant, and thereby had a daily tutorial on how to become a mechanical engineer. I remember a man bursting into his office during the war in a state of high dudgeon. He advanced on Lov, and banged his desk shouting:

'When the hell am I going to be allowed to get on with my job'.

Lovesey leaned back and smiled at him: 'Now let me see, what is it that you want to do?'

'You know damned well, I have got to measure the oil flows in all the lubricating pipes on the engine, and yet I cannot get on any engine test'.

'But it's absolutely vital that we have that information', Lovesey replied, 'How do you propose to measure it?'

The man sat back and gave a lengthy exposition, with Lovesey interjecting, 'Yes, yes, what a good idea'.

The man calmed down, with Lov thanking him for drawing the matter to his attention and assuring him of his great interest.

The man left completely mollified and happy. Since I knew that he had little hope of getting this routine information, because all the engines were heavily committed, I asked Lovesey,

'What are you going to do about that?'

'Bugger all', he replied, and turned back to his papers.

Almost daily the Chief Tester, Stan Orme, and his assistant, Alf Arnold, would appear first thing to report on the state of the engine tests. Both were well over six feet tall, whereas Lovesey was a slight man of about 5 ft 6 in. They knew there would be only one test Lov would be interested in, and they spent a good deal of effort making sure they knew which one that was. Sometimes they slipped up, and got their priorities wrong. Lovesey would rise in his wrath and demand,

'Can't I rely on you to test the right engine, or must I come on to the test beds and do it myself?' He would start to take off his jacket and would have to be forcibly restrained in his chair, while they promised that he would have his test done immediately. He was held in great respect and affection by all, and was really kindness and good nature itself.

Both he and Rubbra gave their whole life to Rolls-Royce, and their outstanding talents were an inspiration to all. When, in March 1971, I was asked to return to Derby to take responsibility for the RB211 engine, whose problems had just caused the world-shaking crash of the company, I telephoned them both, asking them to help me. Although well over 70 years old, and retired, they both joined me in my office, and towers of strength they were too, readily accepting the junior man of 1938 as their Chief.

Back in 1938 I soon became very familiar with the construction of the Merlin supercharger and carburettor. The engine had been designed to fit the Spitfire and Hurricane fighters, and its length had been compressed as much as possible to match the fore-and-aft balance on these aircraft. Since the supercharger was at the rear of the engine it had come in for pretty severe design treatment, and the air intake duct to the impeller looked very squashed, with a shape that seemed peculiar to my eye.

I tried to calculate the pressure losses which the air flowing through this intake would experience before entering the impeller, and the answer looked bad. Since it is the function of the supercharger to compress the air, it was obviously a bad thing to have a pressure loss in the intake.

I wished to determine the magnitude of this loss. After consulting with my new staff, we went to see Albert Rigg, an old boy who inhabited his own little corner of the Experimental Shop, surrounded by the tools of his trade. Albert was a very highly skilled craftsman who specialised in sheet metal work. He could make anything in sheet metal from a sketch on the back of an envelope. Not only could he beat metal to make it thinner, but he could operate on a metal sheet with a hammer to make it thicker in places.

We told him that we wished to cut away the heavy aluminium intake casing from the blower, and asked him to replace it with a sheet metal intake so that the air could go directly into the impeller without having to pass through carburettors or turn awkward corners. This was, of course, for test purposes only, so that we could determine, by experiment, the price that was being paid for the standard configuration on the engine. In a short time the parts were made, and the supercharger put on test. The effect was most enlightening, because the blower pumped a higher pressure and increased airflow, from which the losses in the carburettor and air intake could be calculated.

But engines must have a carburettor, so there was nothing to be done about that. They must also have an air intake leading the air from the carburettor to the eye of the supercharger, but this part could be reshaped to reduce the loss. So back we went to Albert and concocted a new shape for him to make. This was a much more difficult task than his original flare. The principle was that air velocities should be kept as low as possible, by making the cross-sectional area of the duct as large as possible, with the air directed into the eye of the blower in a very gentle curve. At the same time, the overall length had to be unchanged, so that the Merlin could still be fitted into the Hurricane and Spitfire.

With Albert's sheet-metal intake a great improvement was effected over the standard Merlin design, and combining this with the original prediction of the improvement to be obtained from the modifications to the rotor and the diffuser, I was confident that a vastly improved supercharger would result.

At this stage, I had no idea what effect this would have on the power produced by the Merlin engine, or on the performance of the two fighters. Nor could I find anybody in Rolls-Royce who could tell me. The subject had simply not been studied. Was it worth while changing the whole design of the supercharger, with all the drawing work, experimental manufacture, testing, and disruption to production? The judgement of the magnitude of this task was quite outside my experience. Fortunately, at that stage, I did not feel it was necessary for me even to suggest it. I was treating the supercharger as my personal toy, and got my satisfaction from improving its efficiency. What was done with it after that was someone else's affair.

But at this stage Hs took a hand. I was sitting in my office one afternoon when he walked in and sat down on the extra chair I had acquired. On my desk was a Merlin rotor, which he picked up and said, 'I have looked at the reports on your work, and I am interested in the proposal to make the vanes on this thing narrower, because that will take some of the stress out of it'.

As the rotor went round at about 28,000 rpm, cutting down the width of the vanes to about two-thirds would make a substantial reduction in the stress. Hs went on, 'As for the intake, I like the look of that too, so we are going to make it all for an engine test'.

Things then began to happen. Rubbra and Lovesey came to see me to get the dimensions of the rotor and diffuser, and the shape of the intake. The Main Engine Design Office went into gear to produce the definitive drawings for the revised engine. Thus were born the Merlin 45 engine used in Spitfires, and the Merlin XX used in Hurricanes and many other aircraft, and for me the impossible had come to pass. I had changed a Rolls-Royce engine designed by the great Henry Royce himself.

About this time, I was visited by the two senior testers, Orme and Arnold, who always seemed to operate as a pair. Both were horny-handed sons of toil, but they came to tell me that they had working for them a young man, G. L. Wilde — inevitably known as Oscar — who was a mathematical wizard, and a good tester to boot. Would I have a talk with him? Although they would be loath to lose him, they felt that better use could be made of him.

I saw him and was much impressed, and longed to have him on my staff. But how did one do this? I consulted Frank Allen who said there was no problem — if Orme and Arnold were willing to part, and I was willing to have him, then it could be fixed immediately. And so it was that Oscar joined me and became a valued and loyal colleague. He was a man of great enthusiasm and imagination, who was eventually to rise to the very top in the hierarchy of Rolls-Royce engineers.

About this time, I began to realise that it was not sufficient to consider the supercharger by itself. The important thing was the engine-supercharger combination, and it was essential to match the output of the supercharger to the demands of the engine. But what were the demands of the engine? Surprisingly, I could find little information about this, and so decided that we must measure the air consumption of the Merlin on test. Oscar said there wasn't a hope of doing this on the experimental beds because the schedule of testing was very strictly laid down; but why didn't we talk to the chaps on production test?

At that time, in early 1939, the production of the Merlin was just getting into top gear, and the rule was that each engine had to do a 2-hour endurance test before despatch. There were plenty of engines doing this routine test, and when we went along to see the chief tester he welcomed us with open arms. We could take what measurements we liked, provided it did not interfere with the passing-off tests. My own men went and made the measurements, and in a few days we had complete sets of air consumption curves for a considerable number of engines, running over the full gamut of varying power outputs.

In the case of the Merlin, the air was first sucked through the carburettor, where the petrol was sprayed in to give the correct mixture of fuel and air. It went on to the supercharger, where the mixure was compressed and, of course, heated by the compression, and delivered into the induction pipe which lay between the two banks of six cylinders with symmetrical off-takes on each side to each of the 12 cylinders. The pressure in the induction pipe was known as the boost pressure and was measured in pounds per square inch. The higher the boost pressure the higher the engine power, because more of the mixture of air and fuel would be forced into each cylinder.

The principle on which all four-stroke engines work is very straightforward. On the first downward stroke, the appropriate mixture of air and fuel — about 15 to 1 by mass, 9,000 to 1 by volume — is drawn into the cylinder through the open inlet valve(s). These valves then shut, and in the following upward stroke the piston compresses the charge. At the top of this stroke, the sparking plug ignites the compressed mixture, and the rapid rise in pressure which results forces the piston down again to give the power stroke. Before the bottom of this stroke the exhaust valves open, and on the next upward stroke the piston forces the burnt gases out through the exhaust pipe. The cycle then repeats itself. Thus there is one power stroke for every two revolutions of the crankshaft; in the case of the 12-cylinder Merlin there would be six power strokes to each revolution of the crankshaft.

In the theoretical examination I made of the relationship between the power output on the Merlin and the quantity of air/fuel mixture which it consumed, I started from the premise that the internal power generated in the cylinder must be proportional to the quantity of air/fuel mixture consumed. But not all the power generated in the cylinder appears as useful power at the propeller shaft. Some of it is used to drive the supercharger at the back of the engine, and some is absorbed by the friction of driving the pistons up and down, the crankshaft round and round, the valve gear and other parts.

The final answer, which was obtained by a combination of theory and experiment, showed that the Merlin generated an internal power in the cylinder of 10.5 horsepower for every pound of fuel/air mixture it inhaled per minute. This figure was independent of the rpm, or of the boost pressure from the supercharger.

On the theoretical side, I deduced a formula which accurately gave the quantity of charge which the engine would inhale under any condition, either on the ground or in the air. Now at last it was that, armed with the various formulae, we could calculate the power that the Merlin would give in any condition of flight.

Prior to this, we had calculated the horsepower from some very suspect and empirical formulae which had emanated from the Royal Aircraft Establishment. These formulae overestimated the power, and caused a constant argument between Mitchell, who designed the Spitfire, and Camm who designed the Hurricane. Both designers claimed that, from the measured speeds of their aircraft, the Rolls engines could not possibly be giving the power that was claimed for it. In fact, both aircraft were 20 - 30 mph slower than expected at about 20,000 feet, a fact that was kept very secret at the time since the war was imminent. Fortunately, the Germans were equally bad at estimating the power of their engines, and their aircraft were also slower than both the calculated and published figures.

The Americans took their usual line, and decided to build a special test bed at Wright Field in Ohio where their engines could be tested on the ground in conditions which simulated those at altitude, and in this way they were able actually to measure the power output of their engines. By the standards of the day this was a huge installation, with refrigerating plant to reproduce the cold air temperatures at altitude, and large exhausters to reduce the air pressure and take away the exhaust gases.

In comparison with this massive attack by the Americans, we had only a few simple formulae which enabled us to calculate the power of the Merlin while sitting at our desks. When, late in the War, a Merlin was actually tested in the Wright Field installation, the measured powers agreed exactly with those we had calculated several years before. From then on we adopted as our motto "The Pen is mightier than the Spanner".

What was far more important, we were now able to reconcile the performance of the Spitfire and Hurricane with the power output of the engine, and were then able to predict accurately what would happen if we changed the power of the engine by changes to the supercharger.

It is seldom economical or desirable to use a supercharged piston engine at full throttle at sea level, because the resulting power would overstress the engine and its cooling system. In the case of the Merlin, the power at sea level was initially limited to about 1,000 hp, and to obtain this power the throttle would only need to be partially opened. As an aircraft climbs to higher and higher altitudes, the atmospheric pressure decreases, and the density of the air inhaled by the engine diminishes. If nothing is done, the power of the engine would fall off proportionately. But by starting at sea level with the throttle partially closed, as the aircraft climbs the throttle can be gradually opened so as to maintain the power output of the engine. Eventually, an altitude is reached at which the throttle is fully open, and this is known as the "full-throttle height" of the engine.

The function of the supercharger is to force a heavier charge of air/fuel mixture into the engine's cylinders. The extent to which it does this is measured by the boost pressure. To give its 1,000 hp, the original Merlin required a boost pressure of between 6 and 9 lb/sq in. The engine was fitted with an automatic boost control which kept the boost pressure constant as the aircraft climbed. It did this by a servo system which automatically opened the throttle as the altitude increased. Thus, the engine automatically maintained its 1,000 hp up to the full-throttle height, which in 1939 was about 16,000 ft (4877 m).

There was another vital reason for keeping the boost pressure constant at a predetermined value, and this was the need to prevent the engine detonating. The ideal situation is that the charge of fuel and air should burn smoothly in the cylinders. If too much charge is forced in by too high a boost pressure from the supercharger, then detonation can begin and, instead of burning smoothly, the charge literally explodes, and causes shockwaves, like those at the nose of bullets, to bounce around inside the cylinders. These waves are of such intensity that serious mechanical damage can be caused to the cylinder head and pistons, which for lightness are made of aluminium, and thus can be relatively easily damaged.

The onset of detonation can be controlled by the octane value of the fuel, which in 1939 was limited to 87. Just before the Battle of Britain, small amounts of 100-octane fuel became available from the USA and this enabled us to open the throttle further on the Merlin and, in fact, to obtain nearly 2,000 hp without detonation. Thus, the 100-octane fuel made a crucial contribution to the performance of the Spitfire and Hurricane in that battle, as did the work of Lovesey, Rubbra, and their teams, which enabled the Merlin to withstand double its design power for short periods without mechanical failure.

To obtain the increased power, the pilot had to override the boost control which was normally limiting him to 1,000 hp. To do this, he had to pull a knob in the cockpit, and break the seal on it. So we always knew when he had done it! But in the Battle of Britain, 1,000 ft of extra altitude or 5 mph in speed could mean the difference between shooting down the enemy or being shot down by him, such was the equality between the performances of the Bf 109 and our fighters.

Thus, with the advent of 100-octane fuel, we were for the time being released from the nightmares of detonation. We could concentrate on improving the mechanical integrity of the Merlin to withstand higher power, which was Lovesey's job, and improving the performance of the supercharger so that the power could be increased and also maintained to higher and higher altitudes, which was my job.

Unfortunately, the results of the work of my team, which I have so far recounted, did not come into fruition in the RAF squadrons in time for the Battle of Britain. In that epic encounter all the Hurricanes and Spitfires were fitted with the original Merlin III, as designed by Royce. Moreover, all the engines that fought in the battle were made at Derby, because the great factories at Crewe, Glasgow and Manchester, which were subsequently to produce more than 100,000 Merlins, were not even built.

We did not discuss it, but I must say that I expected Derby to be flattened by the Luftwaffe in the first weeks of the war. Thank God, Hitler made one of his several crucial mistakes, and Derby was spared to equip the fighters of the RAF.

I still remember the relentless pressure exerted by Hs in those critical months, and the response he got from the workers in the factory, who willingly worked 18 hours a day, seven days a week to produce the engines. Hs would regularly tour all parts of the factory before some of us were even out of bed, and since everybody knew him, and he knew everybody, the effect on morale was great.

It was Hs' custom to hold a technical review with the senior engineers every Monday afternoon starting at 2.00 pm. On his right hand would sit Elliott as Chief Engineer, and on his left Swift as Chief Production Engineer. Directly opposite him would sit Lovesey, Rubbra and myself, and gathered around would be liaison engineers with the RAF to report troubles in service, material experts from the laboratories, HPS speaking for the Experimental Shop, and Dorey for the Installation and Flight Testing establishment at Hucknall airfield near Nottingham.

Hs was a great chairman. He had the happy knack of being able to carve away the undergrowth and immediately get to the nub of the question. He never allowed time to be wasted by individuals arguing together, because he knew his man, and would turn to the appropriate expert.

'Well, what have we got to do, so-and-so?'

He would accept 'I don't know yet', but woe betide anyone who tried to dissemble or cloak his manifold sins and wickednesses.

Once he had an answer, HPS would hold up his hands 'Give me the drawings, give me the drawings', and Swift would be put on notice that a modification was coming on production.

Of course, on occasions we were all nonplussed. Hs would look around. 'I don't know how you can sleep in your beds', he would say, 'Get your jackets off, and bring me the answer'.

The Merlin was a water-cooled engine, and we were always

troubled by minor leaks at the various joints between the engine and the radiator situated under the wing of the Spitfire. This was Dorey's province, and these leaks used to exasperate Hs, who would taunt Dorey by saying he had only to make the plumbing as good as his lavatory!

On one occasion in the early days of the war, someone in the RAF had filled a Merlin cooling system with water which had been fetched in carboys originally containing nitric acid, and which still had traces thereof. Even though the acid concentration must have been very small, the mixture played havoc with the aluminium cylinder blocks. The Aeronautical Inspection Directorate of the Air Ministry decided that, to avoid any possible contamination, there must in future be an official specification for the water used. This specification was the first item on Hs' Monday meeting, and the AID were there in force. Hs sat in his usual place with his head in his hands listening to the prolonged discussion on how to write the specification. Suddenly he looked up exasperated and said,

"I'll write your bloody specification for you. You have got to be able to drink it'.

These simple anecdotes, out of context as they are, now sound trite and elementary. But in the grim atmosphere of the war, they were just sufficiently humorous to give all enough lift to go away and get on with our jobs with zest and energy.

The initial work that I had done on the supercharger and its air intake appeared on production in 1940 in the form of the Merlin 45 for the Spitfire and the Merlin XX for the Hurricane, Mosquito and Lancaster. The effect was to increase the full-throttle altitude of the engine from 16,000 ft with the Merlin III to over 19,000 ft with the Merlin 45. I knew that this particular blower had now reached the limit of its development. Any further improvement would be much more difficult, and could give only a small gain, unlikely to justify a change to production. Where did we go from here?

At that very time, Lovesey and I were called to a meeting at the Air Ministry in London. We were told that Rex Pierson, Chief Designer at Vickers, had designed a capsule which fitted in the nose of the Wellington bomber and in which the pilot and bomb-aimer could sit. The idea was to pressurize this capsule, so that the aircraft could fly at very high altitudes in excess of 30,000 ft (9144 m), with the crew comfortably seated with an air pressure corresponding to 10,000 ft in the capsule. It was one of the first pressure cabins.

The standard engine for the Wellington was the aircooled Bristol Hercules sleeve-valve radial. To boost the power of the Hercules to get the Wellington above 30,000 ft, Bristol had decided to fit an exhaust-driven turbosupercharger, similar to those fitted by the Americans to their aircooled engines.

The high-altitude Wellington project was considered of sufficient importance to justify asking Rolls-Royce to provide an insurance policy by turbocharging a Merlin. This proposal was not as straightforward as it sounded. At Hucknall, under Ray Dorey and Harry Pearson, a great deal of work had been done on the Spitfire and Hurricane by taking the exhaust from the Merlin and ejecting it rearwards through very short exhaust pipes, where it acted as a means of jet propulsion equivalent to about 150 extra horsepower. With an exhaust-driven turbocharger we would lose that effect, and were loath to do so. I argued that, to obtain the necessary power, all we had to do was to raise the full-throttle height of the Merlin from 16,000 to 30,000 ft, and that to do this we needed two superchargers in series at the back of the engine, driven by the same gears that existed on the standard Merlin.

There was one obvious snag. Due to the high compression of the charge, its temperature would become very high, and the old bogey of detonation would rear its ugly head again. Also, the engine power formula indicated that the high charge temperature would actually reduce the power of the engine. The solution was obvious. We had a water-cooled engine, so we would add an extra water-cooled 'intercooler' after the two superchargers which would cool the charge to 100°C before it entered the cylinders. Calculations showed that in these ways we could double the power of the Merlin at 30,000 ft from 500 hp to 1,000 hp. Now the task was to determine the dimensions of the two superchargers.

At this point, a happy thought occurred to me. The Rolls-Royce Vulture engine, which had 24 cylinders and was much larger and heavier than the Merlin, gave, by virtue of its size and capacity, 1,000 hp at 30,000 ft. Since the power of an engine depends approximately on the amount of air and fuel it consumes, obviously the Vulture supercharger had the right capacity to supply the necessary air as the first stage of the proposed two-stage blower for the Merlin. No design effort on this component was necessary.

It was now that the advantage of the two independent ends of the supercharger test-rig paid off. On the one end we fitted the Vulture supercharger, and on the other the Merlin blower. A long sheet-metal pipe connected the outlet of the Vulture with the inlet of the Merlin, and thus we were able to run the two blowers in series, and measure their combined performance. The result was so good that no further calculation or testing was necessary, and we were able to go to Rubbra and start the Main Engine Design Office on the task of combining the two superchargers together as a single compact unit suitable for fitment on the rear of the Merlin.

There remained the design of the intercooler between the blowers and the induction pipe necessary to cool the air/fuel charge before it entered the cylinders. Here the Chief Engineer took a major part, and it was most impressive to stand with him and others at a drawing board while he sketched in the principle of the construction and mounting of this new component. In fact, to go with Elliott into the Main Design Office was a great treat for us all. He was like the Specialist in a hospital, examining each drawing as he passed, criticising points and adding deft touches to solve any design problem. It was all highly educational to me to follow in the wake of such a great designer. The trouble was that he did so infrequently, but spent the major part of his time in his office trying to get abreast of yesterday's problem.

I would add that he was the No 1 gentleman in Rolls-Royce, calm, serene and kind. The rest of us were roughnecks in comparison. I frequently travelled with him to visit the aircraft companies, and it was a pleasure to see him handle such tough and irate designers as Sydney Camm of Hawker Hurricane fame, and Roy Chadwick, the designer of the Lancaster bomber.

The first time I met Camm was with Elliott in the early days of 1940. Camm and his design office had been evacuated from the Hawker factory at Kingston to Claremont House, which Queen Victoria stayed at and loved. Camm occupied the drawing-room — I mean the drawing-room of a past age — which was still beautifully furnished and had a large, comforting fire going. Sydney greeted us in his usual way — which, I found later, was pure fun:

'What the hell are you lot doing here, wasting my time, telling me how to put your rotten engines into my beautiful aeroplanes!'

I shivered in my shoes, for this was *lèse majesté* indeed, talking to the Chief Engineer of Rolls-Royce in such a manner. Elliott, smiling, replied, 'What a splendid office to work in, Sydney. Such an elegant fireplace. So convenient for burning those mistakes in'.

Sydney grunted, and turned to me.

'Who is this chap. I've not seen him before'.

Elliott introduced me. Sydney looked squarely at me and said,

'I just want to get one thing clear with you, young Hooker. The only time I am wrong is when I am persuaded against my better judgement'.

Then he laughed, and we all sat down amicably to get on with the business of the day in the most constructive fashion.

To return to the intercooler, the internal matrix, through which the charge passed in one direction and the cooling water through in another, as it does in a motor-car radiator, posed a problem. There was no heat-exchanger matrix available in the country of high enough efficiency to do the job in the small space that was available. So we enlisted the help of the Engine Department of the Royal Aircraft Establishment.

Very soon, Farnborough's Dr Remfrey appeared in my office at Derby with a small sample of a matrix made in copper sheet, which tests had shown would do the job. I examined it. The thing that worried me was its mechanical strength.

'Oh, it's strong enough to jump on', said Remfrey.

Instinctively, I said 'Show me'. Equally instinctively, Remfrey put the small sample block on the floor and jumped on it. It went as flat as a pancake, to the howls of nervous merriment from the assembled company. Remfrey was very crestfallen, and, since it was the only sample in existence, feared the wrath of his superiors. I said, 'Never mind, tell them that clumsy idiot Hooker did it'.

In fact, the construction and efficiency of the matrix was excellent, and it was duly adopted for the intercooler. In a matter of months, a Merlin was made with the new design of the two-stage supercharger and intercooler. The test results fulfilled our highest hopes, and the engine worked beautifully on the test-bed first pop.

But the proof of the pudding was really in flying the engine. Although we could predict the power at 30,000 ft, we would only know the real answer in the air. In due course, two engines were installed in a Wellington and the first flight was made from Hucknall.

That day Hs sent for me. I went to his office and he asked 'What do you say the full-throttle height of the two-stage Merlin is?'

Nervously, I replied, 'I calculate it to be 30,000 ft, approximately'.

He passed me a piece of paper, and on it was written just 29,750. He said, 'I have just had that figure from Dorey taken on the first flight of the Wellington'. He never indulged in compliments, but was obviously delighted.

At the next Monday meeting, he referred to the new Mk 60 engine, and then said something that had never occurred to us, 'What would happen if we put this engine into a Spitfire?'

It was blindingly obvious that the Spitfire was the true home for the engine, and it had been left to Hs to suggest it. We all sat back aghast and silent.

Dorey said, 'I don't know, but we will damned soon find out. I will start work on putting one into the Spit immediately'.

This was a considerable task, because the engine was 9 inches longer than the standard Merlin, and thus the whole of the nose of the aircraft, with the engine mounting and controls, had to be redesigned. A new four-blade propeller was needed to convert the power into thrust. An extra radiator had to be provided under the wing to dissipate the heat in the water that cooled the charge (and this helped to balance the extra weight at the front). But the job was done in double-quick time, and in 1941 the first Spitfire with the Merlin 61 engine flew at Hucknall and soared to over 40,000 ft (over 12 km).

This was the prototype of the famous Spitfire IX. The new engine increased its fighting altitude by 10,000 ft, and added 70 mph to its top speed. The Spitfire IX was in the hands of the RAF just in time to counter the formidable Focke-Wulf 190, which owed its performance to an aircooled BMW engine, much heavier and larger than the Merlin. The swept volume of the German engine was 2,560 cu in (41.8 litres); our new two-stage Merlin beat it with 1,647 cu in (27.0 litres). Years later Air Marshal Sir Harry Broadhurst, who had been one of our great fighter pilots at this time, told me of his first operational flight in a Mk IX, and of the look of astonishment on a German pilot's face as he climbed up past him with much greater performance.

The new engine went into mass-production. Many thousands were made for Spitfires, P-51 Mustangs, Mosquitos and special Pathfinder Lancasters. Conceived for the Wellington bomber with a pressurized cabin — which never went into service — it became the principal fighter engine in the RAF. It had a major application in the outstanding North American P-51 Mustang fighter, which was the only aircraft that really challenged the supreme performance of the Spitfire.

After the War began, and after a major false start with the US Ford Motor Co, the Government placed a large contract for the manufacture of the Merlin engine with the Packard Motor Co, in Detroit. Full manufacturing details and drawings were sent to them from Derby. Ellor and Barrington were seconded to Packard to assist them in interpreting the English drawings, and to act as liaison engineers with the rest of us at Derby. They bore such a crushing load that Barrington died in the USA and Ellor soon after his return.

The departure of Ellor and Barrington in 1940 left a hole in the staff at Derby. Rubbra was appointed Chief Designer in Barrington's place, and Lovesey was promoted to Chief Experimental Engineer to replace Ellor. To my great satisfaction, I was invited by Lovesey to become his chief assistant, and moved into his office. Now my engineering education really began. His remit to me was: 'You look after the performance of the engine, and I will deal with the mechanical side'.

And so I had the opportunity of sitting in at many sessions with his staff. I learned the diagnostic way he examined the mechanical problems, and propounded the tests and solutions to overcome them. At the appropriate time, he would say to me,

'Come along, today we will go and see Rubbra and clean this job up'.

Then would follow a session with the main engine designers. At these I learned of the constant interplay between design and development as Lovesey, in his very skilful way, would illuminate the problems, and the equally skilful designers would sketch the modifications to the drawings in such a way as to cause the minimum disruption to production — and yet maintain the high standards set out in the Manuals of Design Standards which had accumulated since the days of Henry Royce. So I learned about designing from them, although I could never hope to become an accepted designer, because it takes 20 years of dedicated application to become that.

The word 'engineer' covers a variety of expertises and people of very varying backgrounds. In my experience, the *crème de la crème* of these are the designers and, if it be true that the status of engineers is too low in Britain, then the charge applies first and foremost to designers.

They are enthusiasts who seek after something more than wealth and power. They lead a tiring and exacting life, standing long hours at their boards drawing in two dimensions engine parts that they visualise in their minds in three dimensions. Not only must they create the drawings which can be explicitly interpreted into instructions, which can be made by the many manufacturing processes available in the shops, but they must liaise with the designers on each side to ensure that their parts will match exactly with those of their colleagues, and that the whole can be manufactured and assembled as an engine with convenient access for inspection of the vulnerable parts.

They are fed (often to the teeth) with information and advice from experts in specialized fields such as performance and gas dynamics, mechanical integrity and material properties, and they must work within the limits of stress imposed by the experts.

They are the 'keepers of the Trade', which embodies all the details of past experience so hardly learned. They are indeed an élite body, yet they are almost always quiet and modest, capable of defending their creation with lucid arguments. At the end of the day, they have the most satisfying and rewarding job of all. They can look at an engine and say, 'I created those parts, and they are exactly as I saw them in my mind when I took my pencil and began to draw on a blank sheet of paper, and they work!'

For myself, I frequently look at an engine and think, 'That is how I visualised it', but, however much one might have influenced the design and laid down the general arrangement, the men who created it were the designers. This does not mean that designers necessarily make the best Chief Engineers, although in the case of Royce this was so. An analogy might be that Yehudi Menuhin, with his superb interpretations, would not necessarily make the best conductor of the orchestra, with its many lesser, but still important, 'prima donnas'.

In my enthusiasm, I considered that Rolls-Royce designs were the *ne plus ultra,* until the Ford Motor Co in Britain was invited to manufacture the Merlin in the early days of the War. A number of Ford engineers arrived at Derby, and spent some months examining and familiarizing themselves with the drawings and manufacturing methods. One day their Chief Engineer appeared in Lovesey's office, which I was then sharing, and said, 'You know, we can't make the Merlin to these drawings'.

I replied loftily, 'I suppose that is because the drawing tolerances are too difficult for you, and you can't achieve the accuracy'.

'On the contrary', he replied, 'the tolerances are far too wide for us. We make motor cars far more accurately than this. Every part on our car engines has to be interchangeable with the same part on any other engine, and hence all parts have to be made with extreme accuracy, far closer than you use. That is the only way we can achieve mass production'.

Lovesey joined in, 'Well, what do you propose now?'

The reply was that Ford would have to redraw all of the Merlin drawings to their own standards, and this they did. It took a year or so, but was an enormous success, because, once the great Ford factory at Manchester started production, Merlins came out like shelling peas at a rate of 400 per week. And very good engines they were too, yet never have I seen mention of this massive contribution which the British Ford company made to the build-up of our air forces.

The demand for Merlins seemed insatiable. Starting as the 'hot rod' engine for the Spitfire and Hurricane, it rapidly found homes in other aircraft types, one of the most famous, of course, being the Lancaster bomber.

Roy Chadwick, the great designer of the Avro company, had originally designed the aircraft as a twin-engined bomber called the Manchester which had two 1,800 hp Rolls-Royce Vulture engines. For various reasons, the Manchester was very unsuccessful with two Vulture engines. In late 1940, therefore, in double-quick time, Chadwick redesigned the wings and installed four Merlin engines, rated at that time at 1,250 hp each. The result was the Lancaster, the supreme RAF bomber of the war. Over 7,000 were made and Air Chief Marshal 'Bertie' Harris described it as 'a shining sword in the hands of Bomber Command'.

Another Merlin aircraft was the versatile twin-engined Mosquito, designed by Bishop and Clarkson of de Havilland Aircraft. The airframe was made of wood, and thus the wood constructing industry was harnessed to the war effort. Although originally a bomber, the Mosquito had the performance of a fighter, and flew at high altitudes and speeds. It was thus almost invulnerable to anti-aircraft gunfire, and was very difficult to intercept. It was a most popular aircraft in the Royal Air Force.

A third, and perhaps the most outstanding, adaptation of the Merlin was to the North American Mustang fighter. This aircraft was originally fitted with an American Allison engine, but its performance at high altitude was so improved by the Merlin that this became its standard powerplant. Such was its efficiency that, despite having larger wings and three times the fuel capacity, it was faster than any Merlin-Spitfire at all altitudes. It was most successful in shooting down or 'tipping over' the V-1 flying bombs, when Hitler launched that devastating weapon against London and south-east England in the summer of 1944.

At the outbreak of war, the Merlin had lately been substituted for a less-powerful engine in the Armstrong Whitworth Whitley bomber. This machine had two engines and was slow and ponderous by later Lancaster and Mosquito standards. Nonetheless, it was at the time the only bomber that could reach Italy with a useful bombload, and was used by the Bomber Group commanded by Alec (later Air Chief Marshal Sir Alec) Coryton for that purpose. En route, it had to climb over the Alps, and at that speed and altitude the Merlin had to be used at maximum power, and the cooling was found to be inadequate. A number of engine failures occurred, and Coryton, who was an enthusiastic amateur engineer, waxed very wrathful with Rolls-Royce, as he thought that insufficient attention was being paid to his aircraft and the safety of his crews. He wrote to Hs inviting any of us to go on one of the raids and to see for ourselves what the problems were. Hs read the letter to us at one of his Monday afternoon meetings, and then surveyed us all.

'Are there any takers?', he demanded. There was no scramble, but Coryton certainly got a better service from us.

Throughout the war, the power of the Merlin was continuously increased by Lovesey and Rubbra from 1,000 hp to 2,000 hp. I have described earlier how its power at 30,000 ft was doubled from 500 hp to 1,000 hp by the two-stage supercharger and intercooler. At the maximum engine speed of 3,000 rpm the power developed in the cylinders was divided between the frictional horsepower required to rotate the engine, the power to drive the supercharger and the useful power at the propeller in the rough proportions of 20 per cent, 10 per cent and 70 per cent.

The maximum recommended cruising rpm for the engine was 2,650. In the early days, pilots tended to use this speed for all their long flights, even if they could get the aircraft speed and altitude they required at lower revs. By so doing, they used the engine at part-opened throttle, and wasted fuel. The frictional horsepower lost could be more than halved by reducing the speed from 3,000 to 2,000 (losses are proportional to the square of the rpm), and the power to drive the supercharger was also halved. Thus, the proportions at 2,000 rpm became 10 per cent, 5 per cent and a healthy 85 per cent. In other words, get the throttle wide open and reduce the revs to a minimum by coarsening the variable-pitch propeller and maximum range would be obtained. This caused me to enumerate the simple maxim, 'Use low revs and high boost' in cruising operations. The RAF printed thousands of large posters saying 'Reduce the revs and boost the boost, you'll have enough petrol to get home to roost'.

There was another engine control lever in the cockpit which adjusted the fuel/air mixture. It was labelled at one end of its travel, 'rich', and at the other end, 'weak'. The idea was that at take-off power surplus fuel (rich mixture) was fed to the engine to cool the charge and thus suppress detonation; at lower power the mixture strength could be reduced to the correct value, when it was called 'weak'.

Hs hated this control, and said, 'If you were going into battle, which would you select, rich or weak?' And, of course, pilots did, in fact, leave the control in rich or forgot to pull it back to weak, and many ran out of fuel as a consequence. So the mixture lever was deleted and the control was connected to the throttle in such a manner that the correct mixture strength was obtained automatically.

The formidable foe in the Battle of Britain was the Messerschmitt Bf 109 fighter powered by the Daimler-Benz engine. This engine had fuel injection direct into the cylinders, in contrast to the Merlin where the fuel was fed from the carburettor into the air upstream of the supercharger, and then the compressed mixture passed to the cylinders. The SU carburettor had normal float chambers, and the German pilots soon found that, if they had a Spitfire or a Hurricane on their tail, all they had to do was to put their nose down and dive. If the Spitfire followed, the negative-g would throw the fuel in the float chambers to the top; the engine would be starved, and would cut out. By the time that the power had restored itself, by the fuel returning to the bottom of the float chambers, the 109 would be safely out of range. Our pilots soon found that they could mitigate this unfortunate situation by quickly rolling inverted as they went into the dive, thus retaining positive-g. But they were very critical, and rightly so.

Lovesey set to work and eventually solved the problem with a redesign of the SU carburettor to what was known as the Diaphragm Carburettor. But this took some time, and in the meantime we were visited at Derby by Miss Shilling, who was a famous lady engineer from the Royal Aircraft Establishment.

She brought with her a small metal diaphragm with a hole in the middle, to be fitted into the float chamber. This stopped the fuel bouncing to the top, while the hole passed sufficient fuel to keep the engine running. It was a most simple idea, and remarkably effective. It will ever be known as 'Miss Shilling's orifice'.

Let me now add that the Germans paid a large penalty for their fuel injection. When the fuel is fed before the supercharger, as on the Merlin, it evaporates and cools the air by 25°C. This cooling enhances the performance of the supercharger, and increases the power of the engine, with a corresponding increase in aircraft speed, particularly at high altitude.

By the end of 1942, my own work on the Merlin, sadly for me, had to end. Rubbra and Lovesey, the mainstays of the development, carried on; my supercharger and performance team passed to Oscar Wilde, who picked up the load with great skill and determination.

When I look back, those first four years on the Merlin were the most satisfying, and, I think, the most important of my life, not only because the work had immediate relevance to the RAF in the war, but because they were my first steps down the road of becoming an engineer.

For me, the future was to lie with the Whittle jet engine, and the enormous developments in aviation that stemmed thereafter.

A. G. Elliott (E)

A. C. Lovesey (Lov)

R. N. Dorey (Dor)

A. A. Rubbra (Rbr)

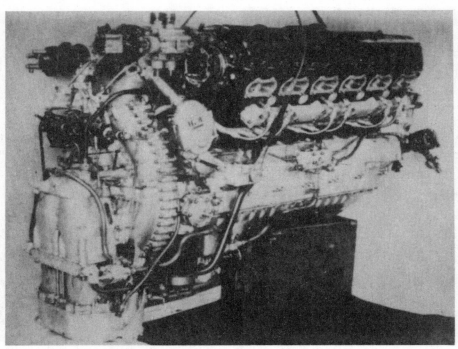

Merlin 45 engine for Spitfire V

Merlin 61 engine for Spitfire IX

Visit to Hawker Aircraft, Kingston-on-Thames, April 1944. This photograph was taken at the Guest House "Coombe Martin", Kingston Hill, by Sydney Camm (see photo at right). The visit, led by Hs, was to persuade Hawker to design a jet fighter, using the Nene engine.
Left to Right: R. L. Lickley, Hawker designer, A. N. Spriggs, Hawker Works Manager, Hs (Later Lord Hives) Rolls-Royce, Roy Chaplin, Hawker Designer, S.G.H., from Barnoldswick, W. Lappin, Rolls-Royce representative, J. E. Ellor, Rolls-Royce Chief Experimental Engineer, R. N. Dorey, Manager Rolls-Royce Hucknall, and P.W.S. ('George') Bulman, Hawker pre-war test-pilot and director.

Dr. E. A. Watson

Dr. J. S. Clarke

John Morley

Lionel Haworth

Chapter 3
Jets

I first met Frank Whittle in January 1940. At that time he was located with a small team of engineers at an old disused foundry at Lutterworth, near Rugby. His firm was called Power Jets, and the work he was doing was Top Secret. I was taken to see his first jet engine by Hayne Constant who, at that time, was the Director of the Engine Research Department of the Royal Aircraft Establishment at Farnborough. Constant had specialized in both centrifugal and axial compressors, and had frequently visited Derby to discuss with me the development of the Merlin supercharger. There was snow on the ground when he took me from Derby to Lutterworth, and I saw for the first time the strange jet engine roaring on its test bed. Compared to the sophisticated design and manufacture of Rolls-Royce, it looked a very crude and outlandish piece of apparatus. Yet, standing near to it while it was running, I felt conscious that I was in the presence of great power. Whether it was useful power or not, I had no idea.

I cannot claim that I was an immediate convert to the jet engine. That took some months, while I did my own analysis of the gas-turbine engine and, more importantly, came under the spell of Frank Whittle's genius and super technical knowledge.

Whittle joined the RAF in 1923 as a 'boy entrant' and within three years his great ability got him to the new RAF College at Cranwell from which he was commissioned as a Pilot Officer. Even in those early days he had come to realise that the monopoly of the cumbersome piston engine in aircraft might be ended, and that far greater powers than could possibly be produced by such engines would be an enormous advantage in aviation. A lighter and faster-running engine was essential, and so his thoughts turned to the internal-combustion gas turbine. Whilst still a cadet he wrote a thesis on this subject, but this was so far ahead of contemporary practice on both engines and airframes that it was regarded as boyish 'science fiction'.

However, the powers that be in the RAF were sufficiently impressed to send him to Cambridge to take a degree in Mechanical Engineering. It was while at Cambridge that he began seriously to design his first jet engine, which combined two very important steps forward. The first was the elimination of the reciprocating motion of the piston engine, which only produces power on one of its four strokes. The other three are utilised for sucking in the charge, compressing it, and exhausting the burnt gases. I once facetiously remarked that the four-stroke engine has one stroke for producing power and three for wearing the engine out! By contrast, the gas-turbine engine produces power continuously by the simple process of compressing air, burning the fuel in the combustion chambers and then exhausting through the turbine which supplies the power to drive the compressor. After this turbine, the gas still has considerable pressure and temperature left, and thus the simple gas-turbine acts rather like a boiler. A boiler produces hot steam under pressure, and the gas-turbine hot gas under pressure.

The second feature, of which Whittle was indisputably the inventor, was to use this pressurized hot gas in the form of a simple jet, the thrust of which would propel an aircraft. Thus, in one stroke, he eliminated both the propeller and the heavy gearing required to drive it. In doing so he swept away the factor which imposed a barrier to further advance in aircraft speed. Unlike the piston/propeller system the jet engine appeared able to propel an aircraft at any speed, and in fact the faster the better.

The great impact that these two steps were to have on aviation was not immediately obvious. Whittle knew, because he had an unrivalled grasp of the fundamentals of thermodynamics and aerodynamics, and he never did anything until he had given it the deepest and most logical consideration. As I came to understand his work, I realised that he had laid down the performance of jet engines with the precision of Newton, a feat whose magnitude he never appeared to appreciate. For the preceding 30 years the performance of piston engines in flight was only known to a very rough approximation based on inaccurate empirical formulae, yet Whittle predicted what a jet engine would do before he had ever made one. Today, 40 years later, his formulae are used unchanged. They are of such precision that it is more accurate to calculate the performance of jet engines, including the most modern fan engines, than it is to attempt to measure it either in flight or in the astronomically costly test plants which attempt to simulate flight conditions on the ground. And this is true from take-off to the speed of Concorde, and beyond. Indeed, the pen really is mightier than the spanner!

Whittle led the world in his thinking, so naturally he was subjected to the full blast of criticism from the sceptics and the ill-informed. Gas-turbines were not new, of course, and for years A. A. Griffith and Constant had been considering them at the RAE. But they aimed to retain the propeller and merely to replace the piston engine by the gas-turbine as the power generator. In addition, Griffith was obsessed by the potential higher efficiency of the axial-flow compressor, as opposed to the simple centrifugal compressor which Whittle proposed to use. Constant also favoured the axial, but he had a more open mind. Sadly, however, these two key men, as principal advisers to the Air Ministry on engine matters, were no help to Whittle, and prevented him from getting financial aid from the Government to develop his engine until the late 1930s, after his titanic struggle had at last got the project going.

Previous gas-turbines, which had all been land-based powerplants, had failed or been ineffective because of lack of knowledge about axial compressors, and especially, combustion chambers. Metals capable of maintaining their strength at the high temperatures in the engine were also in their infancy, although nickel alloy steels were pointing the way forward.

Whittle was well aware of the potential advantages of the axial compressor, but with his infallible clear insight he chose a centrifugal compressor for his engine, on the basis that there was years of experience with them as superchargers on piston engines. They were also robust and strong, and relatively easy to manufacture. But a compressor of the size and performance he required had never been designed, so he set about this task himself and made a first-class job of it. He had had no experience, nor was there any he could draw from, so he was forced back to his own deep scientific understanding. He aimed at about 4:1 compression ratio, and 80 per cent efficiency, and incorporated in his design new and important features at the entry to the compressor and the diffuser. When, some years later, I was destined to take over from him and continue his work, I was never able to improve his compressor — I made it worse on one occasion, but never better.

His first jet engine was made for him for next to nothing by the British Thomson Houston Co, at Rugby. Without their generous help he would never have got started, and we all owe a great debt of gratitude to the Directors and Chief Engineer of that great company, who had such faith in this young Air Force officer and his futuristic ideas.

When I first met him, his first engine was running, and a second was being prepared for flight in May 1941. He had meagre facilities, a very small staff, and the minimum of financial assistance from the Department of Scientific Research of the Government. They had, however, instructed George Carter, Chief Designer of the Gloster Aircraft Co, to design and make the E.28/39 aircraft, as a suitable vehicle for the first flight of this new propulsion unit.

Whittle was up to his ears with trouble with the combustion chambers, and with the reliability of the turbine blades. Both of these matters were outside my field, so we fell to discussing centrifugal compressors, about which subject I mistakenly thought that I was one of the world's experts. But I soon realised that I was talking with my master.

There was no test plant in the country powerful enough to run his compressor independently, and I discovered that Whittle had never seen a real test result on a centrifugal compressor. Accordingly, I took to him the latest and best results from tests on the Merlin blower, which he received with great joy, and began to analyse in his masterly fashion. And so, through the spring and summer of 1940 I visited him at Lutterworth, and saw his engine improving in reliability and performance to the stage where quite long runs could be made at 800 lb thrust.

The significance of thrust as opposed to horsepower was not immediately obvious. Thrust is a force, and it only becomes power when the engine is moving with the aircraft. We at Rolls-Royce were used to thinking in horsepower, and it must be admitted that 800 lb thrust does not sound very impressive compared with 1,000 hp.

One day in August 1940 I asked Hs if he would come down to Lutterworth to see this new engine. I described it to him and he said, 'What does it do?' I replied, 'It is giving 800 lb of thrust'. Hs was not impressed, and said, 'That doesn't sound very much. It would not pull the skin off a rice pudding, would it?'

But I was ready for this, and had done the sum. I said, 'Do you know how much thrust the Merlin gives in a Spitfire flying at 300 mph?' Hs shook his head, 'No, how much?'

'With its present propeller, which is only about 70 per cent efficient, it gives approximately 840 lb', I replied.

Hs leaned back in his chair, and reached back to the push-button on the wall behind him. His secretary came in.

'I am going with Hooker to Lutterworth on Sunday', he told her, and thus it was that he made that fateful trip, while the Battle of Britain was raging in the skies over southern England. This meeting was to transform the speed at which the jet engine was developed, and was destined ultimately to put Rolls-Royce into a commanding lead in the field of aviation gas turbines.

Whittle personally conducted Hs around the plant at Lutterworth and explained to him his progress and ambitions. At the end of the tour Hs turned to him and said,

'I don't see many engines. What is holding you up?'

Whittle explained the difficulties he had in getting certain components made, whereupon Hs said in his typical broadminded way, 'Send us the drawings to Derby, and we will make them for you'. He said nothing about payment.

And so it came to pass that the Derby Experimental Shop began making turbine blades, gearcases and other components for Whittle's programme. In the following months Hs asked me and my colleague Lionel Haworth, from the Design Department at Derby, to keep in touch with the progress at Lutterworth.

On 15 May 1941 Whittle's W.1 engine flew in the Gloster E.28 aircraft, and the flight trials were a roaring success, as well as a source of amazement to those privileged to see them. The strange whistling roar of the engine, and the absence of the propeller or any other obvious means of propulsion, caused a great deal of speculation amongst the uninitiated onlookers. Was the aircraft pushed by the jet or sucked along by the intake? was the question on the lips of the uninitiated. Many thought it was was sucked along 'like a bloody great vacuum cleaner' as one RAF man was heard to say.

When I began to lecture on the new jet engines after the war, this question continually arose. To demonstrate, I used to take with me a blown up balloon, and, at the appropriate time, used to release it when it would be blown into the audience by the escaping air jet.

On one occasion I forgot to blow it up, and at the last moment nipped down to the men's room to do so. I went into one of the cubicles, and was blowing it up when it burst with a loud bang.

An amazed voice from a nearby cubicle called out 'Are you all right in there?' The mind boggled.

Meanwhile, Whittle had been busy designing and making his W.2 engine which, with 1,600 lb of thrust, was to be twice as powerful, and was to be fitted to the first operational jet fighter built by Gloster Aircraft as the F.9/40, afterwards named the Meteor. He ran into new and unexpected troubles with the W.2, in that the compressor surged before the full power was developed. He was unable to get more than about 1,000 lb thrust before the surging set in, and the throttle had to be closed.

Surging is caused by a sudden breakdown in the pressure developed by the compressor, in which case the airflow ceases to pass into the combustion chamber, but reverses and flows backwards through the impeller. Once the pressure in the chamber has been lost in this way, the compressor reasserts itself and the flow reverses itself again back to normality, whereupon the cycle repeats itself.

To see this happen on the engine was quite horrifying. As the throttle was opened the engine would accelerate quite normally until suddenly there would be an enormous bang, and flames would come from out of the intake. The engine and all the instruments would give a large jerk; then the bang would repeat itself while the temperature would rise rapidly, and the throttle would have to be closed to prevent the engine destroying itself.

The phenomenon of surging was well known in compressors, but there was no known means of predicting the conditions of airflow and pressure under which it would occur. The surge line on the graphical plot of performance, to the left of which the compressor behaved in this unstable way, had to be determined by testing the compressor independently, as we had done on the Merlin supercharger rig. But there was no test rig in Britain with sufficient power to test Whittle's compressor, and so he was working totally in the dark.

With Oscar Wilde, I proposed to him that we would build a test rig at Derby consisting of a 2,000 hp Rolls-Royce Vulture piston engine, driving through a 6:1 step-up gear, thus increasing the speed from 3,000 on the Vulture to the 18,000 rpm required by the W.2 compressor. This step-up gear was simply made by putting two Merlin propeller reduction gears in series and driving them backwards. Since each gear had a ratio of 0.42:1, when used in reverse it stepped the revolutions up by the inverse, that is by almost 2.5:1. Thus, two such gears gave more than 6:1 increase in rpm. In this way, we were able to measure the full performance of Whittle's compressor, and I remember noting with envy and admiration that it had an efficiency of 79 per cent, within 1 per cent of Whittle's theoretical figure.

This rig made its contribution to the problem of surging on the W.2, which Whittle was gradually solving by cut and try methods. Its real value came in 1943 when Rolls-Royce had taken over the development of the jet engine at Barnoldswick in Yorkshire, and we were busy uprating it to 2,000 lb thrust in the Derwent I engine. But that story comes later.

The W.2 was designed for the Gloster F.9/40 Meteor fighter, which was ordered by the Air Ministry in September 1940. Coincidentally, therefore, arrangements had to be made for the series production of the engine, for which Whittle's facilities were totally inadequate. The Ministry of Aircraft Production got the Rover Car Co to undertake this task, with Whittle retaining design and technical control of the engine. The only changes that Rover were authorised to make were to be minor ones in order to ease any production problems. Whittle never liked the details of this arrangement, nor did he think (unfairly in my opinion) that the Rover engineering team was good enough to produce his new baby.

The main Rover facilities were fully stretched in producing and repairing Bristol aircooled piston aero engines, and so they had to find and equip another site for the jet work. They chose Bankfield Shed, a disused cotton mill at Barnoldswick on the borders of Yorkshire and Lancashire, midway between Clitheroe and Skipton. They turned this into a jet factory under their Production Engineer, Olaf Poppe, and housed their jet engineering team under their Chief Engineer, Maurice Wilkes, at Waterloo Mill in Clitheroe. As would be expected from their terms of reference, the facilities at Waterloo Mill were very meagre, and those at Barnoldswick were laid out to produce about 20 engines per month. Clearly the authorities were still uncertain about the importance of Whittle's engine!

Through their close connections on motor cars, Rover had sought the help of Joseph Lucas Ltd to produce the sheet-metal combustion chambers and jetpipes. Lucas laid down their facilities at nearby Burnley, under the management of John Morley.

Because of the problems Whittle was having with the W.2, Rover waited long months for the definitive drawings to arrive in order that full production might begin. As time wore on, they decided to ignore their terms of reference, and began taking a hand in the development of the engine themselves at Waterloo Mill. This further strained the relations with Frank Whittle. Perhaps this was understandable, as he saw the control of his brainchild slipping from his grasp.

I have often heard it said — indeed, it was the current view in many influential circles — that Frank Whittle was an awkward and difficult man to deal with. This I absolutely deny. In the more than 40 years that I have known him, we have never had a disagreement. Although Rolls-Royce were destined to take his engine away from him, I, personally, have never had anything but encouragement and generous help from him.

Naturally, after the great struggle and frustrations he had in getting his ideas and engine accepted, he resented the criticisms of those who were now climbing on to his bandwagon. There were plenty of such people, and plenty of criticism when his W.2 ran into such difficulties. Unhappily, he included Rover and Lucas among his *bêtes noires,* though their one objective was to help. Of course, it must be admitted they were babes in arms so far as the science and technology of his revolutionary engine were concerned.

Thus it was that, in early 1942, S. B. Wilkes, Rover's Chairman, appealed to Hs for guidance and help in dealing with this seemingly wayward genius. Rover and Rolls-Royce had always been close friends — according to the advertisements, Rover made one of the finest cars in the world, and Rolls-Royce made *the* finest car. Hs called me to his office, where I met Mr Wilkes, and said,

'Hooker, here, seems to get on very well with Whittle, and knows all about his jet engine. Why don't you invite him to visit Clitheroe to talk to Maurice. He can act as a visiting consultant, although I don't want him to leave his work here on the Merlin'.

And so, I made a number of trips to Waterloo Mill and to Clitheroe. The first objective was to examine the changes that Rover were proposing, and, hopefully, to reject those that were bad, and to persuade Frank to accept those that were good. I found that Rover, in collaboration with Lucas, had made major changes to the fuel system and to the combustion system.

Just before the War, a young man called Iffield had come from Australia to Lucas with the design of a compact high-performance pump of infinitely variable capacity. The device could be run either as a pump or as a motor, and Iffield's original idea was that it would be used as an infinitely variable transmission for a motor car. The engine would drive one working as a pump which would transmit high-pressure oil to a second one at the back axle working as a motor to drive the car. Since the capacity of both pump and the motor could be varied, a highly efficient infinitely variable drive would thus result.

Dr E. A. Watson, the Technical Director of Lucas, realised that Iffield had the ideal fuel pump for Whittle's jet engine, which demanded a variable amount of fuel depending upon the altitude and speed of flight. The pump had an inbuilt servo system, which controlled the stroke of the plungers and thereby the capacity of the pump; thus the control of the fuel flow could be automatic. The system could also be utilised to govern the maximum speed of the jet engine, preventing it from overspeeding and being wrecked.

Naturally, the pump had mechanical problems due to the heavy duty it had to operate at on the engine. One of the early ones was that the balls in the bearing used to crack and split. Herriot, who had past experience in such matters, claimed that the cracks were there before the pump was run, and were due to a manufacturing defect and faulty inspection. Then he added, 'What can you expect when you have young girls handling these balls?' At the meeting to discuss this problem, Elliott, always the soul of propriety, convulsed us by saying in his quiet way: 'What are you suggesting, Mr Herriot. That we should employ married women for this work?'

Watson was a great engineer. He was modest, versatile and extremely sound in his thinking. His breadth of experience and inventions ranged fom miner's safety lamps through ignition systems on motor cars, to the control of gun turrets on tanks. His influence on the progress of the jet engine was considerable. With the enthusiastic encouragement of Oliver Lucas and later of Sir Bernard Waring, he brought to bear the great facilities and expertise of Lucas upon the problems of the complicated fuel system, the atomization of the fuel necessary for good combustion, and the mechanics and thermodynamics of the combustion chambers, which were still proving such a headache to Whittle.

The design of the combustion chamber to give smooth and efficient fuel burning was a 'black art'. There was no theoretical basis to guide the designer, nor any known stable flow pattern for the air. Dr Watson, therefore, decided to employ an expert on combustion, Dr Stanley Clarke, from the Birmingham Gas Company, and to provide him with facilities for experimental work at Burnley. Thus Clarke began his outstanding contribution to the combustion chambers of gas-turbine engines, and the basic designs he laid down were copied all over the world, starting with the United States and, later, the Soviet Union.

The first problem was to obtain an adequate supply of compressed air so that the chambers could be tested independently from the engine. Whittle's engine had ten separate combustion chambers, so it was possible to experiment on a test rig with a single chamber. In the initial stages the compressed air was supplied by a Merlin blower provided by Rolls-Royce at my instigation. This was installed in Clarke's laboratory at Burnley, and, driven by an electric motor, it was able to simulate in a single chamber the engine running conditions. From then on progress was rapid. Clarke soon had stable combustion systems, which were adopted on all Whittle jet engines from 1943 onwards.

Watson, Iffield and Clarke were a remarkable trio — Watson inventive and sage, Iffield also a brilliant inventor, but needing Watson's restraining hand, and Clarke a great enthusiast who drove himself and his team, by practical intuition, to great success. It was the greatest pleasure and privilege to have worked with all three.

The W.2 turbojet ran at 17,000 rpm, and Whittle was anxious to keep the shaft between the compressor and the turbine as short as possible to avoid whirling. Any shaft will whirl or vibrate like a violin string when its rpm is equal to its natural frequency, and he foresaw that this would be a problem on fast-running jet engines. As a consequence, there was insufficient length between the compressor and the turbine to accommodate the combustion chambers, so that Whittle was compelled to go to the reverse-flow arrangement. The air from the compressor is led rearwards past the turbine, and then has its direction of motion reversed so that it returns via the combustion chambers to the turbine.

A much better arrangement was that adopted by Major Frank Halford and his colleague Eric Moult on the first de Havilland turbojet known as the H.1 and later as the Goblin. Halford had been let into the secret of the jet engine at an early stage, and with Moult, under the auspices of the de Havilland Engine Company, had designed and made their own engine. Though the same as Whittle's in principle, employing a centrifugal compressor driven by a single-stage turbine, it differed in that it had a longer shaft of very large diameter, which again avoided the whirling problem. Thus they had sufficient length to use the 'straight through' type of combustion chamber, in which the air passes from the compressor directly through the chamber to the turbine.

Maurice Wilkes had seen this engine, and was impressed by its general arrangement. He wished to redesign the W.2 engine to this format. Whittle, who had given every help and encouragement to the de Havilland team, was infuriated by Wilkes' proposal. He felt, rightly, that there was no time to make such a major change, with the production of the Meteor airframe imminent, and with the knowledge that his reverse-flow combustion chamber had worked very satisfactorily on the W.1 engine in the Gloster E.28 aircraft flight trials. Nonetheless, Wilkes persisted. His Project Designer, Adrian Lombard, of whom we shall hear a great deal more later, produced the modified design drawings of the straight-through engine, and one or two engines were made ready for test by the end of 1942.

This was the unhappy state of affairs I found in mid-1942. At Barnoldswick, Clitheroe and Burnley, Rover had ample facilities for making jet engines. Ignoring the terms of reference agreed with Whittle, they had started down the road of a major redesign of his W.2 engine, whilst complaining bitterly that the original W.2 did not work, and of the consequential lack of definitive drawings to enable them to produce it in quantity. At Lutterworth, with its small Power Jets team and meagre capability, Frank Whittle was wasting his invaluable nervous energy fulminating at what he thought was the arrogance, ignorance and bad faith of the Rover Company, while facing the formidable technical problems that the W.2 was presenting. In retrospect, it is appalling that the Ministry should have allowed such a situation to arise.

I reported to Hs, and said there was no way I could see of getting the two parties on amicable terms, and that the situation was deteriorating week by week. One day in November 1942 Hs called me to his office and said,

'You and I are going to Clitheroe today. We are going to have dinner with S. B. Wilkes, so please be ready to leave at 4.00 pm.

There were only three of us at the five-bob (25p) dinner in that very comfortable old pub, the Swan and Royal in Clitheroe High Street. After dinner Hs turned abruptly to Wilkes and said with a twinkle in his eye,

'Why are you playing around with this jet engine? It's not in your line of business, you grub about on the ground, and I hear from Hooker that things are going from bad to worse with Whittle'.

They were great friends, of course, and Wilkes, smilingly ignoring the jibe, replied,

'We can't get on with the fellow at all, and I would like to be shot of the whole business'.

Hs then said,

'I'll tell you what I will do. You give us this jet job, and I will give you our tank engine factory at Nottingham'.

In as short a time as that the deal was done. The factory at Nottingham was producing tank engines based on an unsupercharged modified Merlin. Rover took it over and produced these engines, which like the jet fighter were named Meteor, for many years. There was no talk of money, and no talk of getting Government agreement to the arrangement. I suspect that Hs had already done that, but I never knew or cared. When two such big men meet together, decisions of this magnitude can be made on the spot.

The next day we made a tour of Waterloo Mill and Barnoldswick. On the way back to Derby Hs told me that he wanted me to take over as Chief Engineer of the jet programme, and to gather some staff together forthwith. He also said that he did not wish me to give up my work at Derby. But I argued that I could not do both jobs, that I had a very competent replacement in Oscar Wilde at Derby, and that the jet engine, in whose future I had come to have great faith, demanded all of my attention at that critical time. Reluctantly he agreed, and then added the most important remark of all,

'That place Waterloo Mill is totally inadequate. We will transfer all the experimental work to Barnoldswick, stop talking about production there, and make it into an experimental and development centre only'.

This decision — which surely ought to have been taken at national level much earlier — changed the whole tempo of the development of the jet engine. Instead of small teams working in holes in the corner, in one stroke nearly 2,000 men and women, and massive manufacturing facilities, were focussed on the task of getting the W.2 engine mechanically reliable and ready for RAF service. The knowledge that Rolls-Royce had taken over, and the personal pressure that Hs was able to apply to all the ancillary suppliers, galvanised everybody into top gear. And, I am glad to say, Frank Whittle was delighted. From then on, he generously gave us every possible assistance.

I felt I owed it to him to have a serious talk. At the earliest opportunity I invited him to Barnoldswick (which I do not believe until that time he had ever visited!). I said to him,

'Frank, you must realise that now that Rolls-Royce have taken over and intend to put their full weight behind your engine, the control of the engine must necessarily pass to us. With the facilities now at our disposal, it is no use you trying to compete. On the contrary, you must join with us, and give us the benefit of your talents and experience. We will march forward together, and I will keep you fully informed and I hope that you will look to me as your man, only too anxious to have direction and advice from you'.

Though this moment must have been a crucial turning-point in his life, he readily agreed. In effect, he said that he would leave the final clearing up of the W.2 to us, while he moved on to improving the breed by subsequent marks of the engine. And that is what happened. He went on to design the W.2/500 and W.2/700 engines, with their elegant and efficient compressor and diffuser arrangements, which we adopted at the earliest opportunity and made standard features on the Nene and Derwent engines.

Frank rounded off his visit by addressing the complete team at Barnoldswick. At this time the jet engine was highly secret. The general public had never heard of Frank Whittle (the first brief disclosure of Allied work in this field was made in January 1944), but I doubt if anyone at Barnoldswick was in ignorance of him. To everyone he was the great man behind it all; but I was almost the only member of the team who knew him. His presence amongst us caused great joy and enthusiasm, which was heightened by his personality and his ability to captivate a large audience.

Although the official takeover by Rolls-Royce was scheduled for 1 April 1943, we did, in fact, move into full control on January 1st. The management and senior engineers in the factory were old Rover employees, and would be required to staff the swopped tank engine factory at Nottingham. They were all given the option either to continue on the jet engine with Rolls-Royce, or stay with Rover. Most opted to go, but, of those who stayed on, by far the most important were Adrian Lombard, John Herriot and Denis Drew.

John Herriot was not strictly a Rover employee. He belonged to the AID (Aeronautical Inspection Directorate) of the Air Ministry, concerned with the maintenance of manufacturing quality in factories producing engines for the RAF. He had had great experience in the development of engines at both the Bristol and Derby factories, and was well known for the energy and determination with which he carried out his often controversial function. He had been allocated to Rover by the AID, and S. B. Wilkes had asked him to take a special interest in the production of the W.2 engine.

Herriot had been appalled by the bickering going on in these crucial mid-war years, not only between Whittle and Rover, but also between Maurice Wilkes at Waterloo Mill and Olaf Poppe at Barnoldswick. Wilkes was responsible for engineering and Poppe for production, and the latter was always complaining about the lack of a firm specification for the engine.

Although Whittle was still struggling to get the design thrust of 1,600 lb, the W.2 would run reasonably at 1,250-1,400 lb. Herriot was anxious to get on with the mechanical development by running the engine for long periods at whatever thrust it gave, and thus to establish the mechanical integrity of the components — the Henry Royce method. In contrast, Poppe had made a number of engines, mostly with detail differences in specification, and these had been languishing at Barnoldswick doing nothing. Herriot and his assistant, Denning, prepared official schedules for testing the engine for 25 hours, 50 hours and 100 hours, and persuaded Poppe to build engines for such tests. He knew the emphasis had to get away from paper towards the new smell of kerosene.

There were four test-beds at Barnoldswick and, in effect, Herriot and Denning took over the control of this important facility in the latter half of 1942. The result seemed miraculous as 25-hour and 50-hour tests were reeled off on a number of engines, first at 1,250 lb and then at 1,450 lb. The total running hours behind the W.2B/23, as the engine was known at Barnoldswick, soared to unheard-of figures. Running hours are a certain measure of an engine's progress to reliability, and although these early hours were done at a reduced thrust, the normal mechanical problems began to show themselves.

When we arrived on the scene in January 1943, Herriot was already well on the way to solving a number of these, and it was a great relief and comfort to me when he decided to stay on and we made him Chief Test Engineer. He was a great organiser, and although he was the first to admit that the technicalities of the engine were beyond him, he often had flashes of insight, born from his past experience with piston engines, which were invaluable. He remained my right-hand man throughout the period at Barnoldswick.

Adrian Lombard (Lom) was a different kettle of fish. He was one of those rare phenomena, a natural-born designer and engineer. He had been trained as a motor-car designer, first at Morris and then at Rover, and although he had had no formal technical or scientific training, he could quickly grasp any theoretical concept concerned with the aerodynamics or the thermodynamics of the engine. And he was a superb designer, ultimately to become the brilliant Chief Engineer and Technical Director of the whole of Rolls-Royce until his untimely death in the mid-1960s.

Denis Drew was a huge man, who originally came from Lucas. He was basically an electrical engineer, but had joined Maurice Wilkes at Waterloo Mill and had taken a wide interest in the problems of the new engine. He was interested in the vibration failures, because the measurement of high-frequency vibrations could most effectively be made by electrical methods using straingauges, a technique which was then in its infancy, but absolutely essential for the development of gas-turbine engines. One could not give him the wrong job, and he was an invaluable member of the development team. We placed under his control the Test Bed Equipment Department which was run by a man called Biker. Equipment for the beds and rigs does not sound very exciting, but it was all new stuff, very different from that required for testing piston engines, and much new thought had to be put into it. The testing equipment is often the weak link in the development process, but Drew and Biker never let us down, and always the equipment was there ahead of the engine.

The main workforce were mostly local people and stayed *en bloc*. We were lucky that Rover had had time to train many of them in their various expertises, particularly the young girls who handled their machine tools with great skill. Many of them lived nearby in a hostel, inevitably called Virgin Villa, and provided the full measure of sweetness and light in the few hours of recreation that were available, because ten hours a day and seven days a week was the normal ration of work. They learned more than their mothers could teach them, and there were no disasters that I ever heard of.

Barnoldswick was a nondescript little town of about 1,000 to 2,000 people. It had suffered from unemployment during the slump of the early 30s, as evidenced by the various cotton mills there were around ready to be taken over for war work. It was situated on the banks of the Leeds-Liverpool canal, between Clitheroe and Skipton. One had to turn off every road to get to Barnoldswick, and it was overlooked by the forbidding brow of Pendle Hill. As the saying went — if you can see Pendle it will soon be raining; if you can't see it, it already is.

To the north and east was the glorious countryside of the Yorkshire Dales and the Trough of Bowland; happy indeed was the day when one could beg, borrow or steal enough petrol for a trip to those beautiful open vales with the tumbling river by the side of the road. It was a part of England where the War never seemed to penetrate, apart from the drain on young manpower for the services. They never heard an air-raid warning blown in anger, and there was no shortage of homegrown food from the local farms — eggs, meat and fish.

We put the workforce and the big manufacturing shops under the command of Horace Percival Smith at Derby, and HPS sent up his right-hand man, Les Buckler, as the manager. Les could operate every machine himself, and had had years of experience as HPS's second-in-command in the Experimental Shop at Derby — a hard and exemplary training if ever there was one. Les Buckler brought with him Les Say to handle the Engine Fitting Shop, Harry Simons to supervise the Inspection Department, and Joe Guest to progress the work through the shops and from Lucas at Burnley.

These men and other assistants from Derby revolutionized the output. Until this time, turbine blades had always been in short supply, and the lack of them was a continuous hold-up in the building of engines for test. Add to this the fact that the blades failed on nearly every test, and it was obvious that the situation needed drastic treatment. Buckler appealed to me, 'Can't you standardize on one type of blade? I am making them in all sorts of material — Hastelloy B, Stayblade, Rex 748, Nimonic 80. I am making them from bars, I am making them from rough forgings, and I even have some forged to size to cope with. If you can cut down on the Heinz varieties, then I can let you have a lot more blades'.

I consulted with the Chief Metallurgist, Harry Gresham, and we agreed that we would standardize on blades made from rough forgings in Nimonic 80. This was a nickel alloy with 80 per cent nickel in its composition and was made by Henry Wiggin at Birmingham — a subsidiary of the Mond Nickel Co. By rough forgings was meant material that had been roughly forged to shape, but still required to be machined all over. It was essential to machine the oxidised skin off the blade, because of intergranular penetration, which was an invisible penetration of the oxide into the surface grains of the material forming little cracks which rapidly extended and failed the blade on engine test.

Lo and Behold, not only did this standardization give us more blades, but it gave us more reliable blades. In fact, we never changed from Nimonic 80 rough forgings for the next decade. Released from the restraints of variety, Buckler set up a line of machines across the shop, each manned by a girl, and each doing its own particular operation, with the result that within weeks there was never a shortage of turbine blades again. This truly remarkable piece of work transformed the building and testing of engines, and left poor old Frank, who for years had lived hand to mouth, green with envy.

Maurice Wilkes and the greater part of his Rover engineering team, naturally, stayed with their parent company, so it was necessary to reconstruct the team with people from Derby. I was given more or less *carte blanche* to choose my team, which was to be modelled strictly according to the Derby format, that is, in three autonomous and separate groups covering respectively design, mechanical development and engine performance.

On performance, I chose Harry Pearson, who worked for Dorey at Hucknall, and had done excellent work in developing the ejector exhaust system on the Merlin. This was a system which directed the exhaust gases from each cylinder rearwards to produce a jet-propulsion effect worth between 100 and 150 hp. Pearson had taken a Physics degree at Oxford, and had a very broadly based knowledge of aerodynamics and thermodynamics. He was also very sound on fundamental principles, and logical in his thinking. I used him continuously as a stalking horse for ideas. Although he was very conservative, once he had agreed I was certain I was on sound ground.

In addition, I took Lindsay Dawson and Geoffrey Fawn, who already worked for me at Derby, anyway. The former was a superficially brilliant young man, not too sound fundamentally, but then Harry Pearson looked after that aspect. He was good-looking, and could be very charming. Full of the zest for life, he added greatly to the good-natured atmosphere which prevailed throughout the factory. Geoffrey Fawn was a different type, with a solid and determined nature. Miscast as an engineer, he nonetheless did sterling work on turbine performance for a few years, until he switched to his natural forté of management. He ended up as Managing Director of Rolls-Royce when the crash came in 1971. Just prior to that he ran the Motor Car Division at Crewe with great success.

In addition, Sharpley Jones from the Carrier Co, and E. Peregrine, who later became a consulting engineer, stayed on at Waterloo Mill to run the facilities there on a research basis. Sharpley Jones was strong on the aerodynamic and thermodynamic side, while Peregrine was an all-rounder with a very fertile imagination.

In consultation with Elliott and Rubbra, we made Lombard the Chief Designer, and decided to stiffen his team with help from Derby. My old friend Ainsworth-Davis, who lived with me at Donington Hall, came up as Assistant Chief Designer, bringing with him the basic Rolls-Royce design standards and expertise.

Freddie Morley also came from the Advanced Project Design Office at Derby. He was a mercurial man of great talent, and rose to become the Chief Designer at Derby. Among the many contributions he made at Derby was the design of the Spey engine, one of Derby's most successful products. Later he was a tower of strength to me when I carried the responsibility for rescuing the RB211 after the collapse of Rolls-Royce in 1971.

One other man of great importance was Ron Kibby, who was put in charge of detail design. In the design of an engine, the designers do the broad-brush work of the general arrangement and specification of all the comprehensive components. The detail draughtsmen then take each part and break it down into its individual components, and draw these again in a manner which permits the shops to manufacture them, adding all the necessary tolerances and material specifications. They are an essential link between the creators of the engine and the men who have to make it. Kibby was a superb draughtsman himself, and the drawings that were issued from his office were models of precision and accuracy. He also had immense energy, and on many an occasion worked all night to complete the details of parts that were urgently required. He, too, rose to the top at Derby, and became the Chief Detail Designer.

For mechanical development, I chose Robert Plumb from

Derby. He was an expert on lubrication, which was one of the problems on the Whittle engine, and also had considerable experience of the mechanical engineering of the Merlin. He was a quiet and modest man, popular with everybody, and he built up a very skilful and dedicated team of young men under him. I was indeed fortunate that he stayed with me all through his professional life, coming with me to Bristol when I left Rolls-Royce. Without his help, the Proteus engine for the Britannia would have broken me.

It was obvious that a very important adjunct of our work would lie in the field of the new materials capable of withstanding the high temperatures which were required for the turbine blades and discs. To cover this aspect, the Chief Metallurgist at Derby, H. E. Gresham, made frequent visits to Barnoldswick, and established there a metallurgical laboratory under the control of his able assistant Douglas Hall. They kept closely in touch with the work that was going on at Henry Wiggin in Birmingham on nickel alloys, and also at William Jessop & Sons in Sheffield on new disc materials. Their reports, prefixed by Gresham's initials HEG, were oft referred to as 'fresh, stale or bad Hegs'.

This, then, was the set-up in the early days of 1943, when we bent our minds to our task. We were a relatively young team. Like Whittle, I was in my mid-thirties and most others were younger than that; Lombard was in his early twenties.

With a workforce approaching 2,000, we had great power. Armed with a letter written in red ink (blood we called it) by Sir Stafford Cripps, Minister of Aircraft Production, which stated that 'nothing, repeat nothing, is to stand in the way of the development of the jet engine', we were able to indent on the local factories for any expertise we required.

And so, regardless of the problems ahead of us of which we were totally ignorant, we forged ahead by the well-established process of running the engine to death, and dealing with the failures on an *ad hoc* basis as they occurred. The results were dramatic. The B.23 (we left off the 'W.2') flew in the F.9/40 Meteor at 1,400 lb thrust on 12 June 1943. It was soon cleared to the full 1,600 lb rating, and in October 1943 it was named the Rolls-Royce Welland I* and put into small-scale production at Barnoldswick, 100 being delivered to Gloster for the Meteor Is. Though this was peanuts compared with our 1,000 Merlins a week, it did at least get the Meteor into the war.

---

*Rolls-Royce named all early gas-turbine engines after rivers, reflecting the idea of steady flow.

The first Meteors were delivered to 616 Squadron RAF on 12 July 1944, fitted with Welland I engines, and the first squadron moved later in July to Manston near the east Kent coast. They flew against the V.1 flying bombs, and the first blow was struck by Whittle's engine when a flying-bomb was destroyed on 4 August 1944. The Meteor was one of the few aircraft that could catch a flying bomb at sea level, and do it without being flogged.

Even the allocation of these modest resources to the jet engine did not receive universal approval in the aircraft industry. The main designers of fighter aircraft, Sydney Camm at Hawker and Joe Smith, who had succeeded Mitchell at Supermarine, were heavily involved in improving the Hurricane, Typhoon, Tempest and Spitfire, and paid no attention to the jet engine. Accordingly, Sir Roy Fedden, Chief Engineer at the Engine Division of the Bristol Aeroplane Company, in charge of radial air-cooled engines, wrote to Air Chief Marshal Sir Wilfrid Freeman at the M.A.P., protesting that a 400 mph (sea-level speed) fighter could more easily be made by designing a larger piston engine. Freeman passed this letter to Hs for comments, and he passed it on to me. From my knowledge of the Spitfire, Hurricane and Mustang, I was able to show that piston engines in excess of 4,000 hp would be required, that is more than double the power of any engine then in production. Since the power output of a single cylinder had reached its limit due to difficulties of cooling, this meant that engines of up to 36 cylinders would be necessary; a complication that no designer would face with equanimity.

On the other hand, if the Whittle engine could be developed to 2,000 lb of thrust from its design value of 1,600 lb, then the Meteor fighter already in hand at Gloster would have a top speed of nearly 500 mph at sea level. This was a prospect that could not be contemplated with conventional piston engines.

Tragically for Bristol, Fedden left the company in late 1942, and his fine development team collapsed. This had a profound effect on the fortunes of the Bristol engines in the post-war era. It was in the early 1950s before a worthwhile Bristol gas-turbine appeared, by which time Rolls-Royce had a ten-year lead. It is very difficult to catch one of the world's fastest operators if you give him such a start.

The reply I gave to Hs on the Freeman letter immediately caused me to start to think about a redesign of the B.23. Rover had already designed and made the 'straight-through' B.26 version of the W.2B, but had not changed the airflow or thrust.

This was a bad mistake, because it is worthwhile making such a drastic change in the mechanical arrangement of an engine only if a considerable improvement in performance and reliability results.

We already knew, by comparing the dimensions of the Whittle impeller in the compressor with that of the Merlin, that the W.2B was capable of passing 25 per cent more airflow provided that the diffuser was suitably modified. At Derby we had the Vulture test rig capable of testing the full-scale compressor. Wilde set to work at Derby to modify the diffuser on the lines of the Merlin, with 20 vanes, and soon produced test results showing a 25 per cent increase in airflow. At the same time, at Barnoldswick we took the W.2B turbine blades and slightly increased their length so that they, too, would pass a 25 per cent increase in flow. These changes were embodied into a modified B.26 which was designated the Derwent I. On test this gave 2,000 lb thrust, or just 25 per cent more than the W.2B.

We retained the new straight-through chambers, and added expansion joints which eliminated distortion and cracking. I also left out the inlet swirl vanes, small curved guide vanes in what aerodynamicists call a cascade, which Whittle insisted improved efficiency. No other centrifugal compressor had such vanes, and because they were made of thin sheet and often broke, damaging the engine when the bits were ingested, they seemed an unnecessary nuisance. Later we found eliminating them reduced compressor efficiency from 78 to 73 per cent, so that to give the specified 2,000 lb thrust the engine had to run much hotter, the turbine gas temperature being 843°C and the specific fuel consumption 1.178. When we replaced the vanes we got 2,000 lb at only 754°C with sfc of only 1.083. But against the advice of Harry Pearson I cleared the Derwent I for production without the vanes, because the engine ran reliably and their omission removed a worrying mechanical problem. We made 500 Derwent Is at Newcastle-under-Lyme before the end of the war, and by the end of 1944 Derwent-engined Meteor IIIs were helping 'Monty' push through the Low Countries to the Rhine.

Chapter 4
The Nene

In 1941 Whittle had been instructed to give the design specification of the W.2 engine, and one of his precious prototype engines, to the General Electric Company, in Boston, USA. This was by agreement between the British and American Governments, and the latter had selected GE because they had experience in steam turbines, and also manufactured the turbosuperchargers which were fitted in vast numbers to American aircraft piston engines. The two main aero engine companies, Curtiss-Wright, who manufactured for the Army Air Force, and Pratt & Whitney, for the Navy, were told to get on with piston engine production. In any case, neither was enthusiastic about the new jet engine's prospects. On the other hand, the giant GE company set forth with tremendous energy to develop the W.2 into an American version which they designated as the I-16. Reports of their progress were exchanged with ours from Barnoldswick. Although GE had more than a year's start on us we were soon running neck and neck. They were first to fly, however; the I-16 was flown in the twin-engined XP-59 made by Bell Aircraft in October 1942. At this time poor Whittle's engine in Britain had all but ground to a halt!

In early 1944 an invitation came from the US Army Air Force's Col Don Keirn for a party of British jet engineers to visit the USA, and see at first hand the progress that was being made. Our party was led by Hayne Constant of the RAE, and included Leslie Cheshire from Power Jets, W. H. 'Pat' Lindsey from Armstrong Siddeley, Moult, Brodie and Clarkson from de Havilland, and myself. We left in April 1944.

We travelled from Liverpool in the US Coast Guard ship *Wakefield,* which had been adapted for troop carrying. On the return trip it travelled almost empty, so we had the luxury of lots of space on board. As it had a speed of 18 knots, we did not have to travel in convoy but zig-zagged our lonely way across the submarine-infested Atlantic. Full alert was maintained at all times, and it was most comforting during the day when from time to time a British aircraft would appear over us to see all was well.

The food was lavish, and very good by our British rationed standards, and one of the most heartening cries was to hear the stewards going through the decks shouting 'Chow time on the *Wakefield!*' We had an uneventful eight-day crossing. After the blackout in Britain it was a thrilling sight, as Boston hove over the horizon, to see the city blazing in light. Later we were to find the shops full of all the good things of life, which had disappeared years before in Britain.

Our first visit was to the GE plant at Lynn, just outside Boston. To my concern I found that they had already made, and were running, an engine of 4,000 lb thrust, called the I-40. I had no idea this was happening, and to add to my dismay, when we visited their factory at Schenectady, the HQ of the steam-turbine division, we found them running an axial turbojet, also of 4,000 lb thrust, designed by Alan Howard. This engine became the TG-180 and led to the J35 and the even more famous J47.

Remember that 4,000 lb is more than the thrust given by a 5,000 hp piston engine/propeller combination. It was clear that the Americans were thinking on a larger scale than we were in Britain, where the most powerful engine was the DH Goblin designed for an eventual 3,000 lb thrust. Then and there, I decided that Rolls-Royce should do something about it on my return to England.

Having been very hospitably and openly received by GE, we left for the West Coast in a military DC-3 provided by our hosts, the USAAF. We spent a short time at Albuquerque, and I wandered down to the sandy banks of the Rio Grande. It was a rather insignificant, turgid, sienna-coloured river, not at all what I expected. My mind went back to those halcyon days in BNC, when Michael Peacock would convulse us by his dramatic rendering of the legend 'When Mexican Pete and Dead-Eye Dick came down from the Rio Grande'. Alas, the gay and gallant Michael was no more, nor were John Brody, Hector Pilling, Alex Obolensky and many others, all killed in the early days of the War whilst serving as pilots in the RAF. Was I not standing on the home soil of Eddie Drake, who gave his life in the defence of Britain in the American Eagle Squadron, and who had become a part of Oxford through the munificence of Cecil Rhodes of South

Africa? These men had helped to wipe out the resolution 'That this House will not fight for its King and Country', and given the lie to the false and insidious eloquence of the Joads of this world. I turned sadly away to rejoin the party. Onwards from Albuquerque via the Grand Canyon to Muroc airfield, now known as Edwards Air Force Base. Flying down the Grand Canyon was an unforgettable experience with its splendid and colourful scenery.

At Muroc, I had my first flight in a jet. The Bell XP-59, powered by two I-16 engines, was really a single-seater, but they had carved a small open cockpit ahead of the pilot in the nose of one of the aircraft, thus transforming it into a two-seater. We were all offered a ride, but when it came to my turn, I was unable to get into the cockpit with a parachute on. It just was not designed for people my size, so I threw the parachute away and had my first flight without one. I was certainly the first man ever to do that in a jet aircraft!

Everyone knows how different jet propulsion is from the piston-engine/propeller combination, but in those early days, the smoothness and lack of vibration and noise were a revelation. Flying at 400 mph in an open cockpit with nothing but a small deflector windscreen was also quite exciting, and that thrilling experience has stayed with me always.

While we were at Muroc, a local rancher invited us to an ox-roasting. The party was set for the afternoon, and we travelled across the desert by car for about 20 miles to get there. When we arrived, the party was in full swing, and a good deal of the ox had already been consumed, washed down with Bourbon and wine. However, there was plenty left, and the hospitality shown to us by all was splendid. I wandered around by the cabins and found one with a cowboy stretched out on his bunk.

'Ever seen a rattle-snake?', he enquired.

I shook my head, and he reached up to a pillow-case that was hanging on a nail above his bunk. He undid the string that fastened the neck, and dumped the case on the floor, whereupon a very large snake began to hiss around in it with its rattles going full blast.

I said, 'Good God, can you rest with that thing hanging over you?' He replied, 'Sure, you have to get used to them out here'.

Later, to entertain us, our hosts got out an old carriage which had crossed the desert in the pioneering days, and harnessed four spirited horses to it. People climbed inside and on the top, and the four horses were released and accelerated away into the desert, followed by loud cries of 'Whoopee'. Eventually the carriage returned for a refill. On the second trip, I was one of about six who got inside, while a large number climbed on to the roof. By this time the horses were even more on their mettle, and once released they took off at high speed in a large arc into the desert. Sure enough, the outfit was now top-heavy and rolled over to starboard, throwing everybody from the top into the desert sand. Inside, where I was, there was chaos as we were all thrown on top of the unfortunates on the right-hand side. It is not nice to have someone of my bulk fall on top of you, but apart from scratches and bruises no-one was hurt badly inside. It was more tragic for the top passengers. In particular, the wife of the Medical Officer at Muroc, who had her back broken and died shortly afterwards. We returned to camp very sadly, although at the time we did not know the extent of the lady's injuries.

The rest of our trip was uneventful and eventually we arrived at Baltimore, en route for home. At that time, British Overseas Airways were operating a trans-Atlantic service with Boeing 314As from Baltimore via Botwood (Newfoundland) to Foynes. These great flying boats could sleep 19 passengers in the bunks in the tail, and had a saloon with a round mahogany dining table, where one spent one's waking hours. I recall it took almost 18 hours for the 1,800-mile trans-Atlantic trip from Botwood to Foynes, and we flew at an altitude of 2,000 - 3,000 ft above miles and miles of deserted ocean. It was July, and after the sweltering damp atmosphere of Washington and Baltimore, the Emerald Isle seemed all that it is cracked up to be. It had an air-conditioned atmosphere! The final surprise was that from Limerick to London, though we flew in a British aircraft, we had the blinds drawn.

Once back at Barnoldswick, I resolved to design a Whittle engine of 5,000 lb thrust. Our current engine, the Derwent I, was running at 2,000 lb, so it was a big step-forward to take, particularly as there was no aircraft suitable for such a powerful engine, and none was even being considered.

In 1940, the development of jet engines was co-ordinated for the Ministry by Dr Harold Roxbee Cox, now Lord Kings Norton, who then held the position of Director of Scientific Research. I knew him well because when I was a student at Imperial College, I had attended his lectures on the design of airships. He it was who formed the Gas Turbine Collaboration Committee, in which all the firms involved in turbine work met at frequent intervals to discuss progress and problems. The first meeting took place in the AID headquarters in Birmingham, and in his opening remarks Roxbee referred to us in prophetic terms as 'the midwives of a new era'. At the height of the controversy about the Lucas fuel system in early 1943, I met with him in London and helped persuade him to support the Lucas fuel system on the basis that, at that time, we could not rely entirely on a gear fuel pump operating at over 1,000 lb per square inch, because of the lack of operating experience at that pressure with fuel as the lubricant, albeit with a small percentage of oil mixed in.

But by the time the decision to build the 5,000 lb-thrust engine was taken, Roxbee had moved on to higher things, and his place had been taken by Group Captain George Watt of the Royal New Zealand Air Force. George was an expert test pilot, and no mean engineer, and being a big man he always took a big view. I telephoned him from Barnoldswick and said,

'George, I want to build a 5,000 lb engine. We must get cracking or the Americans will beat us to it'.

His reply was 'Are you sure the thrust should be as much as 5,000 lb?'

I said, 'Of course not, let us say a figure of 4,200 lb, and we will design for 5,000 lb'.

'OK', he said, 'I will issue a specification for an engine of 4,200 lb, and you can go ahead now. If you get 5,000 lb so much the better'.

I do not remember consulting Hs about this, although I suppose we must have kept him informed of our intentions. But the war was on, and the big boys at Derby were busy helping to win it with the Merlin and Griffon, and were content for us to go our own way at Barnoldswick.

And so Lombard, Pearson, Morley and myself set out to do the project design of the new turbojet, which was later to become the famous Nene. We got down to the task on 1 May 1944, and for the first time were able to start with a real 'clean sheet of paper'. Moreover, at last we felt we had enough experience to know exactly how to design a better turbojet. We set the airflow at 80 lb/sec and designed the best compressor impeller we could, with a diameter of 28.8 in (732 mm) compared with 20.68 in for the Derwent I. We enclosed the impeller in a casing based on the marvellous new pattern Whittle had created for the W.2/500, which was not only aerodynamically more efficient but eliminated cracking.

The turbine disc and rear main shaft bearing had never been adequately cooled, so we incorporated a small centrifugal compressor designed solely to cool these two components. We adopted the straight-through combustion system as on the Derwent I, and Stanley Clarke produced a new design of combustion chamber, which had a low pressure-drop and a high efficiency. We did not ask for a larger fuel pump from Lucas, but just fitted two of the existing C-size pumps as used on the Derwent I, and which were beginning to be very reliable.

Our first study was the B.40, and in the summer of 1944, as the Meteors began shooting down the V.1 buzz-bombs, we refined this into the B.41 and began to release drawings to the shops. We were frankly impressed at the result, because, while we had increased the diameter of the impeller by 40 per cent, we had held the increase in overall diameter of the engine to under 20 per cent, from 41.5 in to 49.5 in, 5.5 in within our target. Dry weight of the first engine was a remarkable 1,600 lb, the design target maximum being 2,200 lb!

At last, on 27 October 1944, the great day arrived when the Nene was ready for test. As usual, the last-minute adjustments to the engine and the test bed had taken all day, and it was approaching 10.00 pm before we were ready to press the starter button. Driven by the big electric starter, the new engine started to rotate and go through the light-up sequence. This consisted of opening the fuel shut-off cock at a predetermined fuel pressure so that a spray of fuel, and not a dribble, went into the combustion chambers, and then ignition was to occur from two igniter plugs (like large car sparking plugs) inserted in opposite combustion chambers.

The positioning of those plugs was always subject to a certain amount of trial and error, and we had got it wrong, because no light-up took place. The whole works had gathered to see the engine run for the first time, and a groan went up when it failed to start. A repeat was tried with the same result.

Dizzy Drew and Ballantyne, our ignition experts, were equal to the problem. Out came one of the igniter plugs, and an oxy-acetylene torch was unceremoniously plunged into the hole! The engine lit with a bang, and some nice flames came from the jet pipe from internal pools of fuel. But in a few seconds it was running beautifully, and all instruments were reading correctly. (Thus, incidentally, was born the almost universally used torch igniter).

Slowly, the throttle was opened, and the thrust crept up to 1,000 lb, 2,000 lb and 3,000 lb, and a cheer went up as we passed the design thrust of the de Havilland Goblin. The throttle was opened wider and when the engine passed the 4,000 lb mark, the cheer must have been heard all over Barnoldswick. It had been a thrilling night and was now approaching midnight, so I called a halt so that we could continue next day. We all repaired to the canteen where the chefs and waitresses prepared a real sausage-and-mash spread. Few people in the factory had much sleep that night.

Next day I telephoned Hs and told him the good news. He replied in what was for him a very unusual way by sending us a telegram. I read 'Congratulations to all. Well done, you have put Barnoldswick on the map'.

When it came to the design of the Nene, Pearson made a last desperate effort to persuade me of the advantages of Whittle's cascade of intake swirl vanes, and so a compromise was made. The engine design had to be such that we could either have them or not, and Lombard was required to satisfy me that a design of vanes could be made which would not fail. The first Nene was completed without the vanes, and the impressive thrust of 4,000 lb was reached on the initial run. But later that night, looking at the instrument readings, it was apparent that the combustion temperature was higher than expected. This was bad news. We would have a struggle to reach the design thrust of 5,000 lb.

Pearson insisted that the engine tests be stopped, and the intake swirl vanes fitted. Reluctantly I agreed, and then went home.

The change was made in the small hours, and next day when I arrived in the factory I could hear the engine running and so wandered over to the test bed. To my amazement and joy, 5,000 lb of thrust was being registered at the same temperature as the 4,000 lb on the first test! The simple little static vanes, which Frank Whittle had computed would be so beneficial, had added 1,000 lb to the thrust of the engine, and improved the fuel consumption by 5-10 per cent. As is usual with the way of the world, I got a 'medal' for leaving the vanes out in the first place, and another 'medal' for putting them back in the Nene. The credit was totally Frank's.

I do not think any of us expected that, from scratch, we could create the most powerful aircraft engine in the world in just five months. But at the political level things were moving somewhat slower. It may be that the 'Dunkirk spirit' still existed in a few places, but the fact remains that not only was there no aircraft in which to fly the Nene but there was nothing even being planned for it! It would have seemed reasonable to instruct several companies to design high-speed fighters and bombers to make full use of this powerful engine, but at Derby we almost began to wonder why we were bothering. Then, suddenly, we were told a new American jet fighter was being made available to us. It was USAAF No 44-83027, the fifth pre-production Lockheed YP-80A Shooting Star, one of four sent to Europe to gain experience under front-line conditions. We very quickly replaced its GE J33 engine by our first flight-cleared Nene and got it flying at Hucknall on 21 July 1945. It was a beautiful machine to fly, but where did we go from there? The answer was nowhere much, though the Nene passed its Type Test in November 1945. On 14 August 1946, more than a year after the Nene's first flight, we got a couple of Nenes flying in the outboard engine positions of a Lancastrian, VH742, in the hands of company Chief Test Pilot Capt R. T. Shepherd.

Although we were now far outstripping him, Frank was delighted with the success of the Nene, and came to Barnoldswick to see it run. We had a celebration dinner at the Swan and Royal at Clitheroe. Everyone bewailed the lack of an aircraft for the Nene, and the suggestion was made that we should scale the Nene down to fit the Meteor nacelle and determine what thrust we could get. Lombard did the design exercise on the tablecloth, and the answer came out at an amazing 3,650 lb. The current production engine was the Derwent I at 2,000 lb, and we were all excited at the prospect of over 3,500 lb from a same size engine, and the great increase in performance that this would give to the Meteor. Currently, it had a maximum speed of about 450 mph; with 75 per cent more thrust, we could predict about 30 per cent more speed, and the goal of 600 mph seemed suddenly within our grasp. Moreover, the RAE had just modified the engine nacelle shape in order to reduce its drag at speeds at which air compressibility effects, or Mach number drag-rise, became significant.

We tried the proposal on Hs at one of his Monday afternoon meetings. He was not amused; after all, Rolls-Royce had just completed the new turbojet production factory at Newcastle-under-Lyme, and it was tooled-up to make the Derwent I, which was then just going into service with the RAF. Hs did not say yes but he did not say no, so that, on a dark winter's night motoring back from Derby to Barnoldswick, Lombard and I decided to go ahead anyway. To celebrate this, we called in at the Station Hotel in Manchester to have dinner, and after a few drinks we had the best the hotel could provide, including a bottle of wine, a rare thing in Britain in 1944. When the bill arrived, I tossed it to Lombard and said:

'You pay this, I haven't got any money'.

He replied, 'I haven't got any either'.

Our hearts sank, and the waiter hovering nearby came over and asked if anything was wrong. We told him of our predicament, and he said 'Haven't you got any money at all?' We searched our pockets and our combined wealth came to just over ten shillings, which he said would have to do. I replied, 'Just a moment, our coats are out there, and we shall have to give the attendant a tip'. So I took a couple of shillings back, and the waiter went off without any fuss at all. I had pictured having to leave my wrist-watch on account, but not a bit of it. Of course, he was only legally entitled to charge us five shillings (25p), the limit for a wartime meal, but we had all forgotten that. Needless to say, on the next occasion we dropped in and settled the matter.

We started the design of the Derwent V, as it was called, on 1 January 1945, and I laid down the rule that it was to be a photographic copy of the Nene, scaled down by a factor of 0.855. Thus no design calculations were necessary, and by 7 June we had the first engine on the test-bed ready to run. On its first test it ran 100 hours non-stop at a rating of 2,600 lb, and later we gradually increased the thrust to 3,500 lb.

By 15 August 1945, two Derwent V engines were installed in a Meteor, and the first flight took place at Moreton Valence in Gloucestershire, which was the home of the Meteor. Eric Greenwood was the Gloster Chief Test Pilot, and I motored down from Barnoldswick. The aircraft took off like a rocket, and disappeared in a clap of thunder. When Greenwood returned he just said 'At last we have a real aeroplane'. He was full of enthusiasm and praise for the new engine. Within weeks he was clocking 570 mph at 10,000 ft, and calculations showed that if we could give him 4,000 lb thrust for a short period, then 600 mph at sea level could be exceeded, and the Meteor would be the first aeroplane in the world to be officially timed at that coveted figure.

The official World Speed Record, which then had to be made

at sea level, stood at 469 mph, made by a Messerschmitt with a Daimler-Benz piston engine just before the war. I always doubted the authenticity of that record, because I calculated that it must have required at least 4,000 hp, but after the war we discovered that the aircraft was not a Bf 109 fighter at all but a small racer given the same number. It was a great propaganda effort by the Germans just prior to the war, and designed to intimidate all.

The next milestone was, of course, 500 mph, and I believed this to have been reached by the Lockheed XP-80A Shooting Star in the USA using an I-40, the 4,000 lb-thrust engine which I saw running at GE in 1943.

And so, by a special test of 1 hour duration, we cleared the Derwent V at 4,000 lb for the speed-record attempt. Two strengthened aircraft were selected to make the attempt at Herne Bay, one to be piloted by Eric Greenwood and the other by an RAF officer, Group Captain H. J. 'Willie' Wilson, whom I did not know. All engines vary a little in performance, so I gave instructions at Barnoldswick that the best two were to be installed in Eric's Meteor, and the inferior ones in Wilson's.

All went well in the trials from Manston over the course at Herne Bay, and when the record attempts were made by the two pilots, sure enough the first news came through that Eric had broken the record at 603 mph, and Wilson had been slightly slower. Science triumphs again, I thought, but it was too soon. A correction came through saying that Wilson had the record after all. It speaks volumes for the consistency of aircraft drag and turbojet performance that both aircraft were within 2 mph of each other. Such consistency was never achieved with piston-engine/propeller combinations.

During these speed records Frank Whittle was at last able to fly a jet. In early October he flew a Meteor I, powered by W.2B/700 engines, at Bruntingthorpe. A few days later he visited the trials at Manston and, at the request of a Ministry of Supply official and while suffering from the effects of a Rolls-Royce party, he flew a Meteor III with Derwent Is.

Thus, in the period from January 1944 to October 1945, the engines for the Meteor had progressed as follows:

(a) The W.2B/23 or Welland at 1,600 lb thrust with a diameter of 43½ in and a weight of 850 lb. The engine had reversed-flow combustion, and followed Whittle's original design conception. More than 100 were manufactured at Barnoldswick and went into service with the RAF in the summer of 1944.

(b) The B.37 or Derwent I at 2,000 lb thrust with a diameter of 43½ in and a weight of 950 lb. This engine had straight-through combustion chambers designed by Lucas, and was produced for the Meteor at the new Rolls-Royce factory at Newcastle-under-Lyme from late 1944.

(c) The B.37 Series V or Derwent V at 3,500 lb thrust with a diameter of 44 in and a weight of 1,250 lb. This engine in the Meteor raised the World Speed Record to 606 mph in October 1945 and to 616 mph in the following year. It was produced in the post-war years at Derby.

With these increases in power taking place, the fuel consumption of the engine was improved. If anything the range of the Meteor was extended by the more powerful engines.

Jet engines were much simpler to fly than piston/propeller engines. In the latter there are at least two controls, the engine throttle which controls the power, and the propeller pitch control which fixes the rpm. There are sundry instruments that have to be watched: boost pressure, oil pressure, coolant temperature and rpm. On a simple turbojet there is only one control, the throttle. The only instrument that needs watching is the jetpipe temperature, which has a maximum marked on it which must never be exceeded. Turbojets are like people: if anything is wrong, the temperature goes up.

I remember seeing the first Meteor at the RAE being handed over to an operational squadron. The young fighter-pilot flew in on a Spitfire, was led over to the cockpit of the Meteor, and briefed for a few minutes, whereupon he climbed into this enormous new twin-engined aircraft with a radically new type of engine, and took off to the war! It was as undramatic as that, and I marvelled at the cool, calm competence of this young man.

The speed and apparent ease with which the Nene and the Derwent V had been designed, made and tested to their full power had profoundly impressed Hs. Neither engine saw service with the RAF until the war was over, and until the end Rolls-Royce continued to produce vast numbers of Merlins. Hs said:

'When the war is over, you will be able to buy Merlins on any street corner for a bob a dozen. We must press on with these jet engines, or we shall have nothing to do'.

The British fighter design teams had been heavily engaged throughout the war on the Hurricane, Typhoon and Tempest at Hawker, and the Spitfire with both the Merlin and the Griffon engines at Supermarine. As a consequence, neither Sydney Camm at Hawker nor Joe Smith at Supermarine had paid any real attention to the jet engine. The Gloster Meteor designed by George Carter was the only British jet aircraft in production when the war ended, although de Havilland's Vampire, powered by their own Goblin with a thrust of 3,000 lb, was cleared for production by English Electric up at Preston.

We made a gallant but unsuccessful effort to get the Nene into the Vampire. The installation work was in the hands of Witold Challier, who worked for Dorey. Challier was an excitable Pole, who was a Don at Warsaw University when war broke out, but walked to Constanza in Romania, and through various vicissitudes arrived at Rolls-Royce, where he gave us invaluable service estimating the performance of aircraft fitted with our engines.

Hs became irritated at the slow progress of the installation, and Challier, resenting the criticism, waved his arms in the air saying,

'There you are, it's all Challier's fault. You say Challier make a miracle, and you don't pay me for that'.

At this we all laughed, and Hs replied.

'The last man that made miracles did them for nothing'.

More laughter, but Challier had the last word.

'And look what happened to him!'

Due to the lack of applications for the Nene, Hs called on Camm and Smith to bring to their attention the potential of this new type of engine, and the rapid progress that was being made with it. In the past, aircraft had been designed to suit the available engines, because it took years longer to get the engine to a stage of reliability than it did to design and make the aircraft. Hs realized that all that was now changed.

'Tell us the size of engine you want, and we will make it to measure quicker than you can make the aircraft', Hs said to Camm and Smith. And if we had stuck to the Whittle-type centrifugal engine I think he was right; but, of course, the wheels of progress were churning on, and it was becoming clear that the axial engine, with its smaller diameter and higher efficiency, would soon take over. Thus, the prophecy that Hs made to Whittle in the early days came true. When Whittle extolled the virtue of the great simplicity of his engine, Hs looked at him and drily remarked, 'Wait until we have worked on it for a while; we will soon design the simplicity out of it!'

Following Hs' tour around the aircraft designers, both Joe

Smith and Sydney Camm came to Barnoldswick to view the Nene running on the test bed. Sydney Camm had with him a project drawing of a fighter aeroplane, later to be produced as the Sea Hawk for the Royal Navy, which featured both a divided air intake and a divided jetpipe. One criticism of single-engined jet aircraft had been that if the air intake was in the nose of the aircraft and the jet discharged from the tail, then the whole of the fuselage was full of wind, and there was little room for fuel and equipment.

Camm's proposal was to take the air in at the junction of the wings and the fuselage, and thus have two ducts leading to the engine. The cockpit and nose of the aircraft was thus unaffected. Similarly, the jetpipe was likewise divided into two, one curving out of the fuselage on each side. Hs always referred to this as a 'birfucated jetpipe', because this sounded more difficult than a bifurcated pipe. In fact, splitting the pipe into two lost practically none of the jet thrust, and gave very little mechanical trouble. Years later, when we were considering vertical take-off, both Camm and myself remembered the 'birfucated' pipe, and this led to the arrangement of the Pegasus engine in today's Harrier.

Joe Smith went back to Supermarine, and with Alan Clifton designed the Attacker, which also was produced only in small numbers. The Nene just did not catch on in England. It is one of the staggering examples of Britain's inability at the political level to get things right in aviation that no government effort whatsoever was made to do anything on a big scale with this world-beating engine. Yet it is probable that more Nene engines were subsequently made than any other jet engine in history — in the United States, Soviet Union, France, China and many other countries.

The American interest stemmed from Phil Taylor, the ex-Chief Engineer of Curtiss-Wright, who were heavily involved in wartime production of air-cooled piston engines. After quarrelling with the Board of his company, Taylor came to England in 1946 and visited Hs at Derby. They were old (rival) friends, and Taylor asked Hs for an option on the licence for the Nene. We had already tried to interest Pratt & Whitney and Curtiss-Wright in the engine but had failed, quite frankly because neither company, drunk with the huge production of piston engines for the American war effort, had yet appreciated the impact of the jet on future aircraft.

Hs agreed to give Taylor the option, and the latter returned to the States, and persuaded the US Navy to have a Nene engine tested in the Navy Yard at Philadelphia. The American Type Test was more severe than the British one at the time, having a duration of 150 hours as against 100 hours, and containing much longer running periods at full power. No American engine had succeeded in passing this test without the replacement of major parts at various intervals. This applied to the GE I-40 engine, which by this time was called the J33. It was rated at 4,000 lb thrust, but was as large and as heavy as the Nene which gave 5,000 lb thrust.

Under the patronage of the Navy, John Herriot took two Nenes to Philadelphia and installed them ready for Type Test. To the delight of the Navy, the engines sailed through the Type Test without incident. The Navy then insisted that their main engine contractor, Pratt & Whitney, should come down to Philadelphia to inspect the engines after test. To Phil Taylor's satisfaction, they also insisted that Pratt & Whitney take a licence from Rolls-Royce for the manufacture of the Nene forthwith, and Bill Gwinn, the General Manager of Pratt & Whitney, and Wright Parkins, the Chief Engineer, came to Derby for that purpose.

In the meantime, Phil Taylor had collected nearly a million dollars for graciously surrendering his option on the licence to Pratt & Whitney, and everybody came out of the deal very satisfied and happy. Ever afterwards, the Nene in the USA was known not only as the J42 (its official designation) but also as 'the Needle Engine', because of its effect on the US engine firms.

And so, full manufacturing details of the Nene engine were given to Pratt & Whitney and the great engine factory at Hartford, Connecticut, was transformed to make it. It is a sobering thought, that the two great engine competitors of Rolls-Royce, which today have the bulk of the world's aviation business, namely Pratt & Whitney and General Electric, both started with British engines — the former with the Nene, and the latter with the original Whittle W.1, given to General Arnold in 1941, before the USA was a participant in the war.

The one-time greatest engine company of all, Curtiss-Wright, did not face the challenge of the jet until it was too late. Then in the 1950s it plunged in with British engines — the Armstrong Siddeley Sapphire and the Bristol Olympus, for both of which they took licences. But it was too late, and the once dominating piston-engine manufacturer is now reduced to the status of a minor sub-contractor. Thus are the sins and omissions of the father visited upon the children.

Meanwhile, the Meteor squadrons were seeing widespread service with the RAF. I remember Sir James Robb, C-in-C of Fighter Command, writing to me saying that, despite its two engines, it only took half the effort to maintain a squadron of Meteors as it did with Spitfires, which spoke volumes for the reliability and simplicity of the jet engine *vis-à-vis* the Merlin.

The Meteors saw action in France in 1945, but were not allowed to go further forward than Eindhoven in the Netherlands in case, I discovered afterwards, one of them should fall into Russian hands. But the Russians knew all about this new aircraft and its engines, and after the war ended they came to Derby to try to purchase a licence for the Nene, or, failing that, to buy some actual engines.

I was detailed to look after the mission, but had to keep them at Derby and not take them to Barnoldswick where the main engine development was still going on. They were, as usual, a charming and lusty lot of fellows and we had some great parties in the evenings at the Midland Hotel. I remember one evening they were all sitting together, obviously telling jokes in Russian. One would have thought that one could speak Russian for ever in that normally very quiet hotel in Derby in 1946 without being understood. I called across to the interpreter and said, 'I hope those stories are clean'.

'As a matter of fact they are not', said a young lady sitting quite independently some distance apart. She turned out to be a Czech dancer who had skipped from her troupe, and was waiting to be collected by some good lady, and to start a new life in England!

With Sir Stafford Cripps at the Board of Trade, the left-wing British Government appeared perfectly happy to sell our latest engine to the Russians, and in September 1946 clinched a deal for 25 Nenes and 30 Derwents, the first few of which the team took back to the Soviet Union and copied exactly in double-quick time. They were produced in colossal numbers for the MiG-15 and -17, Il-28, Tu-14 and many other aircraft. These aircraft were also supplied to the Soviet satellite countries, and North Korea! Over 20 years later I saw VK-1s (Soviet Nenes) being overhauled in Romania.

On my first visit to China in 1972 I was taken to the Peking Aeronautical Institute where they have a display of aero engines. Right in the fore-front was a sectioned Nene engine of which, of course, the Chinese knew I was the Chief Engineer. I inspected the engine carefully and said, 'Yes, the Russians made a very good copy. They even copied the mistakes!' My hosts were much amused at this, and later, when we visited the engine factory in Xian, I found that the Nene was still in large-scale production there in 1975.

By 1947 we had completely mastered the centrifugal engine — in sharpest contrast to the axial type — and at Derby we very quickly added a further half inch (12.7 mm) to the Nene impeller, and made other changes to handle an airflow increased from around 90 lb/sec to a remarkable 130, or a growth of well over 30 per cent. This fine engine, named the Tay, combined all that was best from Frank Whittle and his team, from Rolls-Royce and from our specialist suppliers who produced the essential alloys and accessories. But nobody in Britain had designed an aircraft to use it (if we discount a special version of the Viscount which could hardly have been a greater misuse of this powerful jet). In contrast the Tay was instantly snapped up not only by Pratt & Whitney and the US Navy (and, later, the USAF) as the J48 but also by Prince Poniatowski, boss of Hispano-Suiza. This French company, already making Nenes, called it the Verdon and built it for large numbers of swept-wing fighter and attack aircraft.

The immediate post-war period, like the 1950s that followed, was a time of rapid technological change. Many top decision-takers in Britain were unable to take sensible decisions. As soon as the jet was shown to work, they thought piston engines must instantly be obsolete. As soon as they heard about axial compressors they thought centrifugals must be obsolete. In 1947 our aircraft industry could have made very good use of the Tay. The huge numbers produced elsewhere more than justified Frank's unswerving belief that it was correct to start the jet era with the well-proven centrifugal compressor.

Chapter 5
Axials

By this time, the war was over, and the steam was beginning to
run out of new development programmes. Never, I think, has the
speed of the programmes on the Nene and its smaller brother the
Derwent V been equalled, nor is it ever likely to be again. It was,
of course, due to the team effort, and to the camaraderie and
enthusiasm that existed throughout the Barnoldswick factory.
Men, women and girls worked whatever hours were required
without question, and in a spirit of co-operation beyond
description. That is what used to make Britain powerful and
prosperous.

During this period we had frequent discussions with Frank
Whittle, and always paid due regard to his suggestions and
criticisms. We tried to embody all that was best from his work at
Power Jets, and our relations were of the friendliest nature, with
every encouragement coming from him. The Nene and Tay were
the ultimate expression of his original concept, and he was as
delighted with these fine engines as we were. He was present when
the decision to scale the Nene down in size to the Derwent V for
the Meteor was made; he may well have been the originator of
that idea, but memory fails me on this point.

Hs also paid us frequent visits, despite his arduous labours at
Derby, Crewe and Glasgow on the Merlin and Griffon. Each
Monday afternoon we attended his technical meeting at Derby to
report progress, and we never felt that we were out on a limb on
our own. Les Buckler's close relationship with HPS was valuable;
any manufacturing difficulties were quickly ironed out between
them, and the mighty experimental shops at Derby harnessed to
help us.

At the beginning of the War, Hs had taken on Dr A. A.
Griffith, FRS, who had been head of the Engine Department at
the Royal Aircraft Establishment at Farnborough. Griffith was a

great mathematician and scientist, who since the 1920s had been convinced that turbine engines were the coming powerplant for aircraft. Unfortunately, he was bigoted in favour of the axial compressor, and had reported unfavourably on Whittle's engine, simply because of the large diameter and supposed lower efficiency of the centrifugal compressor. He was a curious loner, whose thinking was years ahead of his time. His fertile brain would produce some radical new idea for an engine, which he would push hard; but once others took up the idea he would lose interest, and pass on to his next invention. He thus had no concept of the team effort which is required to produce a real engine.

At Derby Hs gave him a small office at the Rolls-Royce guest house at Duffield Bank, and he had as his designer Donald Eyre, a superb artist and draughtsman. Eyre had spent many years with Royce, and his project drawings were a marvel of clarity and sophistication. I used to say they sold Griffith's ideas just like Johnnie Walker sold whisky, and with the same soporiphic effect.

My life-long friend and colleague, Lionel Haworth, who became one of the greatest turbine engine designers of Rolls-Royce, fell under the Griffith spell. Derby thus began to dabble in axial jet engines during the War, led by Haworth and Rubbra, and motivated by Griffith. One strange machine, the CR.4 contra-rotating engine, got as far as bench running in 1942.

In the end, a broad-brush version of a more practical engine, the AJ.65 turbojet, was evolved in 1945/6, the nomenclature meaning Axial Jet, 6,500 lb thrust. This engine subsequently became the Avon. It was developed to more than 10,000 lb in the 1950s, powering such famous aircraft as the Canberra and Valiant bombers, Hunter, Scimitar and Sea Vixen fighters, and the Comet and Caravelle passenger jetliners. It was the most important British engine of the 1950s. But at the start of the project the war had only just ended, and since Barnoldswick was the major seat of knowledge on turbine engines, Hs was reluctant to leave the AJ.65 at Derby. He instructed my team at Barnoldswick to undertake the design and development.

Although I was not altogether happy with the proposal for the AJ.65, I did not contest this situation. At that time Rolls-Royce had no real experience in the design of axial compressors, and I hated moving into the unknown on what was obviously such an important innovation in the new field of turbine engines. The main supporters of axial compressors were Constant, now head of the Engine Department of the RAE, and Griffith. The two companies which had toyed with axials were Metropolitan-Vickers at Manchester and Armstrong Siddeley at Coventry. Metrovick had followed the RAE lead, and with Dr D. M. Smith in control had made the F.2 turbojet, designed for 2,000 lb thrust. Although this engine flew in 1943 in the F.9/40 Meteor, its progress had been relatively slow. Apart from its smaller diameter it showed no advantages from the supposed higher efficiency of the complicated axial compressor.

Dr Smith was a very sound and methodical engineer, but had no experience of aircraft engines. Nonetheless, the F.2, which afterwards was named the Beryl, was a gallant first attempt. Smith followed with an absolutely first-class turbojet, the F.9 Sapphire. When the Ministry decided that in the post-war era there was no place for an additional aircraft engine company, and requested Metrovick to withdraw from that field, details of the Sapphire were handed to Armstrong Siddeley.

At Armstrong Siddeley, Pat Lindsey, their brilliant young engineer, had graduated like myself from the development of superchargers on piston engines to a consideration of turbine engines. He designed a test axial compressor in which all the blades could be varied in angle individually, and thus rapidly acquired insight into the behaviour of these multi-stage machines. I had many discussions with him, and was convinced that there were many aerodynamic and mechanical problems to be solved before the axial compressor could be regarded as a sound substitute for the well-proven and rugged centrifugal compressor. The problem was compounded by the proponents of the axial compressor claiming not only a higher efficiency, but also a higher pressure ratio. Whittle's engine had been designed for about 4:1 compression, but for the AJ.65 Griffith was postulating more than 7:1 on paper. The advantages of 7:1 and 85 per cent efficiency over Whittle's mere 4:1 and 80 per cent made the prize very great. So we leaped off into the deep end and landed in such trouble that it took about seven years before the AJ.65 could get a clean bill of health. Seven years, when we had made the Nene in as many months!

We started the design at Barnoldswick, and it was not long before Lombard was in my office saying that there was no way we could meet the projected weight of the engine — in fact, we would be 50 per cent heavier than Griffith's optimistic estimate. At the same time, Harry Pearson was worried about the high pressure ratio, and so I took the decision to drop this to 6.3:1, and told Lom the weight must stay at his design estimate. Morley, who was doing the mechanical design of the compressor, was mindful of the fact that the blades all stuck out like tuning forks, and that resonant vibrations (as had been experienced on Metrovick's F.2) was a major hazard, causing the blades to break off at the roots. His solution was to fix the blades with a pin root so that they were all loose, and hopefully would not vibrate. In the event, this was an excellent proposal, but at high rpm the centrifugal forces on the blades caused the roots to lock-up and resonant vibrations did cause failures. But at least the problem was limited to the high-speed end of the running range.

In the aerodynamic design of an axial compressor, the fundamental dimensions are fixed by the design pressure ratio. In the case of the AJ.65, this actually settled at 6.3:1, and each of the 12 stages of blading was designed to do an equal amount of work on the air in compressing it. Thus, as the air passed from one stage to the next, the height of each blade row was made smaller than the preceding one in order that, as the air was gradually compressed from stage to stage, the velocity with which it travelled along the compressor remained constant. This meant that the outlet area was only about one-quarter of the inlet area.

This arrangement is fine when the compressor is running at full speed at its design pressure ratio. At lower speeds, during starting and acceleration, the pressure ratio is extremely small. In this condition the outlet area and the inlet are completely out of balance. For example, under starting conditions, where the pressure ratio may be about 2:1, the outlet area should only be 20 per cent less than the inlet area. But because the outlet area is, in fact, only one-quarter of the inlet area, the airflow is severely restricted; putting it crudely, the air taken in at the front cannot get out at the back. This causes the blades at the front of the compressor to stall, vibrate, and not infrequently to snap off. The compressor surges and is also very inefficient under these conditions, and this makes the engine extremely difficult to start.

Looked at another way, compressing air is somewhat analogous to driving water up a slope and over a ramp with a broom. One can take almighty strokes, and over the water goes. This is the method adopted by the centrifugal impeller. Alternatively, hundreds of small brushes can be used in quick small strokes gradually forcing the water up the slope. When arranged correctly, this will be much more efficient than the almighty slosh. This is the method adopted by the axial compressor running at full speed, the small brushes corresponding to the large number of blades in the axial 'spool'. If, however, as the top of the ramp is approached the rate of sweeping is reducing (as at part-speed), then some of the water will run backwards to the bottom. This is similar to surging, when the direction of the airflow through the compressor reverses itself and flows backwards.

Clearly, if the big slosh of the centrifugal is not hard enough, or the slope too steep, the water will never reach the top of the ramp and even the centrifugal compressor will surge; but this is much less likely to occur than in the case of the small continuous sweeping action of the axial compressor. The slope, of course, corresponds to the pressure ratio — the steeper, the higher the compression.

Thus, a little thought showed that the axial compressor bristled with mechanical and aerodynamic problems, and so it proved to be. Even GE in America, who had started on the TG-180 axial engine in 1941, took almost six years before it reached fruition. Thus, unknowingly, Hs had been truly prophetic when he told Frank Whittle, 'Just leave it to us, we will soon design the simplicity out of it'.

But we soldiered on as best we could, and in 1946 we had the first AJ.65 engine on test at Barnoldswick. Sure enough, it was difficult to start, would not accelerate, broke its first-stage blades and could only be coaxed reluctantly to 5,000 lb thrust. It was, comparatively speaking, a hell of a mess. In his heart, Hs blamed me personally. Up to that time, everything I had touched had turned to gold, and Hs had come to regard the turbine engine as a piece of cake. Suddenly my life was full of big problems; in contrast, the war had merely been hard work.

Hs knew that my marriage had broken up, and that I was staying in odd pubs, and even sleeping from time to time in my office — a complete wandering Jew. He recognised immediately that the axial engine presented an almighty challenge, and decided to move the whole of the turbine design and development from Barnoldswick to Derby so that the big battalions could take over.

The move was precipitated when Marshal of the Royal Air Force Sir Charles Portal and his entourage visited Barnoldswick and, *en route,* passed through Derby without stopping! Hs' immediate reaction was,

'We can't have that. *Derby* is the centre of Rolls-Royce, not Hooker's bloody garage at Barnoldswick'.

Lombard, Herriot and myself viewed the inevitable move with nervousness. How would we be fitted into the ranks at Derby? We were the acknowledged world leaders of the jet age, and the prospect was not particularly pleasing after the independence that we had enjoyed at Barnoldswick. Though we had no reason to doubt the friendliness of our welcome, there were obviously going to be problems of position and status. I adopted a 'couldn't care less' attitude — 'Tell me what to do and I will do it' — which surprised Hs, and rightly made him suspicious.

I felt fairly secure, because at the height of the success of the Nene and Derwent V, he had invited me, Cyril Lovesey and Ray Dorey to a private dinner at the company guest house at Duffield Bank. He told us that the future of Rolls-Royce would lie in our hands — Dorey as his successor as General Manager, Lovesey as Chief Development Engineer — a position he had occupied for some years already — and me as Chief Engineer. (In the event, only Lovesey survived. Dorey was shunted off as General Manager of the Motor Car Division at Crewe under Llewellyn Smith, and I left the Company).

Why Hs got us together to tell us this I shall never know. It was quite unlike him to commit himself ahead of time, and he had years to go himself, so there was no need to nominate the heir apparent. For myself, I can honestly say that I was struck dumb by the promise that I would be the Chief Engineer of Rolls-Royce. I was already very high in the hierarchy, and the great rapport between Hs and myself seemed to grow stronger every day. I held him in the greatest possible respect and affection, for he had given me great power. For his part, he said later that he regarded me as his son; but when he dangled the plum job before me, things were never the same again. I was intoxicated by the thought, and since I was under 40, the great question that filled my mind was when, when, when? I felt ready for the job and responsibility, and I also felt that I would have the backing of all the engineers in the company. Of course, things are different today. I know many a promising young engineer who will never see 50 again!

I never knew why Ray Dorey fell from grace, but I can say now that it was one of the greatest disasters that ever befell Rolls-Royce. Dorey was cast in the same mould as Hs. A great inspiring leader with tremendous energy and drive, but, perhaps, not quite the same sense of humour as Hs. He was the Manager of our Flight Centre at Hucknall, and built it up from a few wooden sheds to a large and powerful establishment of vast capability.

The original idea of Hucknall was that aircraft fitted with Rolls-Royce engines would be tested there in order to ensure that the total engine installation worked properly, and this included the radiators for cooling the water and oil, the air intakes and the exhaust system, which could be made to act like a small jet propulsion unit. We had found that we could not rely on the aircraft manufacturers to do this work, because they were too busy sorting out their own problems.

In 1939 Hucknall consisted of an aerodrome, a few technical assistants and test pilots, and not much else. During the Battle of Britain, Dorey did a most courageous thing. He rang the Air Ministry and said, 'Send me the crashed Hurricanes and I will repair them'. Considering that he had no workforce to do it, and no experience, it was remarkable that in a matter of weeks he was receiving crashed Hurricane I aircraft with the Merlin III, repairing them, and installing the more powerful Merlin XX, to send them back to the RAF as Hurricane IIs.

He followed this remarkable contribution to the Battle of Britain by installing the first two-stage Merlin in a Spitfire, and thus created the Spitfire IX, which was the most famous of them all. Then he undertook to produce the powerplants for the Lancaster bomber programme, and set up a factory at Ilkeston for this purpose. When we took over Whittle's jet engine, he installed one in the tail of a Wellington bomber, so that we were able to test it under flight conditions without the safety of the aircraft being dependent upon it. In fact, this was the first flying jet test bed.

When the Nene appeared on the scene, Dorey set forth to put four of them into a Lancaster in place of the Merlins. We had calculated that the four-Nene Lancaster would exceed 400 mph and fly well above 30,000 ft. It would thus be immune to enemy action, either from fighters or AA fire. This project was never completed, because the war ended, but he did instal two Nenes in a Lancastrian, leaving the inboard Merlins unaltered. This aircraft would take off with all four engines working; once in the air, the propellers could be feathered, so that the Lancastrian then flew as a pure jet. This Lancastrian was tremendously valuable, because it could take several passengers. Many important people from all over the world were able to get their first experience of jet propulsion — so smooth, quiet and vibration-free, compared to the racketing Merlins.

That Dorey's colossal contribution to the war effort never received any official recognition, will always remain a disgrace to those who serve out such baubles. He was a great man, and when Hs nominated him as his successor, I was not in the least surprised. But it never happened, and Dorey retired to Crewe making the motor cars, and took up farming as a hobby. And so, Hs made his big mistake and sowed the seeds of the creeping disaster that was to overtake Rolls-Royce in 1971.

In the immediate post-war years, when the production of Merlin and Griffon piston engines fell by about 98 per cent almost overnight, the first move was to transfer the production of the Nene and Derwent V to Derby. It was natural that the design and development of these engines should also be centred at Derby, and this transition was made painlessly enough, so that the engineers at Derby could cut their teeth on turbine engines.

At this time, the security cloak on gas-turbine engines had been lifted, and I was asked to lecture at the Derby Branch of the Royal Aeronautical Society. With malice aforethought, I entitled the lecture *Turbine Engines for Beginners.* Hs was not amused at the title, but an enormous audience turned up to hear it, and I had many requests for copies, particularly from the RAF where it was known as 'Squirts for Twerps'. It was not as elementary as the title implied, and all aviation circles were fascinated by the new method of jet propulsion.

The year was 1946, and the strains of the work I had put in for the past eight years, and the emotional crisis of my failed marriage, were beginning to tell on me. One day Hs called me to his office and said,

'I have been watching you lately. You don't look at all well, and I think that you need a holiday. Where would you like to go — anywhere in the world?'

I protested that I was alright, but he insisted; so, of the top off my head, I said,

'I would like to go to South America'.

Hs leaned back in his chair and pressed the button behind him. His secretary came in and he said,

'Book him on the slowest boat you can find to South America'. And then he turned to me and said,

'The Argentine are going to buy some Merlins from us, and we need that order badly as we have Merlins running out of our ears.

So if you do anything to upset the order, I will break your neck'.

I protested, why should I want to do that, and he replied,

'I know you won't be able to stop boasting about those jet engines, and the World's Speed Record, and they are not ready for jets yet. Besides, we need the order badly'.

I promised that I would do all that I could to further the sale of Merlins, but resolved also to take with me slides and material so that I could lecture on jet engines. Meanwhile, his secretary had booked my passage on one of the Holder Lines' meat boats that went from Liverpool to Buenos Aires. This ship had accommodation for about 12 passengers and took 23 days to make the voyage. She sure had found a slow ship, but one that I was to enjoy thoroughly.

There were currency restrictions at the time, so I was given a letter of credit to spend in Argentina, and Hs' secretary thoughtfully provided me with £50 of the Holder Lines' equivalent of money, which could be spent in the ship. I was the only passenger thus endowed, and hence was very popular as the dispenser of booze and tobacco, which were the only things one could spend money on anyway. Gin and whisky were 10s (50p) a bottle.

The other passengers were a mixed bag. There were two young married couples returning to a bank in Buenos Aires, two Argentinians, one of whom had just finished his apprenticeship at Metrovick, and two British Latin-American Volunteer girls who had been in the WAAF during the War, and were being repatriated home. Both had been radar operators.

We had to make our own amusement, and the first thing we did was, with the help of the ship's carpenter, to make a swimming pool on the upper deck. It consisted of a wooden frame with a tarpaulin inside, and water was pumped continuously in from the sea and spilled over the sides. It was a great joy and boon to us all. In the evenings we played cards or danced and sang to the piano music of the Argentinian boy, who was a brilliant player.

The accommodation was a bit scruffy but, being a meat boat, the food was good and plentiful — at least it seemed so after the rigours of wartime rationing. And so we ambled at about 8 knots southwards across the Bay — which was so rough that only two of us survived seasickness — through calm seas to the Cape Verde Islands, which was the only land we saw on the trip. Then on through shoals of flying fish, and the magical dawns at the Equator, to the River Plate.

When we docked at the Embarquero in Buenos Aires I was met by the Rolls-Royce agent, Angeloglou Levante. He was a quiet, thick-set man in his early 50s, and a very shrewd businessman who had made a considerable fortune as an agent for Reynolds chains, Ferodo brake linings and many other British engineering products. He was newly appointed as an agent for Rolls-Royce, and was rightly looking forward to big business in the aero-engine field, with the projected sale of Merlins in the immediate offing.

At this time, Argentina was very rich, although it consisted of a two-class society — very wealthy and very poor. Peron and Evita were in full control, and had made lots of hay out of the war. The country was by and large very pro-European, being mainly a mixture of Spanish, Italian, German, French and British. Being very polite people, they did not like the brash manners of the Americans, nor were they pleased at the US support for Brazil, who challenged Argentina for the dominating position in the South American continent.

I was taken off by Levante, and installed in the Palace Hotel, which was the most luxurious in Buenos Aires and, certainly, the best I had ever stayed in. Quiet, dignified and superbly appointed, it was another world after the gloom and rationing of post-war England.

I was fascinated by the foyer, which was run with superb military precision by the Head Porter. He stood like a ramrod in immaculate uniform at his desk, and ruled with a rod of iron the many bell-boys who stood unobtrusively around, equally immaculate and at attention at strategic vantage points in the huge foyer. It seemed to me that he spoke all the world's languages with equal fluency. People would go to him and he would converse with them in their native tongue; then he would bark out orders in Spanish, at which one of the bell-boys would spring into action. I had never seen the like before, or since.

Having done well out of all sides during the war, Argentina's shops were full of every kind of luxury. The only shortage appeared to be motor cars and spare parts, particularly tyres. Any old banger was highly prized, although the main transport was by British-built trams. All traffic drove on the left, but while I was there the edict came to change to the right, and for a period the population drove with Gallic fervour on both sides of the road — with the added complication that the trams, being on rails, could not be changed over.

When I left England, I had been provided with a letter of credit, since there were rigid controls on the export of sterling. The rate of exchange in 1946 was 16 pesos to the pound. As I write, the exchange rate is more than 3,500, despite the fact that the pound has depreciated to one-fifth of its 1946 value, which only goes to show the ghastly way that beautiful and fertile country has been run during the past 30 years.

I think that their prime mistake was their attempt to blackmail Britain on the price of beef after the war. Their major export had always been beef to this country, but during the war this trade almost disappeared, so they began to eat the beef themselves. After the war, when trade resumed, their price was so high that we refused to buy, and instead developed the meat supply from Australia. In the meantime, rationing went on in Britain until the early 1950s, so our imports were slow to pick up.

At 16 pesos to the pound, my room in the Palace Hotel was costing me £30 per week, which was very expensive in those days. So I conferred with our Service representative, Reggie Longinotto, whose job it was to look after the Rolls-Royce aero engines that were in use in those parts — principally Merlins in Lancastrian and York civil airliners.

I asked him how much he paid to live at the City Hotel.

'About 350 pesos per week for the room alone,' he replied.

'You can't afford that, can you?' I asked.

He said that it was hard going, so I asked him why we did not rent one of the Apartementos advertised in the local paper, and share the expense. He agreed to try, and we searched the adverts, and selected a flat in the Edificio Modart in Corrientis, which is the Piccadilly of Buenos Aires. I sent him away to negotiate the deal, and he came back and said we could not get the key for a month.

I said, 'Did you try him with 100 pesos?'

No, he had not thought of that, so I sent him back again, and he returned with the key of what proved to be a magnificent flat at a cost of 400 pesos per month. This changed our financial outlook more than somewhat, and we now had ample cash to investigate the bars, restaurants and night-life of Buenos Aires, of which there was an enormous variety.

The flat was the service type, and in the foyer of the Edificio a coterie of waiters was always available. One telephoned down, and they would dash in with all the necessary tableware and provide everything for any occasion. They would fetch the food hot from the neighbouring very high-class restaurants — and every other establishment was one of these — produce wine and, in general, join in with great joy and goodwill with anything we wished to organise. It was even better than Oxford!

Buenos Aires was teeming with all the luxuries that Britain had eschewed in the war years: bright lights, night clubs, food and wine, chocolate, silk stockings and fine clothes, watches and jewellery, and all sorts of beautiful leather goods. There was, also, a surfeit of German frauleins, who had obviously been sent to Buenos Aires to get information on the sailing of ships to Europe during the war, and with the collapse of Germany were now left high and dry. It was no problem to set my heart against them.

Apart from the German girls, I saw no signs of the 'white slave' racket for which Buenos Aires was so ill-famed. On the contrary, the locals were as straight-laced as in most Catholic countries, except on the dockside area, where the usual dives were to be found.

We did not lack friends, because Reggie had already made a number through his connection with the airlines, and I had kept contact with the two young married couples and the two WAAF girls from the boat. And so we set out to sample the night-life in a city where it was customary to dine at any time between 11.00 pm and 1.00 am, having restored one's strength in the afternoon siesta.

I kept in close touch with our agent, who had a dark general store, rather like a ship's chandlers, on a street called Alsina. He sat in state in an inner sanctum, and was visited by quiet gents who slid in and out on palm-greasing expeditions, I more than suspected. Nonetheless, he was a most hospitable and entertaining man. His great joy was his motor cruiser on the River Plate, and he loved to take us for the weekend on the river. The cruiser had two 80 hp diesels, and was equipped *en tout confort* for about six people. There was a crew of two, one of whom managed the boat while the other did the cooking and waiting.

It was very pleasant to cruise slowly among the many tributaries of the giant delta, and then to tie up for the night when drinks and dinner would be served at darkness, around 7.00 pm. It was springtime in Argentina, and the weather was lovely and soft. The river was the usual yellow colour, and not very inviting, but the banks were covered in lush semi-tropical growth, with here and there a little thatched wooden house on stilts where the few very poor peasants lived.

We discussed the sale of Merlins, and the proposed aircraft. Levante told me that the centre of this activity was up-country at Cordoba some 500 miles away. How did I get to see it? He said we must get the permission of General San Martin, the GOC of the Fuerza Aérea, and that he would arrange for me to meet him forthwith.

I met the General, who spoke English, and we took to each other immediately. He welcomed my proposed visit to Cordoba, and I set forth with Johnnie Bruton, who was Levante's young partner, and an Argentine citizen although of British parents and education. It was necessary to go by night train, which left Buenos Aires at 8.00 pm. The railway system had all been built by the British, and indeed was British-owned until the war. Thus, except for the fact that the carriages and dining cars were bright and clean, and there was a surfeit of attendants in spotless uniform, one might have been travelling on the LMS to Derby.

Dinner, Italian style, was excellent, and there were plenty of good Argentinian and Chilean wines at cheap prices. The Argentinians are quiet and very polite people, but after dinner, when some had withdrawn, conversation began to buzz. I did my best to encourage this by inviting passengers to drink a glass of wine with me, which they willingly did. Presently, one young man began to sing the melody 'Besame mucho', and followed this, in my honour, with 'Greensleeves'. By magic, a waiter appeared with a guitar, and the party was on. But then, I never could sleep on trains. Even more pleasant were later trips, when, on appearing on the platform at Buenos Aires, I was greeted with loud 'Olés' by the dining-car attendants!

It was always dark on these journeys, so one could not see the flat countryside as one passed through Rosario *en route* for Cordoba. On arrival, we booked in at the Bristol Hotel, and were conducted by the Aeronautical Institute to the factory. The conducted tour started from bedrock at the smelly shop where the glue was made from horses' and cows' hooves, went on to the place where the plywood was ripped from tree-trunks and glued together, and finally to the shop where a few wooden, small aircraft were made.

I said to the Manager,

'Can I see the aeroplane with the Merlin engines in it?'

He replied, 'We have not started to make that yet'.

'Can I see the drawings, because I understand it is going to be similar to the Mosquito'.

'I am sorry', he replied. 'But we have not started on the design yet'.

It became clear that the place was in no way equipped to make even a small number of such a sophisticated aircraft, and I thought, so much for Hs' dream of selling them large numbers of Merlins. I did, however, make one last desperate effort by offering to get from Derby full details of the Mosquito powerplant installation, so that they would only have to do the wooden airframe. They accepted this offer with alacrity, and showed me the one aeroplane they had made, just like a Mosquito but fitted with two Pratt & Whitney 1,200 hp air-cooled Twin Wasp engines.

This was the IAe.24 Calquin (Royal Eagle). It was brand new, and had only flown once, but they insisted on my going on the second flight. The test pilot, Roberto, was a devil-may-care chap, and we roared off into the mountains north of Cordoba. The Calquin shook and vibrated in no uncertain fashion, but charged along at about 250 knots at low altitude through the beautiful valleys and mountains in the most exhilarating fashion. I enjoyed the flight enormously, but little knew that I was destined to be the only passenger ever to fly in the machine, for reasons which I shall recount later.

We returned to Buenos Aires, and I informed Hs by cable that there was not much substance in his dream, and asking for details of the Mosquito powerplant to be sent forthwith. It was typical of the haphazard way things went on in the Argentine, that our agent was uninformed, and equally deluded and disappointed. In due course, the drawings were despatched from Derby by air, but the aircraft crashed *en route* and everything was burned. A second set was duly sent, but by this time the situation had changed dramatically.

It had been decided to hold, in Buenos Aires, the first aeronautical exhibition ever held in South America. I thought this was the opportunity to put on show a Derwent turbojet. At first Hs refused, saying it would prejudice the Merlin sale, but later relented when I said that the chances of that were negligible, and we might as well look to the future.

Finally, he sent an engine by air, and it arrived in the nick of time on a Friday, when the exhibition was due to open on Sunday. No amount of talking would persuade the Customs officials to let us have the engine, so I went to General San Martin who barked out orders, and in no time I was in a lorry surrounded by armed soldiers *en route* for the Customs. Here there was an enormous hullabaloo, but the Customs officials were swept aside and we left with the three packing cases in which the engine sub-assemblies were contained. The exhibition hall was in the centre of Buenos Aires. Reggie and I worked all the Saturday night, assisted by a fitter from Derby who had been sent with the engine, assembling the Derwent on the stand.

The show was due to be opened by President Peron at 10 am on the following day, and the ceremony would have been incomplete without the Calquin. And so, the famous wooden aeroplane from Cordoba was flown by Roberto down to Buenos Aires and landed along the dockside, from whence it was towed by hand through the town amid the cheering crowds to the front of the exhibition.

Peron duly opened the show, and came with General San Martin directly to our stand where I spent some time explaining to them both how a jet engine worked. The time was coincidental with the second attempt at the World's Speed Record made by a Meteor, and I predicted to them that 1,000 km/h would be attained. In the event, Group Captain Donaldson took the record at 991 km/h, but that was near enough.

To say that the Derwent stole the show is to put it mildly. Hundreds of people surrounded the stand all day, and the questions came thick and fast. When I got off the stand at midnight, I was completely exhausted; but the fish had been hooked. Subsequently a licence to manufacture the Derwent I was requested, and the negotiations for the purchase of 50 Meteor aircraft opened up.

The dream of selling Argentina Mosquitos and Merlin engines was not completely ended, because an RAF squadron arrived to demonstrate the Mosquito to the Fuerza Aérea. I went with the British Air Attaché, Air Commodore Beiseizel (inevitably known as Bicycle) to this demonstration, which was at an airfield somewhere in mid-Argentina. We flew in his RAF Anson, and before we left the sergeant pilot whispered to me, 'I expect he will get us lost'. And he did. After we had exceeded our flight time by about 15 min we had to turn back under the navigation of the sergeant, and finally arrived. I was astounded to see that there was a steady stream of locusts, seemingly unending in numbers, drifting across the airfield; to me, flying seemed very hazardous.

But the RAF took off, and put on a marvellous show. On landing, their windscreens were plastered with a layer of dead locusts. What was worse, their radiators were plugged solid with the insects which, with their wings sheared off, just fitted the honeycombs like plugs. But no harm came — nor did the sale of Mosquitos go through.

There was a sad but comical ending to the wooden Calquin prototype in Buenos Aires. The engineers at Cordoba wanted it back to continue the flight trials, so again it was towed through the streets and admiring crowds to the Embarquero for takeoff. In the meantime, Roberto's father had died, and so he was in deep mourning. The deputy test pilot therefore took control, and climbed into the cockpit in front of what seemed to be the whole population of Buenos Aires, cheering their heads off.

Amidst this encouragement, he started his takeoff run down the dockside. He was thoroughly committed when, out of a siding, puffed very slowly a freight train at right-angles to his path. The pilot had just time to throttle back when he hit the train with a sickening crash, and engines, propellers and bits of aeroplane flew everywhere. A terrible groan arose from the people, only to change to cheering when the pilot staggered out with nothing worse than cuts and bruises. The bits of the aircraft were kicked into the gutter, and were still there when I left a few weeks later. This seemed to typify Argentina.

As I have said, despite Hs' exhortation, I had gone prepared to lecture on jet engines, and did this to the Fuerza Aérea in Buenos Aires, and to the Institute in Cordoba. It was on one of the trips to Cordoba that I met M Dewoitine, the celebrated French aircraft designer. It appeared that Dewoitine had left France under a cloud after the war, and was living with a new young wife in a splendid villa on the outskirts of Cordoba.

To amuse himself, he had converted one of the rooms to a drawing office, and was designing a single-jet aircraft using what he knew about the Derwent engine. I joined with him in this work, and together we proposed a machine which was subsequently named the Púlqui (Arrow). It was made after I left and was taken over by Kurt Tank, the German designer of the Focke-Wulf 190, who had skipped from Germany and arrived up at Cordoba. I never heard what happened to Dewoitine, who, although wealthy, was far from happy in the isolation of mid-Argentina.

Thus, the threads came together, and apart from the 50

Meteors that Gloster Aircraft sold, Rolls-Royce made a lucrative deal for the licence for the Derwent V, and the supply of the machine tools to manufacture it. In the event, the Argentinians never made a single engine, but this was typical of the *laissez-faire* attitude which was taking the whole country down the drain.

A. A. Lombard (Lom)

Fred Morley

Harry Pearson

Dr. R. (Bob) Plumb

Barnoldswick – John Herriot and S.G.H. with their welcome guest Air Commodore Frank Whittle.

The Welland 1 – *entered service with No. 616 Squadron R.A.F. in July 1944.*

Derwent production line at Rolls-Royce Newcastle-under-Lyme.

Nene 10.

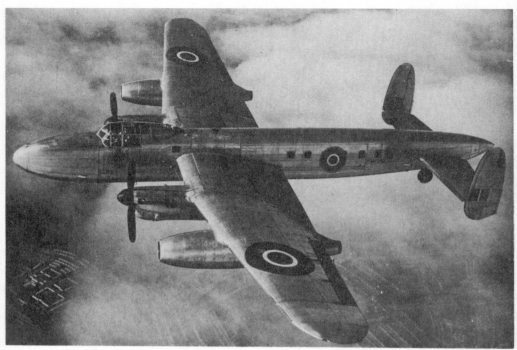

The first Nene–Lancastrian.

After signing Nene licence at Hartford, Connecticut.
From left – Bill Gwinn, General Manager, Pratt & Whitney, S. G. H., Wright
Parkins, Chief Engineer, Pratt & Whitney.

Chapter 6
The Break and a New Start

In September 1946 I was instructed to leave the Argentine and go to New York to assist the negotiations with Pratt & Whitney. With sadness I took leave of many friends and boarded a DC-4 of Panagra. Unpressurized, we flew at about 2,000 ft over varied scenery via Montevideo, Rio, Belem and Jamaica. We spent many hours rumbling across the impenetrable forests of the Matto Grosso to Belem, where the runway had been hacked out of the jungle four years earlier as a staging post between the US factories and Africa. During the refuelling, I braved the stifling heat and humidity to stroll to the edge of the jungle; it really was impenetrable.

After about a week with Pratt & Whitney, I returned to Derby and was told by Hs to get up to Barnoldswick, because the Avon was in 'a hell of a mess'. Throughout 1947, while we strove to cure the Avon's deep-seated ills, Hs looked ahead to the time when the lusty infants we had reared at Barnoldswick would be recognised as the main company products by bringing them to Derby. He did not mean to dispose of Barnoldswick, but to reduce it to the status of an experimental shop for making components and running special prototype engines. The Derwent V was already in production at Derby, and Elliott, Rubbra, Lovesey and (just back from Packard) Ellor were fast becoming gas-turbine engineers. In particular, the new Avon was to be moved to Derby lock, stock and barrel.

Obviously the independence we had enjoyed 120 miles from Derby would vanish; and we wondered just what was in store for us. For my own part, I saw that I could not remain Chief Engineer of Turbine Engines. I asked Hs directly about this. He was embarrassed, and uncertain how to be fair to my team whilst supporting his 'old guard' at Derby. The first thing he did was to appoint Rubbra and myself Assistant Chief Engineers of the company. These titles had not previously existed, but titles counted for little in Rolls-Royce; what mattered were the departments and resources one directly controlled. There was no question of Lov and Ellor working for me, and I was pretty much back where I had been in 1938.

I taxed Hs with his promise that I should be Chief Engineer. I told him that if he put the job up for election I should win easily. He replied 'You're not ready for that job yet. You can't control your own affairs, let alone this great firm'. In retrospect he was probably right. My marriage had irretrievably broken down, and the great strain of this, added to that of the Avon, was showing in my life-style and demeanour. So I went back to Barnoldswick and sulked in solitary confinement, while engineers around me were transferred to Derby and shared out amongst their corresponding departments.

I did little but mull over the unfair treatment I was receiving, and bemoan my coming loss of authority, and with it the last vestiges of my self-respect and confidence. I felt very sorry for myself and resolved to play no part in the transfer, and to await events.

With my sulking in the background, it was early one Monday morning in June 1948 that my office door at Barnoldswick burst open, and Hs walked in. He must have left Derby at the crack of dawn after fulminating over the situation all week-end. There was no trace of the usual twinkle in his eye, and his face was stern and set. I rose and stood beside my desk and we faced each other. Without preamble he barked 'This jet job is too important to leave here in this garage. I am determined to move it to Derby. What are you going to do about that?' My heart lurched, and my stomach turned over.

I was facing the great man, for so many years my close friend and mentor, whose word was law in Rolls-Royce. A smile from me and a soft word would have turned his wrath, but I couldn't do it. With studied insolence I replied 'I am glad that you find it important now. Tell me what *you* want me to do and I will do it'. The first remark implied that he had only just recognised the importance of gas turbines, which was not true, and the second was a parody of what he had often said to me since I joined the firm: 'Tell us what we have to do and we will do it ....'.

His face went grim, and I knew that the moment of crisis — a moment of great drama for me — was upon us. He said 'I am not satisfied with that answer. Furthermore, I won't have you interfering with my plans with a chip on your shoulder'. Feeling physically sick, I plunged headlong to destruction: 'It's the only answer you are going to get from me, so why don't you sack me?' He exploded in a rage I had never seen before: 'I won't put up with you. Go home now. Wait until I decide what to do with you. There is nothing for you to do here'.

With a bravado I was far from feeling, I spat at him, 'That is a fine return for 11 years of hard and successful work for you. Send me home now and it will be the last time I will ever enter a factory controlled by you'. He, too, was visibly shaken, and shouted, 'I don't care about that. You go home, and leave the address where I can get in touch with you'. I replied, 'You can't get in touch with me. If you want to say anything more to me, write to my bank'. Barely keeping back the tears, I pushed past him and left him standing in my office, silent and alone. The whole scene and the words that passed are etched on my mind. We had never had a cross word and I had worshipped him.

Full of grief and depression I left Bankfield shed, never to return. I returned to my digs in Ilkley to consider the black-looking future. I was still under contract to Rolls-Royce, so there was no immediate financial worry, but I wallowed in self-pity. Then, on the Friday morning, I received a letter in Hs' own hand; 'Dear SGH, I am very upset about our meeting on Monday. Please telephone me so that so we can arrange another talk together'. I called him at once. He said 'Where are you? I will come up to see you on Sunday morning'. I replied 'No, Hs, I will come to Derby to see you'. Thus on the Sunday we shook hands in his office.

Hs said 'No recriminations! I have been thinking. How would you like to be in charge of all our research work? There are a lot of new problems in turbine engines, and I intend to set Derby up with the latest and most powerful equipment to tackle them'.

It was, perhaps, ungrateful of me not to be thrilled. 'You know, Hs, research in Rolls-Royce has been called 'very slow development'. It has always come a very poor second to main engine development.'

He replied, 'I am going to change all that, and I promise you that you will get a fair crack of the whip'.

So I settled for the offer. I moved in to share an office with Rubbra at Derby, and simply stuck (Research) after my title of Assistant Chief Engineer.

But I knew it wasn't going to work out, because, deep inside, I had no intention of trying to climb back up the ladder at Derby.

Instead I telephoned my friend from Oxford days, Reginald Verdon Smith.

Thus, on my 41st birthday, 30 September 1948, I made an appointment with Hs and told him that I wished to leave. He was as upset as I was. 'I don't know what's gone wrong, Stanley. I have always treated you as my son, and you have never come into this office and asked for anything without its being granted'. He asked me what I intended to do: I am sure he was not a bit surprised when I said I was joining Bristol and he told me I must serve out my three months' contract doing penance. Without another word, I turned and left his office and walked out of the Derby works for ever — as I then thought.

I walked sadly down Nightingale Road to the Midland railway station. I should have been ashamed of myself, for I had bitten the hand that fed me, but at the time I could not see it that way.

I went back to my rooms in Ilkley. Fortunately for my sanity I had already met the lady who was to become my wife, Kate Maria Garth. Starting with nothing but the clothes we stood in, she built up a calm and happy home which has continued to this day. Her love and understanding helped me through this most difficult period, yet without resentment she always allowed my work to come first, and subjugated her life and her artistic talents to my well-being.

However, the three months in limbo was far from wasted. I have always had the gift of being able to work alone, and with time to reflect on the future of gas turbines I did many calculations on possible future engines for fighters and for bombers or transports. In 1948 the concept of aircraft flying at high jet speeds over non-stop distances of 5,000 miles (8000 km) or more was a pipe-dream, but one capable of realization.

In such aircraft the weight of fuel at take-off is bound to be four, five or six times the total weight of the engines. But in a fighter the weights of the engine and the fuel are much closer, and as the engine has to be carried all the time (while the fuel is progressively burned off) its weight is of much greater importance.

In Britain and all the other jet-producing countries the main production engines were of the Whittle-derived centrifugal type, but it was inevitable that this would be replaced by the problem-ridden axial. I believed that the heady days of producing new engines in six months were over, and that future development timescales would last as many years (today ten years is commonplace). One of the basic advantages of the axial was its potential for high pressure-ratio, today as high as 30:1. The greater the compression, the lower the specific fuel consumption (fuel consumption per unit of thrust). Even in 1948 I could see no reason why a single axial compressor should not reach 12:1 pressure-ratio. Dr D. M. Smith at Metrovick had run a 9-stage spool which showed that a temperature rise of 20°C per stage was achieveable at an efficiency of 87%. Thus with the AJ.65 Avon we settled on a 12-stage spool designed to reach 20°C per stage, giving a pressure-ratio of 6.5:1 at 85% efficiency. To obtain 12:1 I calculated 17 stages would be required, and I then calculated the extra weight of this engine and compared it with the saving in fuel for different aircraft ranges.

We had often bettered Whittle's baseline consumption of 1.05 (lb per lb-thrust per hour) at Barnoldswick, and with the 6.5:1 axial had reached 0.84. I calculated that the 12:1 compression engine should achieve 0.74. But A. R. Howell at the new NGTE (the National Gas Turbine Establishment formed near Farnborough by merging the nationalized remnants of Whittle's Power Jets with the Engine Department of the RAE) had shown that a temperature rise per stage of 30°C was possible. This would cut the necessary number of stages by one-third, thus the Avon could get away with eight and the 12:1 engine with only 12. This opened up new and exciting prospects for reduced engine weight.

Taking the centrifugal Nene as weighing 1,800 lb at 5,000 lb thrust, I calculated that a 5,000 lb Avon ought to weigh only 1,600 lb. If the number of stages were reduced to eight, it would weigh only 1,200 lb. In fact, the Avon began life at far greater weights, but six years later my team at Bristol built the simple Orpheus which gave 5,000 lb for weights well under 1,000 lb. The 12:1 pressure-ratio engine would weigh 2,000 lb but this would come down to 1,600 lb if we could manage with only 12 stages.

Armed with these figures it was easy to work out that for a typical fighter range of 600 miles (say, 1000 km) the weight of engine plus fuel would be around 5,000 lb for 6.5 pressure ratio (the Avon standard), and only 100 lb lighter with an engine of 12:1 ratio. On the other hand, if the range were doubled, the difference came out to nearly 2,000 lb because of the difference in fuel burn. This comparison of engine(s)-plus-fuel weights was not the whole story, because, while the fuel weight decreases during each flight, the engine has to be carried throughout. But the first conclusion was that for fighters the simple engine of about eight stages paid off, whereas for bombers and transport aircraft with a range greater than 3,000 miles the high pressure-ratio engine was worthwhile, and the greater the pressure-ratio the better.

This type of work was right up my street, and not only did the three months pass quickly but I even earned a couple of hundred pounds by writing articles for the technical press. We had no car, so Kate and I spent hours walking over Ilkley Moor, which we both loved. Previously I had enjoyed the enormous privilege of a new Rolls-Royce, but when I left I returned the car. Ordinary new cars were for export, and anyway at that time I could not have afforded to buy one. Yet my enforced exile was a happy time. I cast off the blues at leaving Rolls-Royce, though I was still full of resentment, and prepared to start a new life in Bristol.

The related families of the Whites and Verdon Smiths, of the City and County of Bristol, made history in transportation by land, sea and air. Sir George White, the first baronet, provided the world's first electric tramway systems for Bristol, Coventry, London and then Dundee. In 1909 he took a winter holiday at Pau, in southern France, and was excited to see flying machines. He brought to England from Paris a young Romanian designer, Henri Coanda, who was years ahead of his time with a ply-skinned aircraft with ducted-fan jet propulsion. Coanda advised Sir George in forming the British & Colonial Aeroplane Company, a pioneer aviation factory, and designed some of its first products in the form of very advanced monoplanes. The headquarters was at ivy-encrusted Filton House, north of the city near the terminus of the tramways. Coanda finally left there in 1914, and more than half a century later I was to bring him back on a nostalgic visit to his original office!

Sir George died in 1916, just as the company was growing rapidly, and making a great contribution to the war effort with the Bristol Fighter and about to be renamed the Bristol Aeroplane Company. His son, Sir Stanley White, became managing director, and Sir William Verdon Smith financial director and later chairman. It was against this background of prestige and family-controlled industrial power that Sir William's son Reginald came from Repton to BNC in 1931 to read law. Knowing nothing of his background I remember Verdon as a tall, immaculate young man, somewhat shy and reserved but with a reputation for having a great brain. After getting first class honours in the final law exams, he went on to be awarded one of Oxford's most famous prizes, the Vinerian Prize for Law. Through our mutual liking for golf and bridge, we became good friends.

When I left Oxford in 1935 I heard no more of him until, one day in 1944, he telephoned me at Barnoldswick. I was disconcerted that he should even have heard of the place, because it was highly secret. He asked if he might come and see the work I was doing, and I replied that that would be very difficult, because it was shown only to those who had a need to know. I was completely bowled over when he said 'That's OK, as a director of the Bristol Aeroplane Company, I've already cleared the visit!'

Thus it was that, when in September 1948 I felt in my bones I ought not to try to climb back at Derby, I telephoned Verdon at Bristol 3831. We met for dinner at the United Universities Club in London, and the deal was struck for me to join the Engine Division at Bristol in January 1949. To my surprise I found that he had kept right up-to-date on what I was doing. Later he introduced me to his father and Sir Stanley as 'the man who put the power into the Merlin'.

For the first year at Bristol I saw little of Verdon, because I did not want to trade on our friendship, but in mid-1950 he made me Chief Engineer of the Engine Division, and with this gave me back my self-respect. Had it not been for his unstinted support I do not know what might have become of me, even after I joined Bristol. I was near despair when the Proteus turboprop came within an ace of breaking the whole company — because the Aircraft Division relied on it also — but we just crawled through and weathered the storm. Thereafter, I hope that the Orpheus, Olympus and Pegasus jets repaid my debt to him, though here too these great programmes needed many courageous decisions on his part. Lesser men would have wilted under the responsibility he bore during the Britannia crisis, for his father was dead, and his cousin George White was a happy-go-lucky chap who indulged in his favourite hobby with the Motor Car Division, and left the main business to the 'Headmaster' as he called Verdon.

When the cash-flow crisis caused by delayed Britannia deliveries was at its highest, in 1958, the chief designer of what by then had become Bristol Aircraft Ltd, Archibald Russell, asked me — as his opposite number in the lately formed Bristol Aero-Engines — to go with him to present to Verdon the splendid Bristol 200, first of all the modern aft-engined trijet passenger liners and intended for BEA. We gave a good presentation, after which Verdon surveyed us in silence. Then Russell, with his impish humour, said 'Give me a million and we won't do it!' Verdon laughed, but the relief on his face showed. By this time he was Sir Reginald Verdon Smith, an absolutely masterful public speaker, and dedicated to the welfare of Bristol.

Around 1963 he was chairman of the board of Bristol Siddeley Engines Ltd, whose formation he had masterminded, and chairman-elect of Lloyds Bank, following in the steps of his father. Sir Arnold Hall was BSEL managing director, I was technical director and Brian Davidson commercial director. One day Brian brought to our attention the fact that the company was making excessive profits overhauling Sapphire turbojets for the RAF, under a contract we had inherited from Armstrong Siddeley. In those days it was the rule that the costs of early overhauls of a new type of engine were estimated normally on the high side. After sufficient experience had been gained, the actual costs were carefully examined by the Ministry and a price for subsequent overhauls mutually agreed, based on these real costs. But in the case of the Sapphire the Ministry and Armstrong Siddeley had failed to carry out the detailed review of actual costs, and so the original high-price contract was still running years after the engine had been in service.

This was most embarrassing news, especially as it was something BSEL had inherited and had known nothing about until Davidson did his own careful checks. Verdon ruled that the Ministry must be informed and that BSEL must repay several million pounds, an offer which was accepted by the Ministry. Since the latter and BSEL were equally to blame, no one anticipated that the Public Accounts Committee would create a supposed great scandal and criticize Verdon personally. He was the personification of rectitude in all his dealings, but Wedgwood Benn, who was the current Minister of Technology insisted that Verdon must resign from all his public affairs.

The splendid career of a great man, who had unstintingly given his great gifts for the welfare of others, particularly to the education of young people, was thus ignominiously curtailed in an atmosphere of spite and injustice.

Meteor III with Derwent I engines.

Derwent I

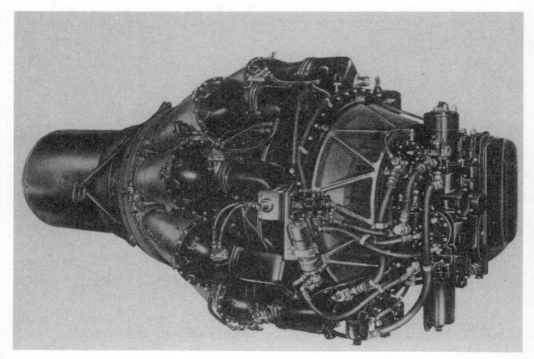

Derwent V

Derwent V cutaway

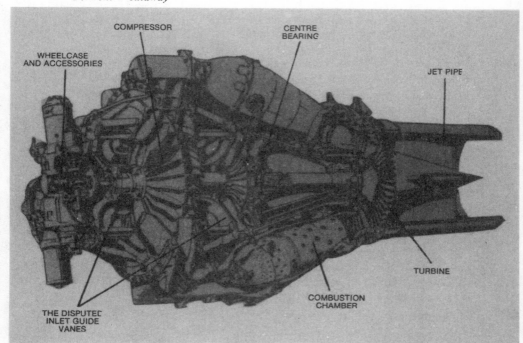

Avon engine prototype.

Alan Newton.

Ernest Eltis.

ROLLS·ROYCE LIMITED

TELEGRAMS
"ROYCAR, DERBY"

DERBY

TELEPHONES
DERBY 2424 (12 LINES)

IN YOUR REPLY PLEASE
QUOTE

17/6/48

Dear SGH

I am very upset as a result of our meeting the other day. I would very much like to have another talk with you. If you will ring me at Derby we can fix a time.

Sir Reginald Verdon Smith   *Charles Marchant*

From left: S.G.H., Air Marshal Sir Ronald Ivelaw-Chapman (with Olympus compressor disc), Air Chief Marshal Sir Alec Coryton, Managing Director Bristol Aero-Engines Ltd., Air Chief Marshal Sir Ralph Cochrane.

Production Proteus engine.

Proteus engine cutaway.

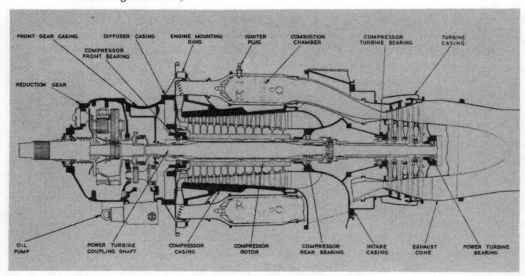

FRONT GEAR CASING   DIFFUSER CASING   ENGINE MOUNTING RING   IGNITER PLUG   COMBUSTION CHAMBER   COMPRESSOR TURBINE BEARING   TURBINE CASING

COMPRESSOR FRONT BEARING

REDUCTION GEAR

OIL PUMP   POWER TURBINE COUPLING SHAFT   COMPRESSOR CASING   COMPRESSOR ROTOR   COMPRESSOR REAR BEARING   INTAKE CASING   EXHAUST CONE   POWER TURBINE BEARING

Chapter 7
The Proteus

I joined the Bristol Engine Division on 3 January 1949, full of optimism. The company was still producing large numbers of the excellent Hercules and Centaurus sleeve-valve aircooled radial engines designed by the great team under Sir Roy Fedden, who had left the company in 1942 in exactly the way I had left Rolls-Royce. Partly for this reason it had lagged behind in the development of turbine engines. It had started with the Theseus, a complex and heavy turboprop, from which it was painfully moving on to a later turboprop, the Proteus. On the drawing boards was a promising turbojet, the Olympus, but the company had yet to sell a single gas turbine. I considered there was a 10-year lag behind Rolls-Royce, a daunting prospect when one considered the power and speed of reaction of Rolls-Royce.

I was determined to provide Rolls-Royce with some serious competition, but in retrospect I think that this would have been very difficult to do had not the Korean war shaken the British government out of its complacency. Recognizing that the RAF was desperately short of new equipment, while the aircraft industry had years of leeway to make up through lack of orders, the Ministry of Supply ordered the Rolls-Royce Avon axial jet to be put into production by the Bristol company as well as by Napier and Standard Motors. Thus, by *force majeure,* the Bristol shops were equipped with the machine tools and techniques for mass-producing modern axial engines. Moreover Bristol established the links with the specialist suppliers of turbine materials, parts for fuel systems, combustion chambers and others parts that were new to their experience. Thus, just as did General Electric and Pratt & Whitney learn to compete with Britain by making British jet engines, so did producing a Rolls-Royce engine set Bristol on the road which, by 1960, saw them providing neck-and-neck competition with the giant at Derby.

My new colleagues, however, were an unknown quantity. Frank Owner, Chief Engineer, had set up what he considered the logical organization of his department. He had four senior engineers reporting directly to him. Stanley Mansell was the Design Engineer, responsible for drawings and instructions to the shops. Brother Harvey Mansell was Research Engineer. Roche Swinchatt was Development Engineer, responsible for all piston and turbine engines. Jimmie Fell was Procurement Engineer, responsible for progressing the shops and getting engines built and modified as specified by Design. My own job was still unspecified, but that did not bother me as I wanted to get to know the Proteus and as-yet unbuilt Olympus, as well as the engineers lower down the ladder.

The four senior engineers and I used to meet each morning at 10 o'clock for coffee in Frank's office for a discussion for which there was no agenda and no minutes. After Frank, Swinchatt was by far the most powerful personality. The Mansells were retiring, and Harvey seldom uttered a word. A typical statement by Swinchatt would be, 'We failed the con-rod on the Hercules on test yesterday. What are you design gentlemen going to do about it?' Therein lay the big difference between the two companies, because at Derby Lovesey would have spent a long time examining the failure and diagnosing its cause, and would approach Rubbra on Design only when he had positive and logical recommendations to make. In fact, at Bristol the Design Office was dominant and could act unilaterally, whereas at Derby it was part of the team and never acted except in co-operation with Development.

I felt no inferiority at joining this team, and internationally was better known than any of them, but decided that I must first, as Hs would have put it, 'crawl on my belly' to Swinchatt. He took the remarkable view that 'the turbine job' would never be any good, and that the future lay with the big Centaurus piston engine. In this he was supported by managing director Norman Rowbotham, and also Johnnie Attwood, general manager in charge of production. These three presented a gigantic 'headwind' to Frank Owner, who completely failed to get any enthusiasm for gas turbines. Frank used to say at meetings of the Divisional Board when completely frustrated, 'Gentlemen, you can be dead three years and the corpse will not smell'.

I went to see the Proteus on test and was horrified. Even at half-power of 1,500 hp the outside combustion-chamber casings were glowing red in places, and they were obviously much too small in diameter for their job. There were difficulties in every part of the engine, and it was clearly miles away from the reliable 3,000 hp promised for the giant Brabazon and Princess transports. I went to see Swinchatt, who exclaimed 'What did I tell you — the bloody thing is a hopeless mess!' I asked why we did not get Clarke of Lucas to help us redesign the combustion chambers, and I must say Swinchatt immediately got Clarke on the telephone. Lucas quickly started work on a new combustion chamber, and when in due course these were forthcoming the combustion problem was fixed. It was a great pleasure for me to see my old friends Drs Watson and Clarke poring over our problems, and to know that John Morley would be sending us good combustion chambers in the numbers we needed.

It was very soon evident to me that far too few of the company's engineers were working on turbine engines. Almost all were still developing the Centaurus, for the Ambassador, Sea Fury, Brabazon 1, Brigand, Beverley and sundry other types, all of them short-term programmes. While I began gentle missionary work to get engineers at least interested in turbine engines, I spent much time analysing test results. At Barnoldswick I had soon discovered that trivial differences in clearance between fixed and rotating parts could allow compressed air or hot gas to escape from its pre-ordained path and not only reduce performance but even damage or distort the engine. Thus, I laid down the rule that every test-bed measurement should be analysed as completely as possible, to determine all the component efficiencies, mass flow, pressure-ratio, flame temperature and similar parameters. Thus every variation from engine to engine, and from test to test, could be noted, and in most cases the reasons diagnosed. But in the testing of the Proteus any kind of analysis of the figures was to say the least haphazard, not because the engineers were slap-happy but they were young and had no experience or guidance. The Proteus was a turboprop with one set of turbine wheels driving the compressor — which was a complex mixture of axial followed by centrifugal — and a second mechanically independent turbine driving the reduction gearbox and propeller. It was more difficult to analyse than a turbojet because its output was partly jet thrust but mainly shaft power to drive the propeller; but I produced a series of formulae suitable for the analysis of the Proteus, and these soon became known as 'Hooker's cookers'.

One day my peregrinations around the offices led me to a tiny den in which three men were working. This proved to be the complete gas turbine project office, less than one-tenth the size of that at Derby. But I was immediately impressed by the drawings of one of the three, Charles Marchant. An ex-apprentice, he had risen by sheer ability to become Chief Project Designer — albeit at that time of a very small team! He had imagination, the eye of a natural born designer for good mechanical construction, and quiet determination. He was to prove a Godsend to me and to Bristol. Even younger was Gordon Lewis, doing calculations on gas dynamics. Like me he had attended the Engineering School at Oxford. Considering the little opportunity he had had at Bristol, I was astonished at his knowledge of aero- and thermodynamics as applied to gas turbines, and he also had an impish sense of humour. I spent many happy hours with him and Charles discussing turbojets of the future, and I was convinced that in that little office I had struck gold.

Time passed quickly and I soon became influential. I tried to be a loyal colleague to Frank Owner, and he in turn treated me with great consideration. He was a man of great intelligence, well-read, a brilliant pianist, possessed of a good sense of humour and a great command of English, both written and spoken. Yet he was capable of acting like an ostrich and putting his head in the sand, though he must have known the day of reckoning would come when the giant Brabazon and Princess would need their Proteus engines. Meanwhile, this abysmal engine sank ever deeper in the morass, failing its compressor blades, turbine blades, bearings and many other parts, even at totally inadequate powers well below 2,000 hp. One day we were walking across for lunch and he said 'You know, Stanley, when we designed the Proteus I decided we should make the engine with the lowest fuel consumption in the world, regardless of its weight and bulk. So far we have achieved the weight and bulk!'

In those days I used to say that the biggest obstacle to Bristol's progress was a Bristol lunch! In each factory the top man had his own little private dining room. Maître d'Hotel of Frank's was Harry Powell, who was aided and abetted by Swinchatt who made sure that the standard did not drop an inch. We would start with hot canapés, while we partook of sherry (Swin and Harry preferred Guinness). Then we would sit down to a multi-course lunch, ending with cheese, fruit and coffee — and on occasions brandy. The whole lot would last from 12.30 until at least 2.30, about twice the time we took at Derby.

One Thursday afternoon in mid-1950 Frank and I were summoned to Rowbotham's office. I had hardly seen him since I joined the Division, and to cap it all Verdon was there also. Verdon made it clear that things had reached such a pass with the Proteus that something drastic had to be done. Accordingly I was being appointed Chief Engineer, and Frank was to retire to a small office and dream about the future. I was thunderstruck. Of course I had hoped one day I would be given more executive authority, but suddenly to be landed with the whole lot was beyond belief. Frank argued with all his eloquence about the iniquity of the proposal, but to no avail.

We retired to discuss between ourselves the next move. Could an acceptable compromise be worked out? I was willing to give in most directions, but insisted on untrammelled authority over engineering. I felt that the eleventh hour and fifty-ninth minute was upon us, and that vast changes in personnel, organization, speed of reaction and integration of engineering effort must be made immediately. Frank was inhibited by his long-standing loyalties, but I was not thus constrained. In the event, Frank was no more able to accept the new order than I had been at Rolls-Royce, and soon left to join de Havilland Engines. I much regretted the circumstances, and we parted without animosity.

During this period, and on many other occasions, I was much sustained by my friend Air Commodore F. R. Banks. At the time, he was Director General of Engine Research and Development at the Ministry, and had known me since my beginnings at Derby, where we often discussed supercharger development in Germany and the USA.

I made immediate changes. I called on Swinchatt and told him he had to take full responsibility for piston engines; furthermore, they had to move out of Experimental and into Production, where there was plenty of room. Henceforth Production were to be responsible for their own modifications, though we would retain Design Control. Swin was pleased with this arrangement, because it relieved him of responsibility for the hated turbine engine. Stanley Mansell I stood on one side to act as consultant on design matters, and immediately appointed Charles Marchant Chief Engineer, Turbine Engines. Harvey Mansell was also moved, and Neville Quinn appointed Chief of Research and Engine Performance.

The Technical Office had always seemed a complete shambles.

Although the departmental heads had their own little offices around the main office, the latter was just a big space where their staffs were all mixed up together with the designers at their drawing boards. I ordered that the whole place be partitioned off into large offices each dealing with one topic. Thus, all the stress engineers were assembled in one office with their chief in a private annexe; and the same went for performance and for mechanical development. At first stunned, the entire engineering department reacted favourably, and morale began at once to improve.

I began immediately to hold Hs-style weekly progress meetings. To impress on everyone the seriousness of the situation I held them on Monday evenings from 5 to 8 pm, and anyone who was absent without good reason placed his job in jeopardy. I gave them an offer they could not refuse: 'Work until it hurts, or get out'. (Today such high-handed tactics would be impossible; our trade unions have seen to that.)

The research equipment for turbine engines was woefully inadequate and badly utilised. There was just one enormous piece of plant consisting of a set of 26,000 hp variable-speed electric motors fed from the mains through rectifiers. These were housed in a great new building called The Gin Palace. The rectifiers and gearboxes were most unreliable, and caused endless hold-ups to the very infrequent tests made in this plant. Fortunately we had a super man in charge of all electrical equipment, Bill Irens, later Chairman of the South West Electricity Board. He had long urged that the rectifiers be replaced by a more modern system, but nobody had listened. I told him to go ahead, and soon we had that basic requirement for turbine component testing; reliable electrical power. David Brown redesigned the gearboxes, but the whole plant was too big and unwieldy for the scale of work required. Moreover, there was also a 3,000 hp plant which was doing virtually nothing, and I had this converted for compressor testing and it is busy on this work even today.

There were some rudimentary combustion-chamber rigs, but I decided to hand all that work to my old friends Watson, Clarke and Morley in Burnley. Lucas was being pushed out into the cold by the decision of Hs that Rolls-Royce should do its own combustion work, and they were delighted to join with us at Bristol on the same terms that had existed at Barnoldswick. I gave them responsibility not only for chambers but for fuel systems also, and within a very short time we were level with Derby in these vital areas. Morever, it enabled us at Bristol to concentrate our efforts on compressors and turbines and the main structure of the engine.

We began taking on more engineers, and there was a drift of experienced people from Derby. First to come was the present vice-chairman and chief executive of Westland, Basil (now Sir Basil) Blackwell. A former Cambridge Wrangler in Mathematics, he was clearly destined for high office. I gave him a job of testing turbines, using compressed air flow from The Gin Palace, and analysing the results. With Basil's energy, our turbine rigs were soon as good as any in the world. I put Gordon Lewis in charge of compressor design and performance. A third young engineer, Pierre Young, was put in charge of overall engine performance. A Cambridge maths man who had come from Armstrong Siddeley, Pierre had been working in a small shed, and I would probably never have met him had he not been brought to my notice by Neville Quinn. These three brilliant workers were installed in the same office, that they might spark one another off, and with Quinn's guidance our aerodynamics and thermodynamics were soon in excellent shape.

I was overjoyed when Bob Plumb wrote from Derby asking if he could join us. Quiet, yet a marvellous tutor to young engineers, he was one of the finest mechanical engineers in the world and had worked with me all his professional life. I at once appointed him Chief Development Engineer, Proteus and Olympus, which predictably put a few older noses out of joint. Plumb's impact was immediate. One of the great problems with the Proteus was that, all the time the engine was running, oil was being blown out of the reduction gear casing. All our attempts to cure this had failed. On the evening he arrived I outlined the problem to Plumb, while he studied the drawings. Soon he suggested a cause and described the modifications necessary for a cure, and these worked perfectly. He was a tower of strength, without whom it is possible we should never have got the Proteus into production in time, with results for Bristol beyond contemplation.

One day even Adrian Lombard asked if he could join me! We met in Gloucester and agreed terms and conditions. But I told him 'You will have to face Hs; it won't be easy for you'. At this Hs saw a very big red light indeed, and immediately made Lom Chief Engineer, a job he held with enormous distinction for over 15 years until his tragic early death from heart failure. Had he lived I am confident the RB211 would never have been so gigantic a failure, and the bankruptcy of Rolls-Royce would have been avoided.

I do not wish to suggest that the old engineering team at Bristol, which had achieved tremendous success under Sir Roy Fedden on piston engines, was devoid of talent or resources. In such matters as the design of castings, mountings for the engine or its auxiliaries, and other mechanical matters the standard was excellent. It was in the new and specialized knowledge of turbine engines that they were lacking. One area where Bristol was outstanding was in its tradition of producing complete fully cowled powerplants. The powerplant design office was ruled by Bob Hunter, and I was able to leave the entire installation side of the Britannia engine in his capable hands, and to the Rodney Works which specialized in sheet-metal construction. Another excellent team worked in the stress department, which I placed under young Keith Chamberlain; they lacked only experience in advanced turbine alloys.

Back in the early 1920s Fedden had recognised — ahead of anyone else in the industry — the vital importance of metallurgy in aero engines. The Division's metallurgical lab, under James Gadd, was one of the best in the world. Gadd had always been responsible to the Chief Production Engineer, but he asked if he might join my staff. This was readily agreed by Rowbotham, with the proviso that Gadd's team should continue to check materials for production.

Thus we soon had a good organization with which to tackle the troublesome Proteus. This complex turboprop had originally been designed to power the giant Brabazon II and Princess flying boat, in which it was buried in the wings and fed by ducts from the leading edge. This went well with the engine's reverse-flow layout, the axial compressor being arranged back-to-front with the inlet near the turbines and the air passing forward through the axial spool to a centrifugal compressor at the front, which delivered the air radially outwards to the combustion chambers arranged around the outside of the axial compressor casing. By 1950 the engine had already been redesigned once, and the resulting Proteus 2 was intended to weigh 3,050 lb and give 3,200 shp plus 800 lb jet thrust. In the flesh it weighed 3,800 lb, and was unable to give more than 2,500 shp, apart from which it was riddled with problems including frequent failures of compressor, turbines and bearings. I was not convinced there was a market for the two giant aircraft (there was not), but the new Britannia was the most important new long-range airliner in the country, and apart from its importance to BOAC, it looked like being a bestseller all over the world as the successor to the Lockheed, Douglas and Boeing piston-engined airliners.

When I became Chief Engineer in mid-1950 I had already decided that the Proteus had to be redesigned yet again, to produce a good engine. I gathered my Three Musketeers, Lewis, Blackwell and Young, and told them that, as we had to get 3,200 shp, they should shoot for 4,000 shp. I then told Charles Marchant to aim for a total weight of only 3,000 lb. Thus was born the Proteus 3, later called the 700-series. It had a new 12-stage axial spool plus one integral centrifugal impeller, with a pressure-ratio of 7:1. This was driven by a two-stage HP turbine, the two-stage LP turbine being quite independent and driving only the propeller reduction gear via a long shaft through the centre of the compressor. The engine first ran in May 1952, the month in which the Britannia first flew on Proteus 2 engines, and on its first test fully met all its specification figures. It was nearly 1,000 lb lighter than the Proteus 2, yet was offered to the aircraft designers at 3,475 shp plus 1,000 lb thrust, soon upgraded to 3,780 shp plus 1,180 lb.

When we studied the prospects for redesigning the Proteus it was evident that there was an overwhelming case for throwing out the whole reverse-flow configuration. A straightforward layout would have been much simpler, lighter and more efficient, and would have suited the Britannia admirably. However, the commitment to power the Brabazon and Princess made such a redesign impossible, because it would have required redesign of the engine installations in both aircraft, with their air inlets in the wing leading edges. As it happened both aircraft were soon cancelled, so we could have produced a straight-through Proteus anyway. To add the crowning touch of irony, it was solely because of the reverse-flow configuration that icing troubles were encountered which delayed the entry into service of the Britannia by two years.

Despite this, the Proteus 3 was still a major step forward. It flew in a Britannia in August 1953, and was Type-Tested for civil operation in August 1954. But in the meantime we had to battle on with the Proteus 2, more than 100 of which had been ordered for the prototypes of the two giant aircraft, the Brabazon and the Princess. It was a time of great stress and anxiety for me. Not only was the earlier Proteus 2 engine deficient in power by 1,000 hp and 1,000 lb overweight but every day some new serious trouble would rear its ugly head. I never expected to see ten of them running at the same time in a Princess, or even four in the prototype Britannia! By dint of hard work, particularly by Plumb and Marchant, we cobbled them through the flight-clearance tests, and one day I was mightily relieved to learn that the Brabazon programme had at last been abandoned, taking 48 Proteus 2 engines out of the Engine Division programme.

The Princess continued, however, and it was a nightmare to attend Saunders-Roe's progress meetings at Cowes. They were only too aware of the Proteus 2 troubles, and quite fairly but relentlessly hounded me at every meeting. It was such a strain I used to lie in my darkened hotel room instead of attending the customary dinner on the evening before the meeting. We got through somehow, but until we were able to demonstrate in 1953 that we had a totally different animal in the Proteus 3 I felt stretched to exhaustion. Fortunately for us, but unhappily for Saunders-Roe, the Ministry and BOAC were by this time beginning to realize that to carry the world's air travellers you need a modernized DC-6B and not a Princess. So the second and the third Princesses never flew, and another 40 Proteus 2s were taken from our programme. I must say what a spectacular sight the giant boat was as it soared across the Farnborough air show with all ten engines running; but, as it passed into the distance, I breathed a prayer of relief and grabbed a stiff double whiskey.

Thus, we were finally left with just the Britannia, which was an eminently sensible aeroplane and a task of great responsibility. We did over a year of flying on the Proteus 2s but in August 1953, just three years after the Proteus redesign was agreed, we got four flying in the second Britannia. At last we had an excellent engine, every part of which had been redesigned on my instructions apart from the reduction gear. This was an 11:1 ratio gear with straight-tooth spur gearwheels to reduce the 11,000 rpm of the power (LP) turbine to the 1,000 rpm of the big DH propeller. It was the only part of the original engine I liked, and it had never given a moment's trouble. Plumb kept reminding me of our troubles at Derby with the Trent, Clyde and Dart turboprops, and how we had had to change to helical gears. I kept re-examining the design, and could see no reason to change, though I did authorise Plumb, as an insurance policy, to get a set of helical gears designed and tested.

One morning in February 1954 Doc Russell visited me with a delegation from KLM, potential customers for the Britannia which at this time appeared to have the world at its feet. I briefed them on the engine, and then they went off to fly in the No. 2 aircraft. Would I like to come? Not today, Russ, because there were things I had to do, and I had flown in the aircraft anyway. So off they went, and less than an hour later shiny G-ALRX was a wreck on the mudflats of the Severn estuary.

Cruising over Herefordshire one engine's input pinion, in the reduction gear at the front end of the long propeller shaft, had stripped its teeth. Freed of all load, the big LP turbine had oversped, almost instantaneously breaking from its shaft and flying with the energy of a battleship's shell through the cowlings and arriving in fragments on the ground. Mercifully it missed the fuselage and the wing tanks, but it did pass through the engine oil tank and the oil caught fire. The fire raged for 19 minutes as chief test pilot Bill Pegg headed back to Filton, but with only a few miles to go he judged that the wing spars might soon burn through and with great skill did a belly landing. The mud instantly covered the windows, and Russell thought they had actually gone deep under water. Fortunately nobody was hurt, but the aircraft was a write-off, largely because of misguided efforts to pull it off the mud using nothing but steel cables.

The telephone rang in my office a little after 10.30 that chilly morning and I was told of the crash, and of the fact that it was clearly caused by engine failure. My feelings can be imagined. A short time later the 'phone rang again: 'Lord Hives wishes to speak to you'. The familiar voice said 'I hear that you are in trouble, Stanley. Do you want any help from us?' My spirits soared as I stuttered, 'Yes, please.' 'Right,' said Hs, 'I will send down the First Eleven, who do you want?' I had the nerve to say Rubbra, Lovesey, Lombard, Howarth and gear-expert Davies. Next morning they were poring over the failure in my office. That was the last time I spoke to Hs, and I am very glad it happened. It was typical of the man that, though by this time he was calling me his 'one great failure', he never hesitated in his act of superb generosity to a competitor in trouble.

When we surveyed the failure it was clear that a resonant vibration had been set up which had swiftly eroded the gear teeth. Spur-gear teeth engage one by one with an impulsive force, and when the frequency of tooth engagement is equal to the natural frequency of vibration of any part of the gear train, trouble will result. Helical gears, with diagonal teeth, engage more smoothly with a sort of shearing action, and are free from this trouble. So Plumb's wisdom was fully vindicated. Thanks to him we had several sets of helical-tooth gears on the shelf, and we were able immediately to build these into Proteus 3 engines and go on testing. Once these were fitted we had no more gear problems, though as a double safety insurance we added an automatic fuel cut-out which shut the engine down instantly if the torque in the LP drive-shaft fell to zero, as it would upon failure of the reduction gear. This device has never been triggered in many millions of Proteus 3 running hours to the present day.

We had no trouble Type Testing the first production model of Proteus 3, the Mk 705, for the Britannia 102 airliners for BOAC in 1954-55. But though the basic engine was fine, it was still able to bite us once more, in a totally unexpected manner. In 1956 a Britannia 102 was on final tropical clearance, flying over central Africa. Passing through clouds at about 20,000 ft the engines suddenly began to hiccough and stop, one by one. The Britannia drifted gently down, and the captain had no difficulty getting all engines restarted at a lower altitude; but what was the cause?

It took us a little while to identify what the problem was. With the aid of television cameras mounted inside the engine cowlings we were able to see that ice could adhere to the inner walls. When it reached sufficient thickness, it could break away and enter the engine compressor. The quantities were so large as to produce a compressor stall, or extinguish the flame in the combustion chambers, or cause both these effects simultaneously.

It proved difficult to locate the atmospheric conditions under which the ice could build up in this way. The conditions were not the same as those under which ice formed on the aircraft wings, so that the test aircraft was not always successful in locating an ice-laden atmosphere. In the tropics where the sea level temperature is about 40°C, the ambient temperature reduces to zero at about 20,000 ft. At this altitude ice crystals can be found in the air because of the enormous amount of water evaporation at sea level. BOAC could easily have avoided these conditions by deliberately choosing to fly at a different altitude but again we were not able to persuade them to do this.

We quickly devised glow plugs which were fitted in a number of combustion chambers. These were heated by the burning gases and, when the flame was momentarily extinguished, the plugs continued to glow long enough to re-ignite the fuel/air mixture. Thus the engine suffered only a momentary bump, and full cruising power was restored at once.

These glow plugs were entirely effective and never failed to relight the engine. The aircraft was totally safe, and the only evidence of severe engine icing was a brief flicker of the cockpit instruments. However, we were unable to persuade BOAC to put the Britannias into passenger service with this palliative. The major flight test programme thus continued for two years to find a means of preventing the build up of ice inside the cowlings. Eventually a series of modifications to the cowling ducts overcame the problem, and the aircraft had a long and profitable service life.

Such was the apparent ignorance of our atmosphere that BOAC's main argument was 'If it ices up in the tropics, what will it do over the North Atlantic?' We were forced to spend almost two years flying about looking for ice despite the fact that the problem had already been encountered in the only place where it existed. In cold regions, with sea level temperature of 0°C, there is extremely small evaporation, so there is little ice and that is near the ground and no problem to the Britannia. In temperate regions the icing is at around 7,500 ft. But in the tropics, with sea level temperature up to 40°C, there is massive surface evaporation and roughly eight times more atmospheric ice, and it is found at just the 20,000 ft level at which the Britannia cruised in such a climate. Piston airliners at much lower levels had never encountered it, and neither had the jets at around 40,000 ft. Even the Britannia could avoid it by flying slightly lower or slightly higher, with hardly measurable penalty in fuel burn, and in any case switching on the igniter plugs eliminated the problem even at the worst icing levels. BOAC seemed determined to turn what was really a molehill into a mountain, until the Britannia had become of such interest to Fleet Street that one observer commented 'If it blows a fuse we hold the front page.'

The impasse between BOAC and Bristol delayed the entry into service of this splendid aircraft by more than two years, and gravely damaged its propects in the export market. In the meantime the stocks of aircraft and work in progress at Bristol caused a cash-flow crisis which came within an ace of bankrupting the whole company. Only the cool courage of Verdon and the financial skill of William Masterson kept the company afloat.

Suddenly Israel's airline, El Al, came to the rescue. They simply ordered three long-range Britannias and put them into widely publicized service between Tel Aviv and New York. On the first supposed direct flight out of New York we waited with bated breath to see if they would land at Rome to refuel. They didn't. Next day the *New York Times* had a vast ad showing a big world and a much smaller world, and the headline 'Yesterday our Earth became this much smaller'.

Subsequently the Britannia had the reputation of being the fastest, smoothest, quietest and safest propeller aircraft in the world. It gave many years of service to BOAC, the RAF and a small number of other operators, but the delay caused by BOAC was just sufficient to cause many other important airlines, such as TWA, to wait for the shorter-ranged but faster 707. Only about 80 Britannias were sold; just enough to save the Bristol Aeroplane Company. The programme was not helped by the decision of BEA to ask Vickers to build a duplicate of the Britannia, the Vanguard, which sold only half as many and proved a financial disaster to Vickers. This certainly converted me to the belief that there had to be mergers in the British aircraft industry.

As for the Proteus, the years of toil and tears receded as it established itself as a reliable and efficient engine. But I shall hate it to my dying day because of the way, whenever we thought we had the problems licked, a new one would suddenly emerge — at the worst possible moment. Yet this engine pioneered two non-aero uses for powerful gas turbines: propelling warships and generating electricity. It was Peter du Cane of the Vosper Company who came to see me about putting three Proteus into motor torpedo boats he was designing for the Royal Navy. He reckoned with 10,500 hp he could get a speed of 55 knots (well over 100 km/h). Three of these Brave-class boats were built, and with them we learned how to instal aero engines in ships, with sea-water separators in carefully designed inlets and jetpipes facing aft to add thrust. We changed many materials to avoid corrosion, and W. H. Allen of Bedford did a new reduction gear to drive the propeller shaft. The whole installation worked so well that 20 years later major navies changed over to gas turbines, with Rolls-Royce (having absorbed our Bristol team via Bristol Siddeley) right in the lead.

As for electricity generation, it was Bill Irens, by now Chairman of the SW Electricity Board, who saw the advantages of using on-the-spot gas turbines to make up local shortfalls in power supplied by the grid. The very first gas-turbine station was built at remote Princetown, near Dartmoor Prison, to feed 3.5 MW (megawatts) into the grid at times of peak demand. The station was unmanned, and was simply started and brought on line by a telephone call from Bristol. When it was getting short of fuel or oil it automatically rang up the controller! From this stemmed hundreds of bigger stations powered by single or grouped Avons, Olympus and many other gas turbines.

In turn, this led to worldwide use of high-power gas turbines for many industrial applications. Chief among these is pumping oil and gas along great pipelines.

I must, however, mention one good thing the Proteus did for me. We very nearly sold many Britannias to Trans-Canada and Canadian Pacific, and I spent much time in Canada on lecture tours. Each time I went to Montreal Dr Eric Warlow-Davies would throw a dinner party for me. Warlow came from Tasmania as a Rhodes Scholar, and was at the Oxford engineering school with me. Tall and spare, he was a determined disciplinarian who could inspire those around him. He joined the LMS railway at Derby, but at the beginning of the war I weaned him away to Rolls-Royce where he soon established himself as a brilliant mechanical engineer whose forté was investigating failures. No scratch or frettage was too microscopic to escape his attention, and he possessed the sixth sense of being able instantly to recognise whether such a mark would lead to a dangerous failure. In 1942 he was sent as Quality Engineer to the Merlin factory near Glasgow, and four years later went with Denning Pearson to Canada to oversee the Merlins in DC-4M airliners. In the early 1950s he set up the Rolls-Royce (Canada) factory outside Montreal to build Nenes for T-33AN Silver Star jet trainers. He did not like this, because running the whole plant cut him off from his first love, engineering.

At about midnight, after one of our (highly liquid) dinner parties, Warlow asked me if I could fit him into the engineering team at Bristol! I welcomed him with open arms. He joined us in early 1954, and our new managing director, Air Chief Marshal Sir Alec Coryton, instantly took to him. They shared a brusque manner and a passionate interest in veteran motor cars. It was agreed that Warlow would become Chief Engineer for current programmes, then the Proteus and Olympus, while I became Technical Director to work on future projects and such theoretical aspects as performance, research and planning — and notably also the icing problem on the Proteus. It was an harmonious arrangement, and Warlow lifted a giant load from my shoulders not only with the Proteus but also with getting the great Olympus into service with the RAF.

Chapter 8
The Olympus

When I arrived in Bristol in 1949 the Division had just completed the project design of the Olympus, an axial turbojet more powerful than any previously built in Britain. The project had already passed to the Main Design Office, supervised by two good designers, Alec Henstridge and Sam Blackman. I was relieved to find that I thoroughly approved of the basic design, though I knew from my Ilkley studies that it was rather large and heavy for the design thrust of 9,750 lb.

It was the first real two-spool engine in the world. The Rolls-Royce Clyde was the first two-shaft engine, having an LP axial compressor followed by an HP centrifugal, but the Olympus was the first to have two axial spools in series, each driven by its own turbine. As in the Proteus, the LP drive shaft passed down the centre of the HP spool. The advantage is that the overall pressure-ratio can be higher than anything possible with a single spool (in 1949), and I have already explained in the Axials story why it is not possible just to go on adding axial stages to the same spool. When a two-spool engine is started, the starter accelerates the HP spool only, and this runs up to speed and gets a good airflow going. The LP system accelerates much more slowly, and this eliminates the tendency for the early stages to stall.

To achieve a pressure-ratio of 12:1 one can take an LP spool working at 3:1 and add an HP spool with a ratio of 4:1. Compressors of such modest pressure-ratios were even then known to be stable and efficient over the whole running range from idling to take-off. But an additional problem is the presence of a sluggish boundary layer along the walls of the compressors, particularly on the inner surface at the roots of the blades. As the air passes from stage to stage through the compressor the layer starts at the inlet at zero thickness and gets thicker and thicker. The more stages of compression there are, the thicker the sluggish boundary layer, and the more does it restrict the effective outlet area. With a two-spool engine the boundary layer can be extracted between the spools, and the HP spool can start off with zero boundary-layer thickness, resulting in more efficient and more stable compression.

Bristol Engine Division was developing the Olympus at Ministry expense to power the great Vulcan bomber, the monster tailless delta whose project design owed much to Sir William Farren at A. V. Roe, who as W. S. Farren had taught me at Imperial College. The importance of the Olympus to the RAF and the UK deterrent force was obvious, but to me it was clear that this super turbojet would at one great leap put Bristol at least level with Rolls-Royce. I had plenty of time to study its design, and though the concept was excellent there were many details I did not like. I suggested to Frank Owner a number of possible detail changes, and ran into a brick wall. Frank would say 'That is a matter for the Design Engineer', and on each occasion I found Stanley Mansell unreceptive and obstinate. But at least the prototype engines were built quickly, and the first was ready for test in mid-1950.

When the first run was a few days off, an American, Roy T. Hurley, came to see me. He was then President of the mighty Curtiss-Wright Corporation, the major engine contractor in piston-engine days to the entire US Army and Air Force. Even in 1950 Wright was still pouring out vast numbers of powerful Cyclone engines in various sizes, and was getting ready to mass-produce the pinnacle of aircraft piston engines, the Turbo-Compound. This was to enjoy a long run as top engine on the world's long-haul air routes, quite apart from big military orders, but by 1950 Hurley and his board were in what they rather suddenly saw as a dangerous position. Unlike rival Pratt & Whitney they had not been dragooned into making turbojets, and their position was that they had millions of dollars in the bank but no capability in the coming field of gas turbines.

Hurley was ex-Ford Motor Company, and a very strong and energetic man. He had formed the view overnight that he must buy time and technology by getting a licence in Britain. Forthwith he had booked on the *Queen Elizabeth* and, Rolls-Royce being tied up with Pratt & Whitney, he had come direct to Bristol. We discussed the Olympus, and at the end of the day he asked if he could take out a licence. I took him along to Norman Rowbotham, not really believing he meant it. They got down to brass tacks, and Hurley then departed, saying he would return in two or three days to sign the documents.

The very next day I heard with horror through the industry 'grapevine' that Hurley had gone straight to our competitor Armstrong Siddeley and was negotiating a licence for their Sapphire turbojet, which was running neck-and-neck with the Avon. Rowbotham called Hurley in high dudgeon, stating that we did not do things like that in Britain, leading a company up the garden path and then nipping off to one's competitor. Hurley replied 'It's OK, I'm going to buy both licences'. And he did just that.

Hurley came back to sign on the very day the Olympus was to run for the first time. Here was the world's most advanced and most powerful engine about to be started by testers who had no experience of any jet engine. I knew they would spend days cautiously running the engine in, treating it with the greatest respect. I decided to visit the new Olympus testbed and take the throttle myself, thus protecting the testers by accepting full responsibility. They stood around me while the starter button was pressed. The first Olympus ran up to speed, lit and started perfectly. I waited only a few more seconds and then banged the throttle open, an action which will cause any jet engine to stall unless it is in tip-top aerodynamic shape. The testers stood aghast, horror on their faces, but the Olympus slammed up to full power without the slightest hiccough or hesitation, and there for all to see was 10,000 lb thrust. I closed the throttle, bringing the engine back to idling, and then repeated the slam acceleration to full power, and again the engine responded perfectly.

I can vividly remember the tremendous feeling of exhilaration this gave me. What I did not know was that Rowbotham and Hurley had come onto the bed and were standing just behind me. It certainly was a dramatic moment for everyone, and it clinched the deal with Hurley on the spot.

He returned to Wood-Ridge, New Jersey, and planned his company's conversion to turbines in two stages. First he would mass-produce the Sapphire as the J65, at 7,000 to 8,000 lb thrust — and, after a thousand times the expected trouble in Americanizing the engine, he did just this. Next, he intended to build the J67, an American version of the Olympus. I told him he must quadruple the size of the Wright experimental shops, but he was up against the reactionary disinterest of Chief Engineer Bill Lundqvist, who was convinced the Turbo-Compound would go on for ever. He was also up against the US Air Force, which stipulated its next turbojet must have a thrust of 13,500 lb. We at Bristol considered this fractionally more than the original Olympus 100-series could be developed to give (in fact, it wasn't) and Wright thereupon decided to embark on a bold redesign of the J67 to give more thrust, and this was the final nail in their coffin.

First, they made the mistake of exactly following the USAF Specification. Sir Sydney Camm used to say 'Follow the spec. and you are dead!' For one thing, in those days engines had a habit of coming out overweight and deficient in power, and it was sound practice to aim at a power appreciably above that demanded. At Bristol I did just this, and succeeded in getting Ministry support for the Olympus 6, later produced as the 200-series, with a design thrust of 16,000 lb. We kept the external size and shape about the same, and even slightly reduced the peak diameter, but cut away the inside to increase the cross-sectional area of the airflow path, so that we could greatly increase the mass flow. At the same time we managed to get so much work out of each stage of compression that we cut back the LP spool from 6 stages to 5, and the HP spool from 8 to 7, without lowering the pressure-ratio.

We kept in close touch with Wright, and each week the J67 would get bigger and heavier, though it was still aimed at only 13,500 lb. I did not have the courage to take the bull by the horns and tell Hurley and Lundqvist to drop it and take our Olympus 6, because after all we were to some extent beginners too. When the J67 at last got on the bench it was entirely uncompetitive with Pratt & Whitney's J75 — and from that moment on Curtiss-Wright ceased to offer any competition in jet engines. Personally I believe we could have got them to have based the J67 on the Olympus 6. Had we done so we would have given Pratt & Whitney the sharpest possible competition, which the USAF likes, but, as it was, both British penetration of the US market and the great Curtiss-Wright company slowly faded away.

Although we did not recognise it at the time, this was a major turning-point in world aviation. Had the engineering capability of Bristol been allied to the vast manufacturing capability of Wright, the future would not have been left to Pratt & Whitney and GE, and Britain would have retained an enormous part of the world gas turbine market quite apart from anything carved out by Rolls-Royce. But, not only do I doubt that this could have been done, for emotional and political reasons, we were also desperately handicapped by the failure of the Bristol manufacturing team. Early in the J67 licence deal Hurley had 19 Olympus engines on order, so that he could get a real development programme going at Wood-Ridge. After a few dozen broken promises it got so that nobody believed the promises of delivery any more. Curtiss-Wright never received a single one of those engines. Even the supply of engines for our own purposes at Bristol was pathetic and always late by anything over a year. It drove me mad with exasperation to see the lead we had gained over Rolls-Royce turned back into a lag.

The total failure of manufacturing forced Verdon into the unpleasant task of retiring Rowbotham and Attwood in 1951. He appointed as managing director Air Chief Marshal Sir Alec Coryton, who had had a distinguished career in the RAF and Ministry of Supply. He had great powers of leadership, and would listen and consider all viewpoints before reaching a decision. His athletic figure and bristling moustache were often seen in the works, and he was fond of barking at a machine operator 'Show me how you do that!' The man would oblige, whereupon the boss would take off his jacket and say 'I'm going to try to do that'. Turners and fitters would crowd around, eagerly waiting to see the boss scrap the piece. It delighted the work-force and Coryton was popular with everyone.

He had the stature to stamp on the internecine warfare. When he arrived, Production ruled the roost, but there was constant friction between them and Engineering. This was constantly fuelled, on the one hand, by the total failure of Production to keep any of their delivery promises, and on the other by criticism of the engineering design caused by continual failure of the early Proteus engines. Coryton simply welded us into a single team, which got stronger and stronger as mutual trust and respect grew.

While the battle of the Proteus raged, the Olympus simply soared ahead. After running at the 9,750 lb level, it had reached 11,000 lb by the time it flew in a prototype Vulcan in September 1953. The Mk 101 production engine began to come off a revitalized manufacturing line in 1955 at this rating, and while the production Vulcan B.1 and B.1A bombers were being delivered we succeeded in improving the Olympus not only to be tougher and even more reliable (from the start it was the most reliable engine in the RAF) but also to give more power. We produced the Mks 102 and 103 and ended this generation of Olympus with the

104, which gave the 13,500 lb the USAF had wanted and which we had not dared to predict!

Early in the flight development of the Series 100 Olympus our Divisional Chief Test Pilot, Walter Gibb, easily took the world altitude record at 63,668 ft with a Canberra fitted with two prototype engines, and later the same aircraft exceeded 66,000 ft. It always seemed a pity that the Olympus-Canberra was never bought for the RAF, because that would have given us the world's best high-altitude bomber and reconnaissance aircraft. Meanwhile, we romped ahead with the Olympus 6 and cleared the Mk 201 version for production to power the Vulcan B.2 at a rating of 17,000 lb. Just as this was happening, in 1957, the Ministry decided in its wisdom that Britain only needed one big jet engine and it picked the Rolls-Royce Conway. Accordingly they withheld all support from the Olympus, and moreover instructed Avro to redesign the Vulcan to take the Conway. To give them credit, Avro were very reluctant to do this. The whole thing was said to have been done on financial grounds, and we knew of no attempt to assess the technical merits of the two engines.

At this point Verdon showed immense initiative and courage. He went to the Ministry and said that Bristol would develop the Olympus 200-series at its own expense. Ah, said the officials, we know what that means; we shall have to pay for the development in the production price. Verdon explained that we were prepared to sell the Olympus 200 for the same price as a Conway. This was no small gamble. In those days the development bill for such an engine was in the order of £5 million a year, and the production cost some £50,000 a copy (today it would be more than ten times greater). Thus, assuming a three-year development programme, we should normally have had to add £20,000-odd to the price of each engine on a run of 500 engines. One major hiccough in either development or production costs and Bristol would be bankrupt.

In the event the Olympus 200 went like clockwork, and we far exceeded our design figures without spending anything like £10 million. Likewise Production rose to the occasion and churned them out at a keen price. The Conway, on the other hand, became more and more expensive, partly to pay for changes to suit the civil DC-8 and 707-420, of which a handful had been sold, and partly because the production price was much higher than expectation. We were thus not only able to keep Verdon's bargain, and keep this splendid engine in the Vulcan, but we made a healthy profit. Even more, we went on to produce the 300-series engine rated at 20,000 lb, more than double the original design figure, by adding a zero-stage to increase the mass flow. These became the standard engines of the RAF's Vulcan B.2 force, which stayed in use 25 years to 1983. These were the trusty machines which bombed the runway at Port Stanley in what were by far the longest bombing missions in the history of air warfare.

More than this, the Olympus went on, as I shall relate, to power the TSR.2 and Concorde. Other versions are the standard engines of the Royal Navy's warships, including such giants as *HMS Invincible,* while hundreds of others generate electricity all over the world. Had it not been for the exceptional nerve of Sir Reginald Verdon Smith the pundits in the Ministry would have scrapped the whole programme back in 1957. As for the Conway, the last few engines in Victor tankers are now being retired, and the engine gained no further applications.

The Minister at the time was Reginald Maudling, and I remember a very painful and acrimonious meeting in Coryton's office as we fought to explain why we felt the Olympus should not be killed off. Eventually Coryton said it was lunchtime, and stamped angrily out, leaving me alone with the Minister. I asked him 'I suppose you wonder how we got into this mess?' He replied 'No, but I wonder how I got into it.'

In general an engine's power is related to the mass flow through its HP spool and combustion system. Though the Conway looked larger than the Olympus, because of its bypass duct, its HP spool was smaller, so it had less potential for further development. In 1960 two extremely large and important new aircraft were being planned in Britain, both to achieve Mach 2.2, the limit for aluminium airframes without compromising structural life. One was the RAF's new strike and reconnaissance aircraft, TSR.2, and the other was the SST that matured as the Concorde. These projects were regarded as inter-related, the TSR.2 being earlier in timing. This enabled the RAF programme to underpin and read across to the later civil SST. It was eventually decided that both would be powered by versions of the most powerful Olympus.

Back in 1952 English Electric's designer, Freddie Page — later Sir Frederick Page, chairman of the British Aerospace Aircraft Group — came to ask me about prospects for replacing the Avon with the Olympus in advanced versions of Canberra and Lightning. The Avon used in these aircraft was clearly going to run out of steam long before the bigger Olympus, and moreover the latter's higher pressure-ratio, for remarkably low weight, gave a much better specific fuel consumption. I told Page that the Olympus was good for Mach 1.8, but that above that Mach number the aluminium compressor would have to be redesigned in titanium because of the very high temperature.

Thus in 1958 the embryonic form of TSR.2 was born. This was the start of a so-called 'weapon system concept' which, in my view, has cost the RAF and this country dearly because of resulting delays and escalating costs, resulting in fewer aircraft for vastly greater prices. One of the demands made for TSR.2 was that the aircraft should be able to fly at its maximum Mach number of 2.2 for a full 45 minutes. This meant a total redesign of the Olympus in high-temperature materials able to soak at the Mach 2.2 ambient conditions (which had previously been met only for about a minute at a time, outside the USA). It was also evident that the engine would need a lot more thrust, as well as a reheat system (afterburner) capable of being fully modulated over the entire range of augmentation, instead of being a mere on/off device as had previous British afterburners. This in turn led to the demand for a complicated system to control the nozzle as it varied in area over a range of 50%, with variable profile leading, in the Mach 2.2 regime, to a large expanding final section to accelerate the supersonic jet.

Also demanded was an operational radius of 1,000 nautical miles. I met the Vice-Chief of Air Staff, Sir Geoffrey Tuttle, on the Folland airfield at Hamble. I asked him 'Geoffrey, why do you insist on a 1,000-mile range? It is clearly a number carved out of the sky. Do you realize that the final 100 miles will cost you something like a million pounds a mile for engineering development?' (That was certainly an underestimate.) He waved his arms in a gesture of despair, and we just went on with what proved to be pouring effort and money down the drain. I had already formed the view that the fresh arrivals of brilliant and dedicated young RAF officers in the Operational Requirements branch tended to justify their existence by changing, usually upwards, the numbers cranked into official specifications. As they stay for five years, while each major programme today takes 10, continuity is lost. Though it is nothing like as ludicrous as the life of governments — to say nothing of ministers — this short timescale makes it impossible to collaborate with the same experienced team throughout a major project.

I am totally unconvinced of the merits of multirole all-can-do aircraft, and even less convinced of the need for everything to do Mach 2. The Harrier has proved so useful because it escaped the British-style weapon system concept. The engine came first, and there was no question of Mach 2. Thus there was always a body of opinion in the RAF that this is a very pedestrian and not very useful aircraft. This opinion ceased to be fashionable after the Falklands campaign.

Do not think that I, or anyone at Bristol, did not do our best to produce good engines for TSR.2. In this programme even the Olympus did its best to bite us, when one blew up during ground running under the Vulcan flying test-bed. After much effort we identified a bell-like 'ringing' vibration of the large-diameter HP shaft, energised by the high-frequency pulsations of jets of cooling air. This was fully cured soon after the first flight on 27 September 1964, but though the TSR.2 and its engines matured swiftly, and gave every promise of being a world-beating all-British aircraft, the whole programme was cancelled in April 1965 along with all the other new British aircraft for the RAF, as the Labour government's answer to the problem of the RAF being — in their own words — 'dangerously overstretched and seriously under-equipped'. Fortunately this wholesale bout of cancellations brought to an end ten years of the worst mismanagement of the RAF's equipment and of the British aircraft industry that could possibly have been arranged.

The one lasting effect of the TSR.2 programme on the British aerospace industry, was that it was used by the government of the day to enforce mergers between what had been rival companies. This is discussed in a later chapter.

The last and most challenging application of the Olympus is the Concorde SST (supersonic transport). This mighty programme, which like so many non-American endeavours failed to reap commercial rewards, was begun in November 1956. By then it was obvious that BOAC's refusal to show interest in the all-British Vickers VC7 — commercial version of the V.1000 transport for the RAF — was bound to hand an entire generation of subsonic jetliners to the Americans on a plate. This situation was accelerated by BOAC's decision, soon after disclaiming any interest in jets in this class, to buy a fleet of Boeing 707s! The only possible thing for Britain to do seemed to be to leapfrog ahead with the world's first SST. The Royal Aircraft Establishment at Farnborough was charged with organizing a programme, and under its Deputy Director, M. B. (later Sir Morien) Morgan, it formed the STAC (Supersonic Transport Aircraft Committee). All the chief airframe companies attended at Chief Designer level, as did Rolls-Royce and Bristol Aero-Engines, the company formed in that year from the Bristol Aeroplane Company's Engine Division.

After prolonged study of several alternatives the STAC Final Report of March 1959 recommended an SST to cruise at Mach 2.2, or 1,450 mph, with transatlantic range. Any speed higher than this would result in structural temperatures too high for long airframe life in the well-tried aluminium alloys, the alternatives of steel and titanium posing great problems in inexperience, cost, weight and, in all probability, a long and troublesome programme. To a rough approximation the rise in skin temperature at cruising speed in °C is equal to the square of the speed measured in hundreds of mph. Thus 100 mph gives a rise of 1°C, 500 mph results in 25°C, 1,000 mph causes a rise of 100°C and Concorde speed of 1,450 mph some 210°C. But at very high altitudes the air is initially at some -50°C, and subtracting this gives an actual metal temperature of only 160°C. We felt we would be able to build an SST, complete with rubber tyres, plastic parts and other components, which could soak at this temperature and still satisfy the civil airworthiness authorities.

We looked carefully at a steel/titanium SST cruising at Mach 3, or 2,000 mph, but after analysing the times needed for take-off, climb, subsonic cruise over land, acceleration to cruising speed, deceleration at the destination and the final slow letdown to the terminal airport, the actual saving in journey time on London to New York did not exceed 15 to 20 min — say, 3 hours 15 min instead of 3 hours 30 min. The latter time, for Mach 2.2, was half the best possible with a subsonic airliner, and beyond this speed the law of diminishing returns set in with a vengeance. The one real advantage of Mach 3 was that, while wing lift/drag ratio hardly altered from 7.5 (roughly half as good as a subsonic aircraft), the greater ram compression increases the engine efficiency, which in turn could mean greater range or more payload.

On balance, Mach 2.2 not only looked the better bet but it was all that the British industry dared attempt. (Later the Americans spent vast sums on Mach 3 and gave up). Archibald Russell at Bristol was given the job of heading the design team for a Mach 2.2 SST to carry 130 passengers non-stop from London to New

York. His report in March 1960 showed that the best slender-delta design, which had by then clearly emerged as the most efficient, would weigh 385,000 lb and need six Olympus engines of 25,000 lb thrust each. This was more than had been expected, but instead of boldly going ahead the committee chickened out and instructed Russ to redesign to only 270,000 lb using four engines. He was reluctant to do this; he maintained the original Bristol 198 design was correct. How right he was can be shown by the fact that today Concorde takes off at 408,000 lb!

At this point everyone was too busy merging with rivals to do much designing. Sydney Camm called the process Mixomatosis, but it was clear that the internecine warfare must cease if we were really to compete with the USA. Bristol Aircraft were merged with Vickers-Armstrongs (Aircraft) and English Electric Aviation, which then took over Hunting Aircraft to form BAC (British Aircraft Corporation). Bristol Aero-Engines combined with Armstrong Siddeley, de Havilland Engines and Blackburn Engines to form BSEL (Bristol Siddeley Engines Ltd). It was a time of great turmoil, especially at the financial and managerial level, but BAC and BSEL quickly became fine teams with a great spirit. The SST remained under Russ, and the Olympus under me.

Over in France the nationalized giant Sud-Est under Georges Hereil, which had produced the successful Caravelle short-haul jet, had lately merged with Sud-Ouest to form Sud-Aviation. Chief designer Pierre Sartre and his right-hand man Lucien Servanty thus became opposite numbers to Russ and Dr Bill Strang at Bristol. This was suddenly important when in 1961 the British and French governments demanded that Russ and Sartre work out a common SST design. The French wanted only a short range, but Russ knew the North Atlantic was essential for an SST to sell in the world market. The final compromise of November 1962 saw the French adhering adamantly to a short/medium-range SST weighing 220,500 lb and BAC pushing a long-range (but not transatlantic) version at 262,000 lb. Fortunately pressure from world airlines shifted the entrenched French position and enabled the design to go ahead, initially at a weight of 326,000 lb, and powered by four of a substantially new type of Olympus, the Mk 593. Under the terms of the inter-government agreement we were required to collaborate with the French national engine company, SNECMA, but this was no problem because both SNECMA and Bristol had in fact survived and flourished as engine companies on the strength of the Jupiter licence taken out in 1920 by Gnome-Rhône, SNECMA's main ancestor. SNECMA was still busily making Hercules engines under Bristol licence in 1955.

There has been much criticism of the management structure of the Concorde programme, which will not be repeated, and on the airframe side there were frequent strained relationships; but from the very start we had the happiest partnership with SNECMA. Their two top engineers, Michel Garnier and Jean Devriese, quickly became BSEL's friends, and I cannot recall a single technical difference that was not settled by a single short meeting. The official work (and money) split was Bristol 60 per cent and SNECMA 40 per cent, my team being responsible for the basic engine and the French for the new and complex jetpipe, thrust-reverser, noise suppressor and the convergent/divergent final nozzle which in cruising flight provides a major proportion of the thrust.

At take-off the thrust comes from the engine itself, as in any other turbojet aircraft. At supersonic cruise conditions the situation is very different. First, the air inlet must convert the relative speed of the oncoming air into high pressure in the most efficient manner. The air approaches the Concorde inlet at about 2,000 ft/sec, roughly the speed of a rifle bullet, and must be slowed to a relative speed of 500 ft/sec by the time it reaches the engine intake face. It is first very suddenly slowed to Mach 1, about 1,000 ft/sec, by shockwaves in the inlet, and then diffused subsonically by an expanding inlet duct leading to the engine. This all happens in about one-hundredth of a second, during which time the air pressure rises fivefold, an extremely important factor in achieving the desired thrust and efficiency. Yet at take-off the inlet has to be opened wide to admit the full airflow at zero forward speed, while at cruising speed it must be closed down to provide the greatly reduced airflow needed. This calls for very large movable flaps, ramps and doors, the control of which is scheduled by an automatic electronic system.

Similar problems arise at the nozzle end. In cruising flight the jet has to reach the speed of sound at the minimum-area throat of the nozzle, after accelerating down a converging section; downstream of the throat the rules are reversed, and to accelerate the now supersonic jet the nozzle has to extend to a large final diameter. There must also be a reverser to slow the aircraft after landing and the most effective possible noise suppressor. SNECMA held complete responsibility for the back end, but the complicated inlet system needed the collaborative efforts of the two engine and two airframe partners.

In jet engines such as the turbojet or turbofan the components at the front, where the air pressure is rising, are subjected to a useful forwards force, while downstream of the combustion chamber, where the pressure is falling, everything tends to be blown out of the jetpipe by an adverse rearwards force. It is the difference between these forces that propels the aircraft. But at Concorde cruising speed one gets an unusual distribution of the various forces: from the variable inlet ramp, -12% (rearwards); from the air intake system, +75%; from the engine itself, +8%; and from the convergent/divergent nozzle, +29%. The total, of course, is 100%, but what emerges is that the inlet is ten times as important in thrusting the aircraft along as is the engine, while the final nozzle is almost four times as important. We therefore had to pay very great attention to the inlet and nozzle, though as the engine was the sole producer of thrust at take-off we were not let off the hook!

Shell carried out tests on the Concorde fuel system which showed that at cruising speed the fuel would gradually be heated to 160°C, at which point it would be on the point of throwing down waxes and varnishes which would quickly be fatal to the sliding parts in the fuel control system. Likewise the oil would heat up to 300°C, at which it became acidic and attacked the bearings. But if the speed were to be reduced to Mach 2.0, 1,320 mph, the air temperature would be reduced to only (13.2 squared, minus 50) 124°C, or 36°C cooler, giving an acceptable margin of safety for the fuel and oil and also for rubber and plastic components. It also promised much lower attrition of the airframe fatigue life. It had little effect on aircraft range, and added only a few minutes to transatlantic block time.

Russell readily approved our proposal to reduce cruising speed from Mach 2.2 to Mach 2.0, but the French were very difficult. However when Pierre Young and I argued the case before the Concorde Committee of Directors in Paris the change was agreed. Today, in fact, the usual figure you will see displayed on the digital speed indicator in the passenger cabin is 2.05.

In the meantime, Concorde grew heavier, as most aircraft do. Increased weight means more fuel, which means more weight, which means both more fuel and also bigger engines, which again means more fuel. More fuel also means a bigger wing, which means more weight, and these adverse spiralling effects are difficult to fight. It was especially vicious in the case of Concorde because there could be no reduction in either payload or in non-stop Paris to New York capability (about 200 miles further than from London). It is for this reason that we finally got a working aircraft at a weight of 408,000 lb, which in turn forced us to work harder on the engine to obtain more thrust.

We started by giving the Olympus 593 a zero-stage on the front of the LP compressor to pump more air with a higher pressure-ratio, as well as a redesigned turbine with aircooled rotor blades to allow a higher operating temperature, but there is a limit to this path and we were running out of steam at around 30,000 lb thrust. The Concorde, however, was obviously heading for a minimum requirement of 36,000 lb per engine, and so as a last resort we persuaded SNECMA to incorporate partial reheat (afterburning) in the jetpipe, which could easily give a 20% thrust boost at take-off. Reheat was common, but only on military aircraft. The drawbacks were extra complication in the variable propelling nozzle, possibly higher fire risk and certainly extra noise; on the other hand, more thrust would mean more noise however it was produced. The aircraft design team were reluctant to accept reheat, but it was too late to go back to Russell's six engines. SNECMA produced a superb reheat and nozzle system, and today, though the captain usually informs the passengers when he is switching on reheat to start his transonic acceleration, through the once-feared sonic barrier, it is all a non-event and Mach 2 is as smooth and quiet as subsonic flight.

In 1960 Bristol Aero-Engines was merged with Armstrong Siddeley Motors Limited to form BSEL, as noted earlier. Sir Arnold Hall, once Director of the RAE, came from the Hawker Siddeley board to become managing director. In 1966 BSEL was acquired by Rolls-Royce — probably an inevitable move of which, in principle, I thoroughly approved. At a personal level I was less happy and decided to retire on my 60th birthday, in September 1967.

Prior to this Sir Arnold had become managing director of the Hawker Siddeley Group, and Warlow-Davies had succeeded him at BSEL. Poor Warlow-Davies reigned for only two years before suddenly dying, as did Lom, of heart failure. His successor was Hugh Conway, from Short Brothers. I disagreed with Verdon about his appointment, but I was wrong and my fears proved groundless. I found him a splendid man to work with, full of initiative, energy and good humour. In 1967 he insisted I stay on as a consultant.

As the Concorde programme progressed Pierre Young bore more and more of the responsibility for its engines. He had the advantage of having had a French mother and a boyhood in France, so he was totally bilingual. He was also a brilliant engineer and mathematician, able to deal with aircraft designers or airlines in a tough but completely fair manner. To him goes most of the credit for the absolute success of the Concorde's propulsion system, which has no parallel in airline service. He was assisted by Leonard Snell, once a talented rocket engineer at de Havilland Engines, and Lionel Haworth who when at Derby had designed the Dart and Tyne turboprops.

Haworth had been a friend since 1938 and I was thrilled when he threw in his lot with us at Bristol. He did many enormous tasks in perfecting the design of the Olympus and Pegasus, bringing to bear equal proficiency in mechanical engineering, aerodynamics, vibration, material properties and accurate estimations of weight and cost. I shall never forget his eloquence in explaining to Pierre Sartre how to solve the unprecedented problem of installing the very long and rigid engine in the extremely long nacelle fixed to the highly flexible wing, which in any case varies in dimensions according to how hot or cold it gets in flight. He was a pupil of Rubbra's, and there is no higher praise than to describe him as Bristol's Rubbra.

By 1968 my life had changed. I was now a consultant to what had become the BED (Bristol Engine Division) of Rolls-Royce. Pierre Young was in sole charge of the Concorde engine, and Gordon Lewis was Chief Engineer of the brand-new RB199 augmented turbofan that was being designed in co-operation with MTU (Germany) and Fiat (Italy) as the engine for the MRCA, which today flies with three European air forces as the Tornado. Henceforward subsonic aircraft would invariably have highly efficient turbofan engines, quieter and more economical than turbojets, but the latter kind of engine was right for Concorde because of its very high speed. At 50,000 ft the Olympus 593 gives 10,000 lb of thrust, but as at this speed each pound of thrust is equivalent to 4 hp the total horsepower of Concorde is a staggering 160,000, or about as much as 160 Spitfires. Compared with Whittle's engine of 1943, already a fairly mature machine, the Concorde engine weighs seven times as much and gives 25 times the thrust up to three times the speed, with a much lower specific fuel consumption.

Perhaps most interesting of all is the fact that the overall thermal efficiency of the engines of Concorde in cruising flight is about 43%, which is the highest figure recorded for any normal thermodynamic machine (obviously one cannot include nuclear power).

In its early days the Concorde promised to be even noisier than the extremely noisy 707 and DC-8, and something had to be done to try to reduce its nuisance at least down to that of these older aircraft. Acoustics, and especially noise nuisance, is an extremely complex subject, and I resolved to recruit the best experts I could get to form a Noise Panel to advise us. I approached Professor J. E. Ffowcs Williams, today Rank Professor of Engineering (Acoustics) at Cambridge but then a brilliant young Welshman at Imperial College. I appealed to him to take charge of our Noise Research Department, and he readily agreed despite losing financially on the deal because he had to give up a major consultancy to Boeing.

He quickly gathered Professor G. Lilley from Southampton, Professor Niels Johannesen from Manchester, David Crighton who became Professor of Mathematics at Leeds, and several other brilliant workers in the field. We at Rolls-Royce and SNECMA contributed our own experts. We hoped that, by more fully understanding the relationship between the noise and the source, we would be able to effect the greatest possible reduction in the nuisance caused by Concorde.

At the time the most advanced theory of jet noise had been produced by Sir James Lighthill, who concluded that the noise was proportional to the eighth power of the jet velocity. But one must take frequency into account. If the pressure fluctuations radiating from the source are harmonic, that is if they are repetitive and of equal magnitude up and down about the mean pressure, then recognisable notes will be heard. Middle C is a constant 256 pressure fluctuations per second, and for each octave above or below the frequency is doubled or halved. Low frequencies attenuate slowly with distance, whereas high-pitched sounds carry only a short distance, which explains the deep note of a foghorn.

The human ear is so sensitive it can hear a watch ticking or an Olympus in full afterburner, a range of sound energy in the ratio 1 to 10,000,000. We therefore measure noise power in Decibels (dB), units which are based on a logarithmic scale which makes this vast numerical range manageable. The simple formula is:

$$dB = 10 \log \left(\frac{\text{power of the noise in watts}}{10^{-12} \text{ watts}} \right)$$

Thus, if a noise increases 100-fold, the dBs increase by just 20, the log of 100 being 2. Likewise, if we have two equal noises, and since the log of 2 is 0.3, the two together increase the dBs by 3 compared with either noise alone. The four engines of Concorde put out just 6 dB more than any one of them by itself. Alternatively, if one could replace one Concorde engine by four jets each of one-quarter the thrust, the noise of each would be reduced by 6 dB and raised to a faster-attenuating higher frequency. This was the basis of the multi-pipe silencers used on the first 707s.

Lighthill's theory was based on the assumption that the jet noise was produced by quadrupoles at the periphery of the jet. A quadrupole is an ideal conception of four sources arranged very close together in square formation, each source in antiphase with its neighbours. Thus when one source is producing a positive pressure its two neighbours are producing equal negative pressure, the fluctuations all having identical frequencies. Emitted noise is then a maximum along the diagonals passing through the four poles and at a minimum along the axes at 45° to these directions, thus explaining the long-familiar fact that the maximum noise behind a jet engine being tested on an open airfield is at 45° to its axis, and a minimum directly behind it.

Many measurements had confirmed that noise is proportional to the eighth power of jet velocity, at jet velocities around 1,000 ft/sec. At only half this speed the noise varies as the fourth power, and — fortunately for us — at very high velocities of 2,000 to 3,000 ft/sec the variation is proportional only to the third power.

Moreover, because of the ear's logarithmic sensitivity, it makes little difference whether, in the presence of a loud noise, we add or remove a second noise almost as loud. If we have a 110 dB noise, we can add six extra noises of 100 dB each and still only increase the total to 113 dB, which the ear hardly notices. Thus the main objective for us was to find the magnitude, frequency and position of the sources of the loudest noise. These occur at the periphery of the jet as it issues from the nozzle, and extend about ten nozzle diameters downstream. At this distance, entraining fresh air has reduced the jet velocity by half, removing its importance as a noise source. Members of our panel explained all this in great detail, and organised laboratory and full-scale engine tests so that we could explore the 'far field' noise, which is what would impact on the people near the airports.

The sheer volume of theoretical studies and test results from our academic members in 1965-70 was prodigious. Their contribution enabled SNECMA, where the burden of responsibility chiefly rested, to design a most elegant exhaust system which, for minimum weight and performance penalty, matched the variable nozzle and thrust reverser exactly to the tremendous variation in flight conditions whilst also reducing noise until it was never worse than that of the subsonic jets, such as the 707 and DC-8. Indeed, as Concorde climbs away much faster and more steeply than those aircraft, its noise nuisance is markedly less.

Noise at airports was not the only issue exploited by the once vociferous anti-Concorde lobby. Another was sonic boom, the noise created by the shockwaves as they pass the ear of an observer. In the case of Concorde the boom is heard about 20 miles behind the aircraft. The mechanism is analagous to the bow and stern waves of a ship, and the double boom-boom is similar to that from distant thunder, but it was said that the phenomenon would squash greenhouses, wreck old buildings and break all the windows along the flight path. In fact, no evidence was ever produced to show that the passage overhead of a Concorde ever cracked anything, but except in the Soviet Union — where the view was taken that nobody minds thunder — SSTs have never been permitted to cruise at Mach 2 over land. Indeed, everyone will remember the way every trick in the book was tried to prevent the Concorde from opening a service to New York at all, though for many years Concordes have carried people in comfort across the Atlantic in $3\frac{1}{2}$ hours with never a mention in the media.

Altogether the opposition to Concorde was an interesting social phenomenon. Many people went to surprising lengths to damn the aircraft, one argument being that the engines would eat up ozone in the upper atmosphere and cause widespread skin cancer from the incoming cosmic rays. Obviously, far fewer harmful radiations reach the Earth's surface than those passing through the flight and cabin crews who spend their lives aboard Concordes, and the airlines say that these crews are a very fit group of people!

It has been my great pleasure to make many trips in Concorde, but I shall never forget the opening of scheduled services by British Airways on 22 January 1976. Only one country in the world would receive the aircraft at that time, and so the route went to Bahrein. Our party was led with extreme skill and charm by HRH The Duke of Kent. After an avalanche of champagne and rousing speeches by Ministers we took off and flew at Mach 0.92 across Europe (which, incidentally, itself saves about 40 minutes compared with other jets) until we turned on the reheat at the head of the Adriatic. As we went through the dreaded 'sound barrier' the only effect was that the big digital readout changed from 0.99 to 1.00, but when it got to 2.00 everyone cheered and down the hatch went another deluge of champagne. We arrived after a flight of 3¾ hours, compared with about 8 by the regular jets.

We were delighted to be invited to a banquet at The New Palace by HH The Amir of Bahrein. The fairytale palace was a blaze of lights, and the bodyguard were a blaze of exotic uniforms. We were individually presented; His Highness was a little man with brilliant twinkling eyes, and my spirits rose further as he said 'I am very glad to have you in my country'. Eventually we entered the fabulous dining room, ritually washed our hands and took our places around the gigantic U-shaped table. I was next to the Minister of Foreign Trade, who spoke perfect English. We each had a waiter in full court uniform, each pair of guests being supervised by a steward. We drank fizzy orange, but the dishes were too numerous to study. The one thing that caught my eye instantly was that every few feet was a complete boiled lamb.

I was about to turn to the Minister and say 'How far-sighted and generous of your government to allow us to bring the Concorde here on its first scheduled flight', when he said to me 'What a great honour you have done our country by bringing your magnificent Concorde here on its inaugural flight!' Considering the violent hullabaloo that was going on in New York, and that nobody else would allow us in, it was difficult to find the right answer! The waiters kept our plates well filled but there was no move to carve up the lambs and I began to fear they were only for decoration. So I asked my host how they were cooked, and he told me 'In the old days they were boiled in large pots, but now we use pressure cookers. Would you like to try it?' That was precisely what I was angling for, and it proved to be lovely, yet I was the only one to eat any of it.

It was my first experience of Arabian hospitality. I was deeply impressed by their generous, cultured and highly dignified behaviour. We have much to learn from them.

No engine in history has ever been developed like the Olympus. The original design figure in 1946 was 8,000 lb, yet the Concorde engine gives well over 30,000 lb and has been run with reheat at 40,000 lb, the highest thrust of any production turbojet in the world. It is a comment on the inability of engine designers to think of everything to note that when we first ran the Olympus 593 oil cost $1.50 a barrel, and when it entered airline service it cost $30 a barrel. This, together with the refusal of countries to permit it to fly supersonically over land, killed the Concorde as a commercial proposition, despite the excellence of its design.

Chapter 9
The Orpheus

During World War 2 the Chief Designer of Westland Aircraft was W. E. W. 'Teddy' Petter. He used Rolls-Royce engines in his Whirlwind and Welkin twin-engined fighters. In 1944 he was enticed up to Preston by Sir George Nelson, boss of the giant English Electric company, which had a massive aircraft factory building Halifax bombers for the war and later Vampires, but no design team. His brief was to set the company up as a producer of military aircraft of its own design so that it did not have to rely on a world war in order to fill its vast factories making other people's designs.

Petter had already begun to scheme a replacement for the Mosquito using jet propulsion. Preston was not far from Barnoldswick, and in 1946 he often came to see me, and I encouraged him to think in terms of a twin-engined aircraft with two Avon engines. His design became the Canberra, which swept all before it, and even appeared in America built by the Martin Company as the licensed B-57 version with Wright's J65 (licensed Sapphire) engines. In 1947 he launched a project for a supersonic research aircraft which eventually led to the Lightning Mach 2 interceptor, with two reheated Avon engines. He then quarrelled with the management, mainly because he wanted to have control over experimental manufacture.

It has always been debatable whether it is a good policy to divide a factory into two watertight compartments, one for design, development and research and the other for all manufacturing. Some engineers adhere strongly to the view that, if you leave experimental manufacturing — which is the life-blood of advancing technology — to the Production Department, it will never get done, because the priority will be churning out today's products for customers. But the production people argue that they alone have the contacts with the material and equipment suppliers, and the ability to make the best use of manufacturing facilities.

Rolls-Royce favoured the second view, and I always agreed that engineers have enough problems without taking on the added burden of controlling manufacturing resources. Petter thought the opposite, and when after a long battle he failed to get his way he left Preston and in 1951 became Managing Director of Folland Aircraft, a small company based at Hamble which at that time was owned by my great friend Charles Hill, chairman of the famous Bristol shipping firm. (Later it was absorbed into the Hawker Siddeley Group). At Hamble Petter was monarch of all he surveyed, and he settled down to design the beautiful little Gnat light fighter.

Petter had become convinced that fighters were becoming too large and heavy, and thus too complicated, expensive and difficult to keep serviceable. Later the suggestion was made in print that he was motivated more by the available skills and financial resources at Hamble, but to me he was always championing a sincere cause in his advocation of a much smaller, lighter and cheaper fighter which could outfly any opponent. Many in NATO thought the same way, and both NATO and the British government approved the basic idea.

Thus in late 1952, Petter was determined to build the Gnat, and approached me at Bristol to produce a suitable engine. I was very keen to support him, as I knew from my Ilkley calculations that it should be quite possible to design a simple axial engine weighing about 800 lb and giving 5,000 lb thrust, which filled Petter's requirement exactly.

I had a much more personal reason to go ahead. Up to this point in my career, I had given my effort to the perfection of other people's basic designs, i.e. the Merlin of Sir Henry Royce, the W.2B of Frank Whittle, and the Proteus and Olympus of Frank Owner. I felt that by now I had served a sufficient apprenticeship to embark on my own designs, and I was eager to do just that.

At this point let me emphasise that designing, developing and producing is a team effort. It needs a whole army of highly qualified engineers and administrators, specialists in aerodynamics, mechanical design, the strength of materials of all varieties, combustion of fuel, with the attendant fuel system, and, last but not least of all, a body of competent designers who can incorporate all of the advice the experts give them into one comprehensive whole, which can manufactured by the facilities available in the factory. It goes without saying that someone has to find the money to pay for all this!

The job of the Chief Engineer can be likened to that of the conductor of such a vast orchestra — he has to bend the performance to his ideas and scoring and supervise many 'rehearsals' when the design is in progress. The supporting players are vital, and their contribution is often unsung. They get their satisfaction when the engine runs and flies just as they foresaw. Neither I, nor anyone else today, can be said to be totally responsible for the 'design' of an aero engine.

To return, I knew from my Ilkley calculations that there was no intrinsic difficulty in producing an engine weighing only 800 lb yet able to give a thrust of 5,000 lb. In keeping with the light-fighter concept the engine needed to be simple, without any attempt to attain a high pressure-ratio, because for a short-range fighter the fuel saved would be more than outweighed by the greater engine weight. But it was apparent that providing an engine for the Gnat offered opportunities to rethink axial engine design and introduce a number of novel features.

One was the elimination of the centre bearing. Previous axials, including the Avon, Sapphire and Olympus, had three main shaft bearings, one at each end of the compressor and the third at the turbine. According to Euclid a straight line is the shortest distance between two points, not three, and for this reason it is impossible to keep all three bearings absolutely in line. The main rotating assembly has to be split into front and rear sections joined by a coupling able to allow for small misalignments. In the design of the BE.26 Orpheus we adopted a short seven-stage compressor driven by a single-stage turbine, and it was desirable to eliminate the centre bearing. Doing this in ordinary engines would lead to the main drive shaft suffering from whirling, bending outwards and whipping around like a skipping rope. But we made the drive shaft in the form of a thin-walled tube more than 8 inches in diameter. It was surprisingly light, and had a critical whirling speed much higher than any possible excitation from the engine.

Leaving out the centre bearing and its attendant coupling meant we could also leave out the strong supporting structure, a lubrication system, a sealing system to prevent escape of oil, and, in most engines, also an air cooling system. This simplification saved not only weight but also cost and extra maintenance.

We also devised a new method of construction for the

compressor rotor. The blades were slotted into aluminium discs which were then separated by spacer rings. The assembly was dowelled together for concentricity and fastened lengthwise by steel bolts.

A new method of mounting the turbine on the large-diameter shaft was devised. The disc was provided with precision-machined radial splines, which engaged in similar splines on the face of the shaft. This ensured very accurate concentricity whilst allowing for the radial expansion of the disc and shaft due to temperature and centrifugal force. This was a most successful innovation, and for the first time it was possible to remove and replace a turbine without having to rebalance the whole assembly.

The combustion system was of the cannular type, a single outer casing containing seven flame tubes. These also broke new ground in that the downstream portion of each incorporated one-seventh of the turbine entry duct, complete with the stator blades (called vanes in the USA). This duct conveys the hot gas from the combustor to the turbine. Previously it had been made of a combination of steel castings and refractory sheet-metal parts fabricated by welding. Not only did this part of the engine often give a great deal of mechanical trouble, due to cracking and distortion, but it was heavy, difficult to manufacture, expensive and unreliable. The neat Orpheus design eliminated these troubles in one go, because the individual chambers were merely held together by a simple bolt, which allowed for expansion without stress.

A stroke of good fortune was that cancellation of the Princess programme in 1953 freed an excellent Bristol designer, Bernard Massey, who for many years had led a section working on the giant flying-boat's air-conditioning plant. He was thus able to take on the Orpheus, leaving Marchant and the main design office working on the Olympus and Proteus engines, and the project officially got going in December 1953. I spent many fascinating hours with Bernard at the drawing board trying to get the design down to our target weight of 750 lb. The initial design stage costs little money, but the obvious question was: who was going to pay when the Orpheus moved into the hardware stage, and the thousands of pounds became hundreds of thousands or even millions? Not the RAF, who wanted ever bigger and more costly fighters, of which they could afford fewer and fewer.

Unknown to us, the Gnat proposal had caught the attention of

Col Johnnie Driscoll, USAF, head of the MWDP (Mutual Weapons Development Program) office in Paris. MWDP was a US organization set up to organize projects within NATO, and bring in additional nations who had weak industrial strength. The NATO Supreme Commander was Gen Lauris Norstad, also of the USAF, and he was very interested in light fighters, partly because they could be dispersed widely away from the vulnerable airfields and partly because they were within the industrial capability of many nations, including the rebuilt Italy and West Germany. Driscoll therefore convened a meeting of NATO aircraft companies where they were given details of a requirement for a light tactical strike fighter weighing around 8,000 lb and able to take-off and land in less than 2,000 ft, in what Driscoll called 'cow pastures'. At this time, all jet fighters required a concrete runway of at least 5,000 ft, and as such were vulnerable to the new missiles, which were just appearing.

This NATO requirement was based on Petter's concept of the Gnat, and thus he had the ball right at his feet. However, there was just one stumbling-block. The Gnat had high-pressure tyres, for concrete runways. In vain did I plead with him to change to low-pressure tyres; his response was always that he could not do it, because the larger bays to house the retracted wheels would spoil the drag of his fuselage. In desperation I urged him 'Just say that you will try to do it', but Petter had had a Quaker upbringing and could not stretch the truth in the slightest. So the Gnat was eliminated and the NATO Light Fighter competition ended up between Dassault, Breguet and Nord in France and Fiat in Italy, with British firms showing no interest. France's Sud-Est Durandal and Sud-Ouest Trident dropped out, as did Nord, leaving Breguet to build the Taon (French for horsefly but an anagram of NATO), Dassault the Etendard and Fiat the G91. And the satisfying thing for us was that all three finalists chose the Orpheus as their engine, so Driscoll was able to dip into his pile of dollars and assist us to develop the engine. The MWDP deal was that they would pay for 75% of the costs if the developing country would find the rest. As Whitehall showed no interest, I had to ask Verdon, and he readily agreed to pay for 25% of the cost of developing the Orpheus with company funds. I at once hastened the programme into the manufacturing stage, with Massey assisted by John Dale, an experienced development engineer who had recently joined us from Derby.

At this point I re-established my friendship with Theodor von

Kármán, which had begun at Cambridge in 1934. In 1933 von Kármán had left Aachen, where he had been Professor of Applied Mechanics, for Pasadena, California. Though he was a brilliant mathematician with many interests, his first love was aeronautics and at Pasadena he had rapidly risen to being No. 1 aeronautical expert in the whole USA. He had rendered them great service as Chairman of the USAAF Scientific Advisory Board before and during World War 2, and had been held in great respect by successive Presidents of the United States. But at heart he was a European, and after the war he came back to Paris to act as Chairman of AGARD, the NATO Advisory Group for Aeronautical Research and Development.

He was a batchelor, and at Aachen had loved to follow the German professorial tradition of drinking with his students in the *bier-kellers*. In Paris he was invariably accompanied by an entourage of young, and not so young, ladies, who were chaperoned by his sister. They all adored him, for he was charm personified. I cannot resist telling a story that sums up his philosophy. After a very good lunch he returned to his office to be admonished by his secretary for missing an appointment. He asked 'What does it matter, when I have discovered the secret of a happy life?' 'What is that?' inquired his secretary. 'Why, a Japanese maid, a Hungarian cook and a French mistress.' Plaintively the girl asked 'Don't we Americans get anything?' 'Of course, one would need to have an American washing machine.'

Since the total US investment in the Light Strike Fighter and the Orpheus engine amounted to millions of dollars, von Kármán was asked to serve as overall technical adviser. Because I knew him so well he spent much time with me examining the design and the progress of the Orpheus, to which he finally gave his enthusiastic support. The first engine ran in early 1955, and since every one of the radical design innovations worked like a charm its development was rapid. In January 1956 it was Type-Tested at 4,000 lb thrust, in November 1956 the first production series was Type Tested at 4,520 lb and in May 1957 the first of the Mk 800 series — identical except for a fuel pump of increased capacity — was Type Tested at 4,850 lb. The first development engines all weighed just about 800 lb, and I was particularly pleased that we had got back to the speed of development of the Derwent V and Nene. There was one big difference: while those earlier engines gave about 3 lb thrust for each pound of weight, as did the axial Avon and Sapphire, the Orpheus pushed this ratio up to 6 lb! In fact, it was well into the 1980s before this ratio of thrust to weight could again be equalled, except by the Pegasus which was pretty much developed by the same team, as noted in a later chapter.

In the battle for the NATO aircraft the Fiat contender had an advantage that the irritated French lacked. The company's technical director, the great Giuseppe Gabrielli, had been von Kármán's pupil at Aachen in the 1920s, and so the man he called 'the maestro' gave him every possible encouragement. When it was announced that the G91 had won the competition — and justly so on its merits — the French angrily refused to have anything to do with the programme.

Fortunately the G91 proved to be a sound and well-engineered aircraft which had a very long and popular career. Many were made in Italy and West Germany, and some are still serving in Portugal. The Orpheus 803, rated at 5,000 lb thrust, was made in large numbers both by Fiat in Italy and KHD (Kloeckner-Humboldt-Deutz) in West Germany to power the various G91 versions. Norstad got his wish of an emergent European industry, and the first 100,000 hours flown by the Luftwaffe after 1945 were flown largely on the G91. It is a pity we cannot have a few more Colonel Johnnie Driscolls to knock NATO heads together. He was a likeable genius at getting collaborative programmes going. With Air Marshal Sir Neil (Nebby) Wheeler, I attended many of his light fighter progress meetings in Paris, London and Turin.

Johnnie had been a USAAF bomber pilot in the War, and was proud of his Irish descent. He was a keen, intelligent officer of great driving power, and poured millions of dollars into the Orpheus and the Fiat G91 project at a time when development funds in the UK had virtually dried up. The office of MWDP was an act of great generosity by the American people, and Johnnie and von Kármán were great ambassadors for them. It was a stroke of good fortune for Bristol when the Orpheus was chosen, and I count myself as very fortunate in the friendship that I had with these two outstanding men.

The meetings in Turin at the Fiat works took place only in the morning because after an Italian light lunch nobody was in any condition for further work. On one occasion at the great Fiat works we were summoned to the main boardroom to report progress to the chairman himself, Dr Valletta. The room was enormous, probably 20 ft high, and its giant mahogany double doors were polished like mirrors. We waited with bated breath for the great man to enter. Suddenly, and in total silence, the mighty doors swung open, controlled by a footman in full morning dress, and through them entered the very short and stocky Valletta. But he was clearly a leader, and took charge of proceedings immediately, giving Gabrielli all possible support and encouragement.

Meanwhile Petter, having disqualified himself from the NATO competition, did create a beautiful and exciting little fighter in the Gnat. But it is difficult to sell a fighter that is rejected by its own air force. The Ministry bought six to play with, and this caused great embarrassment when it was found that RAF pilots were queueing up to get their hands on them. Yugoslavia bought two, because it looked like something they might make themselves, and 12 were sold to Finland where they enjoyed long and successful front-line careers. Much later the RAF did buy a two-seater Gnat as a trainer, with a reduced-thrust version of the Orpheus, and millions saw the specially painted group that for many years formed the equipment of the Red Arrows. But it was far-away India that finally decided that Petter, who sadly died quite early in the project, had been right all along. The Gnat appeared to be a tough customer in a dogfight, and also within the technical capacity of Hindustan Aircraft Ltd to build under licence. The same company's engine division took out a licence for the Orpheus, and the engine has remained in production to this day at Bangalore, for the Gnat, for the HAL-designed HF.24 Marut twin-engined fighter, for the HAL improvement of the Gnat called the Ajeet (unconquerable) and for the Kiran II trainer, as well as for booster pods fitted to heavily laden transports taking-off from high-altitude airstrips. Thus, despite the total disinterest of the British Air Staff, Verdon's instant agreement to paying 25 per cent of the development bill proved a fine investment.

To conclude this chapter I would like to acknowledge the help given over many years by the various overseas agents of both the Bristol Aeroplane Company and Rolls-Royce. In the case of the Orpheus the chief intermediary role in France was played by the Bristol agents, the Société Franco-Britannique, whose Gerry Morel and Jean Allais were able to open all doors. Gerry and Jean were patriotic and cultured Frenchmen devoted to the cause of Anglo-French co-operation in aviation, and they played a major role not only in the Orpehus but also in the Pegasus and the Bristol/SNECMA Olympus 593 for the Concorde. In Italy we had the Mercantile Italo-Britannica, whose Major Bill Rogerson was on intimate terms with Fiat. He conducted the early Orpheus negotiations with great skill and success, and remained an essential link through the production of the G91. Sadly, Gerry Morel died from injuries received at the hands of the Gestapo before our projects saw the light of day, but Rogerson and Allais remained great friends, ever generous in hospitality and ever watchful of our interests.

Basil Blackwell.

Neville Quinn.

Gordon Lewis.

Pierre Young.

The two Britannia prototypes.

Don Pepper. *Hugh Conway.*

The first non-aviation applications of an aircraft gas-turbine (1) fast patrol boats HMS Brave Borderer and Brave Swordsman, (2) Princetown peak-lopping generating station, (3) Bluebird. All were powered by the Proteus.

S.G.H. with Olympus 200 LP compressor.

Olympus 200.

S.G.H., Britannia in background.

The Vulcan powered by 4 Olympus engines with the much more powerful Olympus engine for TSR2 slung underneath.

The Olympus-powered generating station at Mahmoudiya, Egypt.

Chapter 10
The Pegasus

In Paris, in 1957, Johnnie Driscoll, having got the Fiat G91 light fighter firmly launched, turned his attention to vertical take-off. Rolls-Royce had already flown the 'Flying Bedstead', which was a metal frame supporting two Nene engines mounted so that their jets acted as lifters, and under the stimulus of A. A. Griffith was busy developing small ultra-lightweight jet engines such as the RB108, so that a useful military aircraft could be lifted off the ground by a number of such engines.

Even in a single-seat fighter, a minimum of eight such engines would be required for safety purposes. The idea of a pilot attempting to monitor all these engines during the dangerous time of take-off beggared the imagination, despite the initial success of the Short SC.1 research aircraft, lifted by four RB108 engines with a fifth for propulsion. Nonetheless, the subject of jet-lift V/STOL (vertical or short take-off and landing) was fast becoming all the rage. Driscoll was one of those who believed in the development of V/STOL close-support aircraft, up with the forward troops where they could replace heavy fuel loads by weapons, and could be dispersed away from main airbases.

Thus the stage was set for Michel Wibault, who between the wars was a leading French designer of fighters and airliners, to ponder a solution to the problem. He was living in some style in Paris as the protégé of Winthrop Rockefeller, who was interested in his project studies. One such was his proposal for a vertical take-off and landing aircraft called *Le Gyroptère*. It resembled a stumpy jet fighter containing a Bristol Orion engine, our planned successor to the Proteus, with the propeller drive replaced by two cross-shafts driving four large centrifugal blowers arranged like wheels at the sides of the fuselage. The blower casings could be rotated so that at take-off the four jets of compressed air were directed vertically downwards, evenly disposed around the CG (aircraft centre of gravity) to make the *Gyroptère* rise vertically. The pilot could then slowly rotate the casings directing the jets rearwards to give propulsive thrust, the lift gradually being taken over by the wing as the forward speed built up.

For my part, the Derby solution of the multi-engined aircraft seemed hardly likely to succeed. The engine control systems had to be automatically connected, so that if one lift jet failed to respond, or failed mechanically, its opposite number on the other side of the CG would be immediately shut down to preserve balance. Thus, at least two engines' worth of spare thrust was needed just for safety reasons. Moreover, after take-off, the lift engines were just dead weight to be carried throughout the flight, before they were all (hopefully) relit for landing. I used to say facetiously "The pilot must press a button for take-off, close his eyes and, if he is alive one minute later, then he will be flying!" Even my friend Frank Robertson, Chief Designer of the SC.1, used to quip (when he was referring to multi engines in order for balance to be preserved) 'Nothing comes down faster than a vertical take-off aircraft upside down'.

Wibault's concept seemed more practical and realistic, though the shafts, gearboxes and centrifugal compressors were cumbersome, inelegant and very heavy. This was my verdict to Johnnie Driscoll when he called me to Paris to discuss Wibault's proposal. But I was strongly in favour of what von Kármán, christened 'vectored thrust'. A vector can be directed in any direction, enabling one engine to be used for both lift and propulsion.

At Bristol, I discussed the concept with Lewis, Young and Quinn. Lewis proposed one large axial compressor to replace the four centrifugals with two rotating nozzles, one on each side.

It was easy to show that, for a fighter-type aircraft, it would be better to replace the complex and expensive Orion by the cheap, lightweight Orpheus. The obvious place for the extra compressor was on the front. The next big step was to make it an integral part of the engine, large enough for its inner portion to supercharge the air entering the original Orpheus compressor, and thus increasing its efficiency and power. The air from the outer part of the large compressor could be ducted to left and right vectoring nozzles, while the hot jet could also be used for lift.

We took our proposal back to Driscoll and von Kármán, who were enthusiastic and urged us to proceed to the design stage. At this crucial moment Driscoll was moved back to Norstad's staff, and Col (later General) Willis Chapman replaced him. Fortunately Chapman could not have been more enthusiastic and positive in his support. We took on Wibault as a consultant, and he and Gordon Lewis were the original vectored-thrust patentees. Sadly, Wibault died soon afterwards and never saw the success that his original idea was to lead to.

At this juncture Sir Sydney Camm took a hand. He had been watching the Derby proposals with growing disbelief, and suddenly sent me a one-line whip: "Dear Hooker, What are you doing about vertical take-off engines? Yours, Sydney". I sent him our first BE.53 (Pegasus) brochure, and then at once busied myself in Olympus work. It was thus a shock when Camm telephoned me a few weeks later, asking "When the Devil are you coming to see me?" I replied "As soon as you like, of course; but what is the subject?" And he said "It's vertical take-off; I've got an aeroplane for your BE.53".

We set off hot-foot for Kingston, where Camm showed us a drawing of the P.1127. It looked very like the Harrier of today and we were thrilled when Camm told us that, despite the inability of the Ministry to show much interest (because manned military aircraft were out), he intended to go ahead and fly a prototype. The Hawker Siddeley Board supported him, and put up the money, just as it had done in 1936 in tooling up to make 1,000 Hurricanes. In 1936, however, at least the company knew the Hurricane would be ordered eventually, whereas in 1958 there was absolutely no reason at all to think that the P.1127 would be ordered, even as a prototype.

On this historic visit to Kingston we met Roy Chaplin, whom I knew from Hurricane days pre-war, and Ralph Hooper and John Fozard. The latter two were brilliant young designers who, after the death of Sir Sydney and the retirement of Chaplin, were to bring the revolutionary P.1127 through the intermediate stage called the Kestrel, to service as an operational weapon system for the RAF in early 1969 as the Harrier. To them and to Chief Test Pilot Bill Bedford must go the credit of producing the first practical VTOL jet.

We started on the definitive design of the BE.53 in 1958. The deal with Bill Chapman of MWDP was the same as for the Orpheus; they paid 75 per cent of the initial funding, and Bristol were to pay the rest. As before, Verdon never hesitated, and this proved one of the most important investments ever made by British private industry. At the same time, had it not been for

MWDP, and Driscoll and Chapman who administered that fund, it could never have happened. Chapman's only proviso was that we should build two flight-cleared engines and allocate these to Hawker Aircraft.

Charles Marchant, having handed over his responsibilities for the Proteus and Olympus to Warlow-Davies and Hughie Green, was able to devote his whole effort to the design of the Pegasus. The engine appeared in the flesh in August 1959, and was handed to John Dale to develop to flight standard.

Converting the Orpheus into the Pegasus presented us with new challenges. Basically we took an Orpheus and added an additional LP turbine driving a shaft passing down the centre of the (conveniently large-diameter) HP shaft to an axial fan at the front. At first this had two stages, but we later added a third stage, all these being overhung like a propeller ahead of the front bearing. The air from this fan was split, the inner supercharging the gas-generator, and the outer part discharging air from the vectoring front nozzles.

Camm, remembering his "birfucated" jet pipe in the Sea Hawk, suggested bifurcating the jet pipe on the Pegasus and using a second pair of left/right nozzles rotating in unison with the first pair. A further desirable feature was to make the HP and LP spools rotate in opposite directions, thus almost eliminating the engine's gyroscopic couple. This is a very important objective for a V/STOL aircraft, enabling it to hover under perfect control.

Thus, the unique Pegasus arrangement evolved and gave its output in the form of four jets, symmetrically arranged in front and rear pairs so that, when the engine was installed in the Harrier, the resultant thrust acted through the aircraft CG. In the first Pegasus the front jets delivered air at only about 2.3 pressure ratio, resulting in a temperature of some 100°C. We called these the 'cold jets'. The two rear jets delivered gas at about 650°C. They handled a smaller mass flow, but we designed the Pegasus so that the front and rear jets gave approximately the same thrust, thus easing problems in the balance and control of the aircraft.

For minimum weight we made the 'cold' ducts and nozzles in glassfibre. Well into the flight programme the test pilot, Bill Bedford, suffered a sudden inflight malfunction on the side unseen by the accompanying chase aircraft. At low level Bedford found he had lost lateral control, and could not stop the aircraft rolling. He managed to eject safely, but the aircraft was wrecked in the crash. It would have taken a long time to pinpoint the cause had not a local farmer near Yeovilton walked in a day or two later saying "Does this belong to you?" He was holding one of the glassfibre nozzles!

We saw at once that in making the nozzle the strong glassfibre had not been taken round into the bolted flange holding it to the mounting ring (which was then not part of the engine but of the aircraft), leading to a fatal weakness. Design in glassfibre demands careful control of accuracy, consistency and the run of the fibres, which alone provide the strength that is absent from the plastic adhesive filler which binds the fibres together.

Subsequent efforts to make reliable cold nozzles verged on the hilarious. Sydney cursed us for being such idiots as to use material he wouldn't have for a lavatory seat, and said his chaps would make us a set of nozzles in aluminium sheet. When we got them we put them on the Pegasus, to run on the testbed, and within two or three hours they were cracking and breaking up because of air pulsations. So we told Sydney we would make the damned things in titanium, but these also cracked. Sydney then washed his hands of the whole affair, but John Dale pointed out that, during all the argument, the rear nozzles, in heat-resisting steel, were working perfectly, even at 650°C. So we went to heat-resistant steel, and the front nozzles have never given any more trouble. Sydney howled blue murder at the extra weight of 50 lb, but as we started the Pegasus at 11,000 lb and went into production at 21,500 lb he didn't do too badly in the end.

Many features of the Pegasus were innovations. The original BE. 53 with a two-stage fan was one of the first engines to have no inlet guide vanes, the first part of the engine encountered by the airflow being the rotating fan blades. When we added the third stage, we found that we could overhang this fan ahead of the front bearing like a propeller and this is today the practice on all turbofan engines. This enabled us to do away with the front bearing and all fixed radial struts or vanes upstream of the fan, and thus also to eliminate the hot-air supply previously needed to prevent ice forming on them. Inlet guide vanes were added to all early axial jet engines to swirl the incoming air in the direction of rotation of the rotating blades, in order to keep the relative Mach number between the air and blade below unity. With engines such as the Pegasus we had fans whose blades were supersonic over their outer portions, the tips running at Mach 1.3 to 1.5. We suddenly recognised that inlet guide vanes had become part of gas-turbine folklore and were no longer needed.

Another innovation was contra-rotating spools. On conventional aeroplanes the large gyroscopic forces imparted by the engine — which in effect is a spinning top — are not noticed because they can be continuously counteracted by the aircraft control surfaces. On the Harrier the airflow over these surfaces can be zero while hovering, so RCVs (reaction control valves) fed with HP air bled from the engine must be used instead. Any attempt to yaw the hovering Harrier, swinging the nose left or right, would have resulted in a powerful nose-down or nose-up tilt, because gyroscopic forces act at 90° to the axis of disturbance. Contra-rotating the two spools overcomes this, and the resultant gyroscopic force imparted by the Pegasus is exceedingly small.

When we ran the first Pegasus in August 1959 it failed to give the 13,500 lb for which we had designed it, and we had to advise Sir Sydney that the thrust would have to be limited for the first flight to 11,000 lb. He predictably went off the deep end, but even 11,000 lb was enough to get daylight under the wheels of the prototype P.1127 when stripped of non-essentials and given the minimum of fuel. In any case 11,000 lb was ample for a conventional take-off using the Dunsfold runway. When I suggested this, Sydney replied "Why should we want to do that?" I put my foot right into it. "To prove", I said, "that the P.1127 has good handling qualities as a conventional aircraft." "All Hawker aircraft handle perfectly," he barked back, "there is no need to waste time on that! The first flight will be a VTO."

Every meeting with Sydney began with a blast at his visitor or the industry in general. He once opened with "Haven't you got a sufficient sense of grief and shame?" I tried unsuccessfully to think of a recent disaster, but he explained "You come here every Monday hawking your crackpot scheme for VTOL with your damned engine, you'll cost the country millions!" It was just his sardonic humour and we were soon down to business.

So in September 1960 Bill Bedford opened the throttle, got between 10,000 and 11,000 lb thrust, and lifted the stripped-down P.1127 off its special grid at Dunsfold. The only concession Sydney made was that the aircraft should be restrained by loose tethers. This was not a good idea, because at the limit of the tethers the P.1127 swung about like a balloon on a string, out of control. But after these halting steps Bedford and his colleague Hugh Merewether got into their stride, and in September 1961 Bedford made the first accelerating transition from a VTO into high-speed horizontal flight. I asked him what it was like during the transition, and he said "The aircraft felt like a brick on ice!"

In producing the first engine the little coterie around me — Marchant, Plumb, Lewis, Young, Quinn and Dale, for example — had come across many new problems. An obvious one was the reliable operation of the four nozzles. We were playing with the entire engine thrust and vectoring it through angles up to 100°, from horizontal to vertically downwards and 10° forward for braking. If one nozzle stuck, the result would be serious and probably disastrous. The nozzles *had* to rotate in unison. We bled HP air from the combustion chamber to power two air motors feeding into a differential box in such a way that, if one motor were to jam, the other would continue to drive but at half-speed. Cross-shafts from the box drove motor-cycle chains passing round the two pairs of nozzles. Normal practice would have been to use a gear-train, but I said I had not seen a broken motor-cycle chain for years, and that this was the lightest and simplest way to lock the four nozzles together.

The nozzle drive had to rotate the nozzles quickly and lock them positively at any desired setting. For example, in making a ski take-off the pilot of today's Sea Harrier quickly moves the lever to 55° and expects to get just that, and neither 54° nor 56°. I cannot speak too highly of the job done for us by Plessey in producing an extremely reliable operating system. Unlike all other VTOL aircraft, the single nozzle lever is the only extra control in the cockpit, and its motion is instinctive and immediate.

Another new problem was the nozzle bearings. We did not expect any trouble with the 100°C front nozzles, but the 650°C rear nozzles were a different story. All four nozzles rotated inside giant ball bearings, but 650°C was a severe requirement for any kind of bearing and special cooling measures were necessary. To our joy, we calculated that the pressure in the cold air ducts would always be slightly higher than in the jetpipe, so that, if a pipe were to be run from the LP plenum chamber to a volute around each rear bearing, it would automatically supply cool 100°C air and keep back the hot gas. Lo, it worked just like that, and the problem of the rear bearing was solved.

We collaborated with Sydney's team on the special RCVs for use in hovering flight. We put these, popularly called 'puffer jets', in the nose, on each wingtip and in the tail, the tail jet being rotatable to give directional control like a rudder. The four puffer jets were fed with HP air from the combustion chamber. When opened, each gave about 1,000 lb of force. The opening and closing of each jet was connected to the pilot's control column, so that, if the nose went down, he would react normally and pull the stick back, thus opening the front puffer to push the nose back up again. And the same for the wing tips and directional control, the pilot always moving the control column as he ordinarily would in normal flight. This feature has greatly contributed to the ease with which pilots can be trained to fly the Harrier.

The earlier Rolls-Royce Flying Bedsteads had been controlled by similar puffer jets, but with an automatic stabilizing system governed by gyroscopes like an autopilot. This feature had been used in the Short SC.1 research aircraft, which had four RB108 engines for lifting only, each of around 2,000 lb thrust. For safety, it is customary to use three automatic systems, in case of system failure. One might fail, two might fight against each other, whereas three provide the essential margin of safety.

Hugh Conway, who had been Managing Director at Shorts at the time of the SC.1, made a special trip to Camm to persuade him — with a long and very technical presentation — to use the three-lane system. I saw Sydney shortly afterwards, and he told me he had said to Conway "We are ignorant buggers here at Hawkers, and don't understand all that science". So the Harrier was left in the hands of its pilots, with what success we all know.

Once the transition from vertical take-off to wing-borne flight had been made, and the P.1127 shown to be a practical proposition, MWDP began, naturally, to reduce their financial contribution. However, further support from MWDP came some years later when the Tripartite squadron of nine Kestrel aircraft was formed. MWDP, the British Government and the German Government each contributed three aircraft. The purpose of this squadron, which had engines rated at 15,000 lb, was to demonstrate the capability of the aircraft to operate under actual field conditions, which it did with great success.

I would like to pay a tribute to Larry Levy, a wealthy American, who had joined MWDP, and had the political clout and dollars to persuade the American, Federal German and British governments to purchase the Kestrel aircraft and set up the field trials. The Tripartite unit began operations in 1964, dispersed as in war conditions, and the trials were literally a roaring success.

The British Government was reluctant to pick up the cheque

for the continued development of the Harrier, because the RAF continued to show little interest. Nonetheless, the programme went ahead. Chapman and Driscoll bowed out, but it must be a source of great personal satisfaction to them to see that the bread they cast upon the waters in 1958-62 returned to the US Marine Corps when they ordered more than 100 Harriers in 1969, under the enthusiastic leadership of Col. (later Lt. Gen.) Tom Miller, USMC.

Obviously, the next step was to increase the thrust of the Pegasus so that the Kestrel could be equipped with a war load, and all the ancillary equipment involved. Accordingly, we followed the usual practice of increasing the mass flow of the fan, and raising the engine operating temperature from 970° to 1,170°C by using air-cooled cast blades in the HP turbine. Thus the thrust was increased, first to 18,000 lb and later, in production, to 21,500 lb.

We also added a small gas-turbine starter, so that the aircraft would be completely independent of ground services. This little gas turbine gave 100 hp (as I recall), and could be run independently of the main engine so that all the electrical equipment could be checked without running the main engine — an important feature for aircraft dispersed in the field.

To the Hawker Aircraft designers Hooper and Fozard, and to the Hawker test pilots Bedford and Merewether, must go the credit for converting the first demonstrator P.1127 into the final weapon as the Harrier. To John Dale at Bristol must go the credit for converting the early Pegasus into a reliable service engine. In fact John spent 20 years of his life developing the Orpheus and Pegasus, and gained worldwide respect for his judgment, and the firm way he ran the Pegasus development programme.

It seems unlikely that such a programme could happen twice — Orpheus and Pegasus — where an engine and aircraft are made and tested ahead of any military specification. But miracles do sometimes happen, and the whole enterprise reaped its just reward in its contribution to the Falklands campaign. No Pegasus, no Harrier and no Task Force.

As for the US Marine Corps, they continue to be staunch supporters of the aircraft, and Lt. General White, Deputy Chief of Staff for Aviation, USMC, recently wrote me a congratulatory letter in which he stated that the Marine Corps intended to re-equip its light attack force with the Harrier II (AV-8B) which is being jointly developed by British Aerospace and McDonnell

Douglas. Such things do not happen by accident, nor without a great deal of determined and dedicated persuasion by men such as Gene Newbold from our American company. Gene came first from Fairchild, went to Curtiss-Wright, and finally joined Rolls-Royce Inc in New York. He dedicated his efforts to the Pegasus and the Harrier, and is held in such great respect by all in the Pentagon that he had the entrée to the low and the high. He continues to be a key man in the efforts we have made to sell the Harrier to the US Air Force and Navy. This is no mean task, considering the great production facilities that exist in the USA, and which will naturally favour the production of American-designed aircraft and engines.

28 May 1982

Dear Sir Stanley,

On the occasion of the highly successful introduction of V/STOL aircraft into combat, we congratulate you on your keen foresight and your steadfast pursuit of the development of the Pegasus engine for V/STOL aviation.

As you know, the U.S. Marine Corps will soon make the transition to an all V/STOL light attack force with the Harrier II. This serves as the highest testimony to your contribution to the goals, of not only the U.S. Marine Corps, but to those of free world aviation.

We wish you a speedy recovery.

Very respectfully,

A. J. WHITE
Lieutenant General, U.S. Marine Corps
Deputy Chief of Staff for Aviation

Sir Stanley Hooker
Chesterfield Hospital
#3 Clifton Hill
Clifton, Bristol
BS8 1BP
England

Chapter 11
The Mergers and my first Retirement

Few can doubt that in the 1950s Britain had too many aircraft companies, and too many military aircraft development programmes. It was inevitable that both should sharply diminish, but perhaps this should have been possible without either suggesting that military aircraft were obsolete or that companies failing to merge should no longer be considered for government contracts.

The pressure on companies to merge grew from late 1957. Westland, the helicopter builder, took over Fairey, Saunders-Roe and the helicopter programmes from Bristol. Hawker Siddeley, by far the largest existing group, progressively swallowed up Folland, Blackburn Aircraft and de Havilland Aircraft. Bristol Aircraft joined with the successful TSR.2 contractors, Vickers-Armstrongs and English Electric, to form BAC (British Aircraft Corporation), which also absorbed Hunting Aircraft. On the engine side Rolls-Royce took over D. Napier & Son, while Bristol Aero-Engines and Armstrong Siddeley Motors merged to form BSEL (Bristol Siddeley Engines Ltd) to provide engines for TSR.2, thereafter taking over de Havilland Engines and Blackburn Engines.

It was a time of great turmoil, rarely equalled in any industry. People in the great pioneering companies of this British industry were passionately proud and loyal to their great names, and powerful emotions had to be eroded if the mergers were to succeed. At top levels of management tough and astute tycoons fought for various interests — their employees, their company names, their aircraft projects, the financial deals and the fine print in the agreements. But at the technical and engineering levels it all took place with scarcely a ripple.

Russell's aircraft design team, led by Bill Strang and Mick Wilde, still reigned intact at Bristol. On the engine side my team received a small influx of valuable talent from Armstrong Siddeley, together with a large increase in knowledge and experience. Only later did I learn how large had loomed the fears of others that the chief engineers, all strong personalities, would indulge in a head-on collision. In fact there was little argument and I carried on as before. Dr Eric Moult of DH Engines took over helicopter engines, a growth area, at his factory at Leavesden, outside Watford. Pat Lindsey, of Armstrong Siddeley, took over the new Industrial and Marine Division at a former ASM plant at Ansty, outside Coventry. We had all been friends since the early days of jet engines, and hardly had a cross word.

Thus BSEL was, from the word go, a happy ship. As Technical Director I was nominally able to direct Moult and Lindsey, but they were so competent and self-propelled that no interference from me was necessary. We contented ourselves with mutual sharing of technical expertise and mutual support to overcome any serious problem.

No better example of this policy could be given than the changes made to the Olympus and Pegasus combustion chambers. I had previously been only too happy to stick to the Lucas system, in which the fuel is fed under high pressure to atomizing jets which spray it in a cloud of fine droplets into the burning region. For many years palliatives had been sought for the most severe disadvantage of this method, which is the fact that it is not possible to maintain the high pressure needed for proper atomization, except at maximum fuel flow. Thus, at take-off the fuel flow is 100 per cent and the fuel pressure may be 1,000 lb/sq in, giving good atomization; but at flight-idling, or low power at high altitude, the fuel flow may be 10 per cent and the pressure only 10 lb/sq in, a hundred-fold reduction. This low pressure results in the burner emitting a spluttering jet containing small, medium and large droplets, which need highly variable periods of time in which to burn. This can wreck the desired fuel distribution and air/fuel ratio, lay down carbon deposits, cause a smoky jet and promote flameout whenever the pilot opens or closes the throttle.

From the beginning, Armstrong Siddeley had concentrated on vaporizing burners rather like a Primus stove or common blowlamp. In their system the fuel was supplied at low pressure and metered into a curved tube like the handle of a walking stick, located in the burning zone of the combustion chamber. The fuel was vaporized by the heat surrounding the short walking-stick tube and emerged as a vapour which mixed readily with the airflow and gave uniform and consistent combustion under all conditions.

Of course the ASM system had its problems, one of which was melting of the metal of the walking-sticks, but brilliant work by that company's engineers — notably former rocket designer Sid Allen — overcame them completely. When we at Bristol inherited the system in 1960 it was free from any significant trouble. I had a careful evaluation made against the traditional high-pressure atomizing burners, and the vaporizing method emerged as clearly superior.

I had no hesitation in deciding that both the Olympus and Pegasus should forthwith be changed to vaporizing combustion, with the assistance of the former ASM combustion engineers. The change not only gave perfect behaviour under all conditions but eliminated visible smoke and gave sundry other valuable improvements.

All liquid fuel must be turned into a vapour and mixed with the correct amount of oxygen from the air before it will burn. It seems obvious that to do the vaporizing separately under controlled conditions is better than squirting droplets into the burning zone and leaving them to do it on their own. Why did it take until 1960 for the blinding light to dawn on me? My defence is that I was so busy dragging Bristol into the jet age that I was only too happy to leave combustion to Lucas.

That great firm, under Sir Bertram Waring, a mighty supporter of the aircraft industry, had from the early Whittle days developed gas-turbine combustion chambers and fuel systems. It did the chambers at Burnley under Clarke and Morley, and the fuel systems at Shaftmoor Lane, Birmingham, under Dr Watson and Dick Iffield. As far as possible it was a case of 'fit and forget' the Lucas system where I was concerned; but equally there was no doubt of the superiority of the vaporizing system.

Whilst we were changing over to vaporizing combustion, in the early 1960s, the technology of the jet engine was poised for a giant new leap. Though 20 years earlier the so-called ducted-fan engine, again first envisaged by Sir Frank Whittle, had attracted only very limited interest, it was obvious from the way Pratt & Whitney beat the Rolls-Royce Conway, simply by going to a much higher bypass ratio in their JT3D turbofan, that the subsonic transport engines of the future were going to have much higher bypass ratios, in the region of 3 to 7, and would thus be much quieter and much more fuel efficient.

BSEL and Rolls-Royce studied such engines but lacked funds to build one. In the United States, however, the USAF organised the CX-HLS programme for a gigantic long-range cargo aircraft, and this led to the Lockheed C-5A Galaxy and to new-generation HBPR (high bypass ratio) turbofan engines at General Electric and Pratt & Whitney. GE got the contract for the C-5A engine, but Pratt & Whitney decided to go it alone and constructed the JT9D engine to power the first of today's wide-body commercial transports, the Boeing 747, 'Jumbo Jet'. Rather suddenly it was a whole new ball game.

Rolls-Royce boldly gambled company money on the design and prototype manufacture of a large HBPR engine, the RB178. After careful planning BSEL planned to join with our existing French partner, SNECMA, in the JT9D programme. In view of what has happened in the past 20 years, this US/UK/France programme would clearly have been an excellent step towards collaboration in the largest projects, but it was not to be.

In 1966 Rolls-Royce ran a demonstrator RB178 engine and to strengthen its hand, the main board at Derby made a successful bid for the entire BSEL assets and business with the result that in October 1966 we were bought up by Rolls-Royce at the substantial price of £63.6 million.

Although I was quite happy with the basic principle of amalgamating Bristol Siddeley with Rolls-Royce, I was sad that these two famous names were to disappear. I was not so pleased with what this entailed for myself and my team of engineers. Derby had Sir Denning Pearson as Chairman and Chief Executive, Sir David Huddie as Managing Director of Derby Aero Engines, and F. T. Hinckley as Commercial Director. I asked Pearson to appoint me to the main Rolls-Royce Board but his feeling at that time was that I was no longer acceptable to the engineers at Derby. My request was turned down and so I decided to retire at the earliest convenient date, which was my 60th birthday on the 30 September 1967. The negotiations to obtain the best possible financial terms for me were aided by two of my friends at Derby, Don Pepper, Director of Personnel, and Trevan Hawke, Financial Director.

Sir Arnold Hall.

Bill Rogerson.

Orpheus cutaway.

Col John Driscoll and Theodore von Kármán.

Fiat G 91.

Gen J. Chapman, U.S.A.F.

Professor Gabrielli.

Gerry Morel.

Jean Allais.

H.M.S. Illustrious powered by Olympus gas-turbines. She carries Sea Harriers (Pegasus), Sea King helicopters (Gnomes) and Sea Dart missiles (Odin ramjet).

Early production Pegasus.

The first Kestrel (Pegasus) in formation with a 2-seater Hunter (Avon).

Two-seater demonstrator Harrier. From left; Fred Sutton, Chief Flight Development Engineer, John Farley, Chief Test Pilot, S.G.H., John Dale, Chief Pegasus Development Engineer, Bill Bedford, former Chief Test Pilot.

On the Great Wall, Sir William Cook, Sir Kenneth Keith and S.G.H. with their Chinese Hosts.

Chapter 12
The RB211 and the Prodigal's Return

When I decided to retire in September 1967, Hugh Conway, who had been appointed to the Rolls-Royce main board whilst remaining managing director at Bristol, asked me to stay on as a consultant. This I willingly agreed to do. Having no executive responsibilities I was able to sit back and survey the various Rolls-Royce engine programmes. The one that stood out like a sore thumb — in size, importance, technical and financial risk, and lack of progress — was the RB211 at Derby.

The RB211 was the giant High By Pass Ratio engine that the main board finally chose to build. The reasons behind the giant HBPR engines now need explaining in more detail. Back in 1958 Pratt & Whitney had shown, in meeting the competition of the Conway bypass jet, that it was possible to add on the front of an existing turbojet a large fan, with a diameter much greater than the rest of the engine, driven by extra turbine stages (or an additional turbine driving a separate LP shaft). Such a fan would both supercharge the rest of the engine, called the gas-generator or core, and also greatly raise the propulsive mass flow and reduce the mean jet velocity, a system which we had also used in the Pegasus in 1958.

In all gas-turbine jet engines the central core can be regarded as a 'boiler' producing hot gas under pressure. In a simple turbojet this flow is allowed to escape through the propulsive nozzle, producing thrust. The higher the pressure ratio and the higher the operating temperature, the greater the efficiency of the boiler — provided, of course, that the efficiency of each compressor and turbine can be maintained. On the other hand, the higher the 'boiler efficiency', the greater the velocity of the jet, the kinetic energy of which is wasted on being released to the atmosphere. The propulsive efficiency therefore falls. Propulsive efficiency is equal to 2Va divided by Vj plus Va, where Va is the velocity of the aircraft (relative to still air) and Vj is the velocity of the jet (relative to the aircraft). In round figures Va may be 850 ft/sec (580 mph) and Vj 2,000 ft/sec, giving a propulsive efficiency of 60 per cent. For Concorde we do better because Va is much greater. The only way to do better with subsonic aircraft is to reduce Vj. If we could get it down to 1,500 ft/sec, by augmenting the airflow, we could raise the propulsive efficiency to 72 per cent, thus — other things being equal — cutting the fuel burn by at least 20 per cent.

With the new breed of HBPR engines which became visible in the first half of the 1960s the first thing to do was to take an existing type of core and add an extra turbine downstream, driving via a long shaft to an enormous fan at the front. This fan, in essence a multibladed propeller, runs at a tip Mach number of about 1.5, so most of the area of each blade is supersonic. It has a design pressure-ratio of about 1.5, so it supercharges the entire airflow entering the core engine by this amount. Thus, if the core had a pressure-ratio of 16:1, a figure within previous experience, the overall engine pressure-ratio became 24:1 when supercharged by the fan, giving a 'boiler efficiency' higher than ever before achieved.

So far we have increased the pressure-ratio and reduced the jet velocity. The third objective was a further major improvement in 'boiler efficiency' gained by running much hotter than ever before. A combustion temperature of about 1,250°C was sought, roughly 150° above the current state of the art.

These were the basic objectives of all the new HBPR fan engines, which were pioneered by the TF39 built by General Electric for the Lockheed C-5A Galaxy for the USAF, and by the Pratt & Whitney JT9D produced mainly at company expense for the Boeing 747. It was clear that such engines would have an enormous impact, especially on commercial aviation. Their great size and power made possible so-called 'wide-body' airliners carrying more than twice as many passengers as their predecessors, for unprecedented long ranges, and with an enormous and welcome reduction in both specific fuel consumption and noise.

By 1967 Boeing's chief rivals, Lockheed and McDonnell Douglas, had offered the airlines large trijets to meet the specifications of American Airlines and other US trunk operators. These needed engines in the 33,000 lb class, compared with 40,000 lb for the C-5A and 747, but the aircraft grew in weight and more thrust was needed.

Sir Denning Pearson (Psn), Managing Director and Chairman of Rolls-Royce, and commercial director David Huddie decided to get into the US wide-body market. The RB178 had been developed for the European Airbus A300 into a very large and powerful engine, the RB207; but this was never built because Psn ordered the entire resources of Derby to be devoted to a smaller engine, the RB211, sized to the requirements of the Lockheed L-1011 TriStar. The final contractual commitment was that RB211 engines would be delivered at a fixed price from September 1971, fully certificated at 42,000 lb thrust. In March 1968, on this basis, the L-1011 went ahead with large launch orders from Eastern Airlines and TWA, plus a specially formed British financial group called Air Holdings whose purpose was to underwrite 50 of the US jets for sale to non-US carriers.

General Electric, in fact, not only secured the propulsion contract for the McDonnell Douglas DC-10, almost a duplicate of the TriStar, but also launched the development of a much more powerful version of their basic CF6 engine, the CF6-50. This fitted the Airbus A300B and also enabled McDonnell Douglas to offer a much heavier DC-10 for long-range routes. Rolls-Royce could see that this would lead to DC-10 sales far outstripping those of the TriStar, but had their hands so full with the original RB211 that they had no hope of funding a more powerful version.

Thus, fairly soon, Rolls-Royce was in an inferior marketing position. They were striving to build an engine of 42,000 lb thrust in competition with a much larger US rival who was offering engines at thrusts up to 49,500 lb. Moreover, whereas both the American rivals had extensive running experience, with the JT9D on the verge of airline service in the 747, the RB211 existed only on paper. Rolls-Royce had additionally been compelled by market pressure to abandon the policy laid down by Hs that no engine should be sold for airline service without extensive military experience. It is ironic that when the RAF got its first RB211 engines in 1983 they were secondhand ex-British Airways!

Obviously, the RB211 was a much greater challenge than Rolls-Royce had ever previously faced. The operating pressures and temperatures were outside the company's previous experience, and the size of the fan blades, casings and rings was more than double anything seen at Derby previously. There were two key features of the RB211 that could be, and were, used by Rolls-Royce to sell the engine to Lockheed instead of a US rival, and used by Lockheed to justify their choice to the airlines. One was the use of three shafts, and the other was the Hyfil fan blades.

The reason for the three-shaft, or three-spool, layout appears later in a Technical Appraisal I wrote in the crucial month of February 1971. By that time the Hyfil fan blade, on which so much hope had centred, was a thing of the past.

This was a bitter blow not just to Rolls-Royce but to Britain. In the early 1960s British workers at the RAE at Farnborough had pioneered the conversion of polyacrilonitrile yarn into fibres of pure carbon so strong and stiff, yet extremely light in weight, as to open up a whole new world of structural possibilities. Carbon fibre became all the rage, one of the main planks in what Prime Minister Wilson called 'Britain's white-hot technological revolution'. But actual applications were hard to find until Rolls-Royce decided that carbon fibre material was ideal for the RB211 fan. The fan was huge by previous standards, over 7ft in diameter. Each pound saved in the mass of its blades could be multiplied many times in reducing the weight of the hub, bearings and main engine frame. Aerodynamic calculations showed that with a sharp-edge 'lenticular' profile the blades could reach surprisingly high efficiencies, at pressure ratios of 1.5 to 1.7 and tip speeds over 1,500 ft/sec (Mach 1.5).

To make each blade vast numbers of strong carbon fibres, thinner than human hairs, were bonded by resin adhesive into thin flat plies which after being cut to shape were stacked in a pile and bonded into one solid mass. The blades were smooth, black and amazingly strong and light. They enabled the RB211 to give the TriStar considerably greater payload than the rival engines with metal fans.

On test the Hyfil blades worked well, and enormous money and effort went into their development and tooling up for mass production. But when prototype fans and complete RB211 engines were subjected to the mandatory birdstrike test, in which 4 lb chickens from the supermarket are fired at high speed into the engine running at take-off speed, the blades proved to have an Achilles heel. The weak resin plastic could not take the sudden impact on the thin leading edge.

As a fallback programme an all-titanium fan had been designed, and with great reluctance this had to replace the new-technology Hyfil construction. At a stroke this wiped out the engine's weight advantage over its rivals.

As for the vital HP turbine, this again went well beyond the previous state of the art. Derby had been one of the pioneers of aircooled turbine blades in the Conway bypass jet designed in the mid-1950s. All Derby blades were forged in a Nimonic high-nickel alloy, able to retain adequate strength at about 900°C. In the Conway the peak gas temperature was about 1,100°C, so the cooling air holes and passages inside the blade had to keep the blade at least 200°C cooler than the surrounding gas. In the RB211 the gas was going to be at 1,250°C. This may not sound a very big increase over 1,100, but the strength of the blade is halved for every extra 25°C!

To make a blade at Derby the rough metal bar from which the blade would be fashioned was first pierced by a large number of long but small-diameter drilled holes. Just where these had to be was found by a laborious process of trial and error, so that, after the rough blank had been forged, the holes were all in the correct positions. To forge the blade it was squeezed while almost white-hot between two dies having the correct shape to form the blade. Finally the whole blade was machined all over to precisely the correct size and profile. The price of each blade was inevitably very high, and the whole process was an engineer's nightmare because microscopic variations between the cooling air holes in successive blades meant that the cooling would be uneven.

At Bristol we had abandoned forged blades soon after 1960. Instead we cast our blades using the famous lost-wax process used 500 years earlier — by da Vinci, for example — to produce precisely repeated sculptures. Casting enabled us to use materials basically stronger than Nimonic alloys, too hard to be forged or machined. We cast our blades to the finish dimensions, with a mirror finish, without any machining apart from precision grinding of the root. Cast blades proved to be much stronger in tension than forged and machined blades, and despite their brittleness and susceptibility to thermal stress we proved on the Proteus that they are superior. On the Olympus 593 and Pegasus we produced large numbers of eminently reliable blades with radial air cooling passages operating at some 1,250°C, much hotter than any production engine at Derby at that time.

Derby was aware of the Bristol experience, and planned to switch to such blades eventually, but designed the RB211 to use forged and machined Nimonic. Predictably, the HP turbine blades were prone to failure. Yet a further problem was that, though potentially an advantage, the three-shaft layout posed severe problems in oil leakage and bearing failure.

This all added up to plenty of problems, but far more serious than these was the fact that, when the first RB211 engines ran, their performance was way down and totally unacceptable.

As the months went by in 1970 it became obvious to me that Rolls-Royce was in trouble over its contract with Lockheed, and yet this was the contract on which the company's future was to be based.

On the financial front things went from bad to worse. On a really successful programme the money paid out on development and getting into production is so enormous that it takes something like 15 years for the programme to move from the red into the black. At the fourth or fifth years many millions of pounds have to be spent on production tooling, raw materials and finished parts which begin to fill the stores with 'work in progress'. But if there is any minor hiccough in development, production is thrown into utter confusion making engines and parts that cannot be delivered to the customer, while the stores fill up with costly parts of which some or all will have to be scrapped.

By mid-1970 it was clear that Derby was deep into this situation and would be unable to fulfil its contractual obligations to Lockheed. The company's enormous assets were no help, because what it was fast running out of was cash and credit to pay the wages and the bills of the thousands of subcontractors and suppliers. The government saw all this and in 1970 at last had to act by removing Psn and Huddie and appointing Ian Morrow to take charge of finance. Hugh Conway was appointed managing director at Derby, and Lord Cole, ex-chairman of Unilever, was appointed caretaker chairman. I pressed Hugh to reorganise the engineering set-up, because obviously it was the engineering problems that had to be put right first. I recalled Hs's axiom 'If the engineers are wrong, then we are all wrong.'

Finally at the end of 1970 Hugh agreed that I should go to Derby to survey the situation. To give him his due, he also insisted I should be accorded the status of Technical Director at Derby. I flew up to East Midlands airport and was met by car and taken to the colossal ultra-modern main office block at Moor Lane, which I had never seen. I was filled with trepidation. Would I be able to do anything useful? Would I be accepted back into the fold?

When I arrived at Moor Lane I was greeted with delight by my old friend Chief Commissionaire Phillipson, who looked more imposing and immaculate than ever. As he ushered me into the main foyer I could hear the voice of Hs saying 'Go to it Stanley, tell us what we have to do and we will do it as easy, as easy, as easy.' When I later went in to lunch, everyone crowded around to welcome me, and Freddie Morley said, 'Welcome back, you old bugger. It has cost us 63 million to get you, but it's worth every penny'. He was, of course, referring to the price paid for Bristol Siddeley.

I had been allocated a small empty office in the main engineering block. The first thing I did was to call in the performance engineers to give me a run-down on the reasons for the shortfall in engine performance. I was disturbed at the lack of data, and the scrappy nature of the analyses. They claimed that the efficiency of the HP turbine was 65 per cent. To that I said 'Rubbish, turbines can't be made that bad. It takes a genius to get above 85 per cent but it also take a lunatic to make one worse than 75 per cent.'

I then enquired about the speeds (rpm) of the three shafts. Again I was bemused to find that these were way off the design values. It is always possible to adjust shaft speeds by altering the areas of the nozzle guide vanes between the various turbine stages which swirl the gas into the turbines. We went to work and calculated the changes in NGV area necessary to achieve the correct shaft speeds. These modifications were instructed to the shops. We got the test results of the first modified engine at the most opportune moment, in mid-February 1971. What follows is the first Technical Appraisal which I delivered to Hugh Conway in February 1971, very slightly abridged.

Technical Appraisal
  1. The RB211 is a high bypass ratio, high-compression ratio, high-temperature fan engine competitive with the Pratt & Whitney JT9D and the General Electric CF6 engines made in the USA.
  2. The take-off thrusts at which the three engines are on offer today are: JT9D, 43,500-45,000 lb; CF6, 40,600 lb for the DC-10 and 49,500 for the A300B Airbus; RB211, 42,000 lb for the Lockheed 1011 TriStar. The specific fuel consumptions and weights of the three engines are competitive. The comparative order of basic size or air consumption is: CF6, 1.0; RB211, 1.10; JT9D, 1.20.

3. The RB211 is unique in that its fan, intermediate (IP) compressor and HP compressor are each driven independently by its own turbine. This arrangement allows the three components — fan, IP compressor and HP compressor — to be driven each at its own optimum speed, and thereby improves the overall aerodynamic efficiency and flexibility. In particular, the independence of the fan speed, and the ability to raise this speed, the fan being the major thrust-producing component in the engine, allows further thrust growth as the turbine entry temperature is raised by future development.

4. As a typical example, the desirable speed relation between the three spools of the RB211 is, in round numbers; Fan, 3,600 rpm; IP, 6,800 rpm; HP, 10,000 rpm.

5. The situation in regard to the thrust of the RB211 as it existed in January 1971 *vis-a-vis* Lockheed was:

   (a) A contractual obligation to produce 40,600 lb take-off thrust up to a day temperature of 84°F.

   (b) Because of weight growth during the manufacture of the prototype L-1011, and because the RB211 was itself overweight (38,441 lb for a ship set as against the original guarantee of 34,566 lb), Rolls-Royce undertook to produce a thrust of 42,000 lb up to 84°F. This proposal was discussed with Lockheed.

   (c) Notwithstanding the weight growth of the aircraft and the engines (much larger, in fact, on the aircraft) it was the opinion of Rolls-Royce that an acceptable thrust for entry into service of the L-1011 would be 38,500 lb up to 84°F. This proposal was not discussed with Lockheed. Summarising: 40,500 lb was the contractual commitment, 42,000 lb was offered, and 38,500 lb was considered acceptable by Rolls-Royce for entry into service.

6. For the start of the first prototype L-1011 flight programme, Rolls-Royce delivered to Lockheed five Batch 1 engines rated at 34,000 lb at a Turbine Entry Temperature (TET) of 1,167°C. For the second prototype, Rolls-Royce delivered six Batch 3 engines rated at 34,200 lb at a TET of 1,202°C, with a contingency or emergency rating of 36,200 lb at a TET of 1,232°C. These engines flew in the second prototype on 15 February 1971.

7. At this stage, it was clear that the engine performance was

sub-standard, in that the TET was too high for a given thrust. Modifications were, therefore, made to engine No. 100011, and on test at Derby in early February 1971 the following figures were demonstrated: 37,000 lb at 1,167°C TET; 39,430 lb at 1,227°C.

8. On another engine, a new design of HP turbine blade discharging its cooling air from the trailing edge was tested, and this improved design reduced the TET at a given thrust by 28°C, or increased thrust at a given TET by 2,000 lb. It is intended to cast this type of blade by the lost-wax process, and to conduct further testing on the bench in October 1971, with a view to incorporating into production engines in mid-1972.

9. Following the successful improvements demonstrated on Engine No. 100011, a further change was been made to the LP nozzle guide vane areas, and this is **predicted** to give 41,500 lb at 1,227°C. This engine will be on test on 17 February 1971.

10. Summarising the performance results (all quoted for the test bench on a Standard Day):

Batch 1 Engine	34,000 lb at 1,167°C.
Batch 3 Engine	34,200 lb at 1,202°C.
Engine 100011	37,000 lb at 1,167°C.
Engine 100011 (February 1971)	39,340 lb at 1,227°C.
Engine 100011 with modified LP NGV (predicted)	41,500 lb at 1,227°C.
Engine 100011 with cast blades (predicted)	43,500 lb at 1,227°C.

11. Actual thrust developed depends directly upon TET. It is anticipated that a TET of 1,227 ± 20°C can be adequately cleared by bench running.

12. In the future, the new cast turbine blade will not only be better aerodynamically but will be cast in a material (MARM 202) which has better high-temperature properties and will allow at least 50°C increase in TET. This will increase the thrust at 1,277°C to 47,000 lb on a **standard day,** and this figure must be regarded as the potential growth in thrust of the RB211 without major redesign.

Thus we had in a matter of weeks transformed the RB211, and could promise not only to restore the missing performance but to go way beyond it. I explained much earlier how the RB211 crisis would never have come about had that great jewel Lombard been at the helm.

192 *Not Much of an Engineer*

While we were doing this, in the winter 1970-71, the tough chairman of Lockheed, Dan Haughton, was commuting every few days between Los Angeles and Derby. He adamantly refused to modify Rolls-Royce's contractual obligations. The situation came to a head in February 1971, just before we got the improved engine on test, when Lord Cole declared Rolls-Royce insolvent.

To describe the whole world as stunned is an understatement. Rolls-Royce was regarded as no more likely to collapse than the Monarchy or the Church of England. But in fact it was a matter of arithmetic. After years of massive outgoings the RB211 was reaching the peak of its cash-flow deficit. If engines, in 1970/71 could have been delivered to Lockheed there would at last have been an inflow of cash, probably enough to stave off disaster.

But the engines could not be delivered because they were deficient in performance and had not yet passed the tests of the UK or US certification authorities. So the works just went on piling up expensive stocks and work in progress until the cash dried up.

For once, the British government acted with lightning speed. Overnight it purchased, for an unspecified price, all the company's assets. I understood this was to forestall foreign creditors from claiming assets on the basis of first come, first served. The government also dismissed the company's board, with the exception of Lord Cole, Ian Morrow and Hugh Conway, who were left minding the shop.

In purchasing the assets the government made one specific exception: it refused to buy the RB211. Nobody else wanted it either! The purchase was made, it was said, purely because of the company's importance to defence in Britain and many other countries. The affair thus came under Lord Carrington, who was Secretary of State for Defence in the Heath government.

He appointed 'three wise men' to give him an appraisal of the technical and financial viability of the RB211. They were Sir William Cook, the former Scientific Adviser to the Ministry of Defence; Sir St John Elstub, chairman of Imperial Metal Industries; and Professor Douglas Holder, who held the chair of Engineering Science at Oxford. Bill Cook had been my colleague at Woolwich Arsenal, and he asked me to join them at the MoD to help prepare the report.

A few days later in February 1971 we were in the midst of our examinations in London when the news came from Derby that engine No. 10011 with new NGVs was running, and that it was showing the predicted performance. At one stroke the thrust for a given TET had been increased from 34,000 lb to well over 40,000 lb. Clearly all that remained was to grind through the many mechanical faults which affected engine reliability. Freddie Morley began to issue his design changes which collectively became 'The Morley Mods', and we were close to having a good RB211.

The Cook Report was favourable, and the British government then made Lockheed an offer they could hardly refuse. Either renegotiate the contract, this time under British law, with one year added to the delivery dates and with an increase in engine price (incidentally for a considerably better and more powerful engine than the original RB211-1), or the programme will be abandoned. Lockheed and their customers were rather relieved, though Lockheed's own financial position was serious and eventually led to an unprecedented decision of support by the US Congress which was carried by just one vote.

Thus, after a long series of negotiations which had no historical precedent, we got the RB211 on the road again, and Lockheed went on with the L-1011. The British government formed a new company called Rolls-Royce (1971) Ltd, and paid for the day-to-day costs of the RB211 programme. It also restructured the board, inviting Sir Arnold Weinstock (at the time the No. 1 tough company troubleshooter) and Gordon Richardson (later Governor of the Bank of England) to join. Sir William Cook and Sir St John Elstub were also invited, and so was I, as Technical Director, so that somebody on the board might know about the engineering position.

Thus I found myself, four years after my retirement, occupying the very chair promised to me by Hs 25 years previously! But elation was the last thing I felt. Under me the great team of engineers, and indeed the whole vast Derby works, was completely demoralized. Many were looking for someone else to blame. I called a meeting of the entire engineering staff and explained the exact situation. I then appealed to their loyalty to the good name of Rolls-Royce to get the RB211 quickly certificated and delivered to Lockheed. I promised 100 per cent support to their efforts and asked any doubters to leave at once.

Nobody left but a few days later I heard that one senior engineer was dickering with the motor manufacturers who had set up a recruiting office in the Midland Hotel. I sent for him and bluntly asked if this were true. He replied that he had not yet made up his mind. I told him, 'Well, I'll make it up for you. I would like you out of this factory by 4 pm this afternoon'. I got the personnel manager to pay him then and there what was due to him. Everyone else decided to stay.

Rather remarkably, within days of first being called up to Derby a few weeks before, I had been able to put my finger on several crucial faults and to have them rectified very quickly indeed. But one cannot truly know a piece of machinery as complex as the RB211 without living with it from the start. So I did not attempt to run the show but left the day-to-day programme to Ernest Eltis, whom I had displaced as Technical Director, but who gave me the most loyal support, and to his assistant (and an old colleague of mine from Barnoldswick) Johnnie Bush. They proved an inspiration to their teams, and worked closely with Chief Designer Freddie Morley and his assistant John Coplin.

I bore the ultimate responsibility, however, and soon decided to invite my old tutors, and perhaps the greatest of Rolls-Royce engineers, to join me to form a kind of Chief of Staff committee. I asked Cyril Lovesey and Arthur Rubbra, both well over 70, to come back into the thick of it. They responded with alacrity, and I cannot describe the comfort in seeing Rubbra poring over the drawings, and to discuss the forthcoming programme with Lovesey. Their vast experience was immediately put to use, and I pay tribute to the way they gave this to the new company, as to the old — and, in Lovesey's case, he gave all his remaining years.

It was all too obvious that the Derby engineers, normally proud and self-confident to the point of arrogance, had slid from bad to worse when their great leader, Lombard, had so suddenly been plucked from them in 1967. His death had left a vacuum which nobody could fill, and I saw it as a major part of my job to rebuild an atmosphere of confidence in the future so that gradually the vacuum would disappear. Always the crucial programme was the RB211, and whenever it could be seen that more manpower was needed I drafted it, leaving the barest skeleton staffs under Metcalfe to look after the Spey, Dart, Adour and other Derby engines.

Thus, between February and the autumn of 1971 the Derby works achieved a miracle in totally transforming the RB211 programme. The modifications needed extended to every part of the engine, but they were carried through with a speed and a spirit reminiscent of the Battle of Britain. The costs incurred were controlled tightly by Ian Morrow, and rightly so because it was RB211 costs that had broken the original company. At the same time I knew we were running a race, and it was frustrating perpetually to be told that a modification was not possible because the finance had not been cleared.

My response was always the same: 'Get on with it, and I will take personal responsibility for the costs'. Such arguments took up a lot of my time, and eventually I went to Ian and said 'I am sure you are as keen as anyone to see the RB211 through to certification, but people are using your name to fight against every step we take. Please give me a million pound credit, to use as and when I think fit'. He readily agreed, and I never had to spend one penny of it, because the knowledge that it was there, enabling me to over-ride any financial blockage, ensured that no more such blockages occurred.

Thus we gradually got the great company not merely on the road again but really humming. Bankruptcy may temporarily shatter morale, but it certainly concentrates the mind wonderfully. Very quickly we got a terrific team working on the RB211. Geoffrey Wilde took over design and development of the troublesome turbine blades. Harry Pearson came back from retirement to oversee performance analysis. Peter Colston, within the hour of each of our decisions, prepared formal engineering requests and delivered them to two miracle-workers, Eric Scarfe (Production) and Trevor Salt (Experimental Manufacture).

In between working with my splendid RB211 team I had to attend main board meetings, which in 1971-72 were devoted largely to establishing the price the government should pay for the company. In the haste of the takeover the wording was that the price should be a 'fair and reasonable one, as if there were a competing buyer in the field'. This phrase drove Sir Arnold Weinstock mad, because, he said, it was impossible to quantify such a vague generalization. Arnold had the reputation of being the toughest of tycoons, and he was unquestionably the dominating personality on the board. I quickly came to admire his rapier-like mind, and his logical and eloquent exposition of each point of debate.

He made a quick test case where I was concerned by asking for my opinion on some obtuse point, and I replied 'Sorry Arnold, I don't know; you design the company and I'll design the engines.' After that he left me out of the arguments on law and finance, but listened with great attention to my reports on technical progress. He used Gordon Richardson as the stalking-horse for the arguments, and the two them, with Ian Morrow, settled point after point of the intricate details of the government purchase and the capital finance needed to run the company. The rest of us sat in silent admiration.

In the autumn of 1972 Ian Morrow had a disagreement with the Minister of Aviation, Michael Heseltine, about the choice of a new managing director, and he resigned. I much regretted this, because Ian was extremely experienced at many aspects of company finance, as well as being a delightful man to work with. He was one of the key men in getting Rolls-Royce (1971) Ltd on its feet.

Back at the start of the RB211 programme Rolls-Royce had given Lockheed an understanding — no more than that — that it would eventually develop the engine to 45,000 lb thrust. The idea was that, as experience was gained with the original engine in service, the throttle should be progressively opened to give higher thrusts. This was still the official policy in 1971, but it seemed to me that, in view of the grave difficulties encountered in reaching the contractual figure of 42,000 lb, there was little likelihood of taking even the improved RB211-22 to 45,000 lb.

At the same time our competitors Pratt & Whitney and General Electric were moving ahead with firm programmes, initially to 47,000 lb for the JT9D, with much more to come, and to 50,000 lb for the CF6-50. These engines were needed for improved long-range 747s, for the longer-range version of the DC-10 and for the European Airbus. All were clearly going to be of the greatest importance. It was later evident that the long-range DC-10 was going to become almost the standard version, far outselling the L-1011 TriStar, while the Airbus could outsell both by a wide margin. Rolls-Royce simply had to have an engine to compete in the increased-thrust market.

I was forced to the inescapable conclusion that we should at least study a second-generation RB211 in which extensive redesign would give higher thrust, better efficiency and other advantages, just as we had done with the Proteus, Olympus and Pegasus. But this time I had no far-seeing Verdon to put up the finance; we were a bankrupt company with money tightly controlled by a government which, along with many other people, would have thought new versions a presumptuous and unjustified extra risk. Nonetheless, though it seemed a pipe-dream, I steadily ploughed ahead with the performance, compressor and turbine engineers — almost as light relief — to establish what could be done.

I set 50,000 lb as the target, and concentrated on the fan, which provides about three-quarters of the thrust. One of the basic design objectives was to make the second-generation RB211 fit the TriStar, including the centre (tail) installation, and if possible we wanted the new engine to be installationally interchangeable. Roy Hetherington, the fan and compressor expert, succeeded in designing a new fan passing 20 per cent greater airflow within the same diameter. We also redesigned the IP compressor to pass more air through the core, but here we ran up against a seemingly insurmountable snag. There was a massive steel aircraft mounting ring in the way, and this was regarded as sacrosanct.

I sent for Freddie Morley, who was up to his neck in design mods for the current engine, and, pulling his leg, said, 'Freddie, I hear that you will not allow us to change the mounting ring, so that we can redesign the IP compressor and raise the thrust to 50,000 lb.' I knew perfectly well that he had never heard of the proposal, and he almost burst a blood-vessel. His response was 'Nobody has told me a f - - - - thing about the f - - - - ring!!' He departed in high dudgeon, to reappear a few days later with a splendid drawing of the redesigned mounting, fully interchangeable with the existing one but giving us the room we needed.

Thus we completed the design of the superb RB211-524 series. It was to be another two years before, under Sir Kenneth Keith, we were at last permitted to go ahead with full development. Today the -524, in several versions, is the standard RB211 for large long-range aircraft, and it not only gives thrust over 52,000 lb but it demonstrates the lowest fuel consumption and best performance retention of all the big fan engines.

One Saturday afternoon in September 1972 I was telephoned by the Secretary of State for Industry, John Davies, and informed that Lord Cole was resigning and that his successor would be merchant banker Sir Kenneth Keith. The next time I saw Gordon Richardson I asked what he was like, and was told 'He is a Big Gun, but you will like him'. And so it was. From our first meeting we have been friends; in fact Kenneth told me he saw only two friendly faces when he arrived at Rolls-Royce's London office, mine and Bill Cook's!

A large man in every sense, he had powers of leadership the company had not seen since the days of Hs, and after years of the doldrums the whole workforce of the company soon realized that at last they again had a great man at the helm. The only sad thing about his coming was that there was not room for him on the same board as Sir Arnold Weinstock, and the latter soon resigned. Kenneth brought with him another Kenneth, K. G. Wilkinson, a fellow board member of British Airways. Thanks to Hugh Conway's disagreement with Ian Morrow we were short of a managing director and Wilkinson filled this job for a time before returning to the airline.

As chairman of Hill Samuel, Sir Kenneth was used to high finance, but had formed the view that £5 million was a lot of money. I told him we had added a zero to his stature, because after a few weeks on the RB211 he soon came to understand that £50 million is peanuts. He took the job on the condition that he had a free hand and direct access to the Prime Minister (then Edward Heath). His task was to restructure the giant firm and make it viable in the long term. He found a lack of discipline which appalled him. He gathered a small handpicked group around him to run the company and said 'Anyone else who sticks his head above the parapet will get it struck off!' Rapidly everyone recognised that a man of courage and decision had taken over. For his part, he learned rapidly, rivalled Hs in his tireless passion for work and visited all the factories and all the big customers. At each factory he had a private and forthright meeting with all the shop stewards and quickly cleared up their problems and grievances. With the customers he replaced their belief the firm would never survive by a new confidence and an eager anticipation for production RB211s. He came for two years and stayed for seven, leading us with panache and verve and defending us from bureaucratic interference. When we gave him his farewell dinner his voice was choked with emotion, because even men as big as he soon come under the spell of the magic of the name of Rolls-Royce.

The RB211 programme might easily have foundered in 1971 had it not been for the steadfast support of Eastern Airlines, one of the major launch customers for the Lockheed TriStars. The President of Eastern was one Sam Higginbottom, who never wavered and thereby acquired some criticism. He eventually left Eastern to become President of Rolls-Royce Inc. in New York, and such is the respect for him and his vast experience in civil air line operations that the RB211 programme in the USA has gone ahead, despite the vicissitudes of the bankruptcy and engineering problems in the programme.

Lt. General Tom Miller, USMC.

Eric Warlow-Davies.

Sam Higginbottom.

Gene Newbold.

Early RB211 on test bed.

Romania, from left: Sir Kenneth Keith, President Ceaucescu, S.G.H.

China, S.G.H. with Vice-Premier Wang Chen.

With Kenneth (Lord) Keith and the portrait of S.G.H.

S.G.H. and family arriving at Buckingham Palace to receive his Knighthood in January 1974.

Chapter 13
Romania and China

Today British Aerospace and Rolls-Royce have close connections with two countries which have Communist governments and which used to be considered to be remote. I was lucky enough to be in at the start with both these foreign connections, which have been rewarding in many ways including that of money.

Our association with Romania arose solely because of the tireless efforts of George Pop. This remarkable man had been born in Romania, studied at the Sorbonne and eventually became a British citizen. He spoke almost every European language fluently — certainly English, Romanian, French, German, Italian and Spanish — and he lived at the ultra-modern Hotel Inter Continental in Bucharest where he beavered away at his self-appointed task of selling British aviation to Romania.

He was given official backing by none other than the world famous Henri Coanda, who before 1914 had been given the title of 'chef technique' at the British & Colonial Aeroplane Company which was the origin of the Bristol Aeroplane Company. After 1945 the new Communist regime in Romania tracked down Coanda and invited their most famous scientist to return to Bucharest. He did so on condition that he was given back the family house, which had been appropriated by the state, and that the street where it stood was renamed after his father, who had been assassinated. The Romanians did more. They appointed Coanda Head of Inventions and Development, with the status of a minister, and he was able to advise on all technical matters.

With his encouragement Pop was able to get things moving, and in mid-1965 we at Bristol received a party of Romanians led by an energetic and extrovert air force officer, General Ispas. They at once expressed an interest in the Viper turbojet, which as an original Armstrong Siddeley design had powered Petter's

Midge prototype at 1,640 lb thrust. By the time we made it a Bristol Siddeley engine it was in large-scale production for such aircraft as the Jet Provost, Aermacchi MB.326 and SOKO Galeb jet trainers and the HS.125 bizjet, at ratings around 2,500 lb. Along with the Viper we had inherited some fine engineers, including Johnnie Marlow, who remained chief engineer on the Viper until he retired, and E. A. Macdonald who took over all compressor research at Bristol. In ten years we took the Viper to 3,000, 3,300, 3,750 and 4,000 lb thrust, and now it is in production with an afterburner at 5,000 lb, and the new Mk 680 version will be more powerful still! Getting on for 6,000 have been sold in countries all over the world.

I had already visited Yugoslavia, a country which had built up a busy aircraft industry with the Viper-powered Galeb trainer and Jastreb light attack aircraft. The factory was at Mostar, in the south, near Sarajevo where in 1914 Archduke Ferdinand was assassinated, triggering off World War 1. The footprints of the young assassin are cast in concrete at the spot. He could hardly have missed, because the street was only just wide enough for one carriage, and I stood there in deep emotion thinking of the millions who died as a result of this single act.

The Yugoslavs merely bought Vipers from us, but Romania wanted to make the engine. So between 1965 and 1975 I had to make many visits to Bucharest. I was always received with the greatest goodwill and soon began to make friends. On the morning of my first visit I was quietly dressing in the Inter Continental Hotel when I was informed that the General was waiting for me in the foyer. I quickly joined him and his entourage, and instantly a large tray of cognac, coffee and sparkling water arrived. After this we moved on to the newest and largest engineering works in Bucharest, making steam and hydro-electric turbines. We retired to the boardroom where a large tray of cognac, coffee and sparkling water was served. After a tour of this factory we moved to the Aeronautical Institute, where I was to give a lecture at 11 am. On arrival a large tray of cognac, coffee and sparkling water appeared, and we chatted amicably, with George as the indispensable interpreter. Suddenly, in walked Coanda, to a round of applause from us all. I found him a quiet, cultured gentlemen, obviously delighted to see people from Bristol. As soon as we all sat down again — guess what? A large tray appeared, soon followed by several more. I am told the lecture was a great success, but my memory of it is somewhat clouded by the lunch which followed, where wine flowed like water and we also consumed considerable quantities of tuica, the local plum brandy. No better first day in a Communist state could be imagined.

Bucharest had held a romantic appeal for me ever since, as a young man, I had read of the affair of Lord Thomson, the Air Minister who died in the R.101, with Princess Bibescu. I loved to walk around the city, though it looked very run down, rather like Paris in 1945. Rambler roses brightened up the wide old boulevards and garden-filled squares, but so many things cried out for attention. On my first visit there were almost no cars, the only transport being trams. I wandered through the great salons of the famous Hotel Athenée, with their faded decoration. I would have liked to stay there, but George decreed that we were expected to use the new Inter Continental, where we might as well have been in Chicago.

Few shops had anything to sell, and there were no window displays. In particular the ladies were having a thin time: only the plainest of dress fabrics and clothing, and no silk or nylon stockings, no make-up and not even face cream. On the other hand, there seemed to be adequate food, and certainly good meat and fish. But I did not have too much time for sightseeing, because I was subjected to many interminable barrages of questioning on the merits of the Viper. On numerous occasions George and I would go to the Technical Import Corporation and have meetings with officials, but in my experience it is difficult in Communist countries to find the man who has the power of taking a decision, and next to impossible to find one who is willing to take the responsibility of actually doing so. But with George's diplomacy and Coanda's backing we gradually moved up the hierarchy, meeting ministers, then the Prime Minister George (Gheorghe) Oprea.

On one visit I was delighted to receive an invitation to meet the Vice-President, Emil Bodnaras. Emil was an old-guard revolutionary who had been an army general, but he was imprisoned for Communist activities and spent eight years exiled in the Soviet Union. When I met him he was nearly 70, but prided himself on keeping his stocky figure in first-class shape. We formed a great rapport together, and he always attended the grand dinners that George would organise for us at the Inter Continental. The first time he came there was a great commotion, with security men searching the kitchens and hotel rooms, and guarding his entrance. The British Ambassador — who, with his staff, was always most helpful to us — also used to attend, and at the end of each dinner we used to arrange for the two great men to sit undisturbed so that they could discuss affairs of state.

Occasionally the Vice-President would entertain me in his own home, which was a modest suburban house (but in a guarded road). It was filled with mementoes of his dealings with the Russians and Chinese. He it was who managed to persuade the Kremlin to take the occupying Soviet forces out of Romania; an accomplishment not equalled by any other Warsaw Pact satellite. He then made many visits to Chairman Mao and Chou en Lai in China, and the close alliance between the two countries certainly led to a respect for Romania in Moscow. He was delighted when I called him "The Winston Churchill of Romania". If only I could have had a tape recorder at our many friendly chats I would really have had an historic tale to tell.

Our intimacy with the Vice-President made George and me VIPs. George had an uncanny knack of self-effacement, only to materialize the moment the negotiations reached a difficult point. He entertained generously, not only people involved in business but also a steady stream of others. Some were old friends whom the revolution had reduced to penury; they would sneak into the plush hotel, have a good meal on George and leave rejoicing with a 100-Leis note. Others would come to George in the coffee room to request help on every conceivable topic, and in a babel of different tongues. Quietly, without any condescension or arrogance, George would get things put right, even though the plaintiffs' troubles were through no fault on his part. We were indeed fortunate that George chose to represent Rolls-Royce and British Aircraft Corporation (now British Aerospace).

Shortly after Sir Kenneth Keith arrived on the scene I asked him whether he would come with me to Romania and Yugoslavia. Hitherto I had never been able to get the Top Brass at Derby to show interest in such an insignificant place (in their opinion) as Romania, but Kenneth replied 'Certainly, when shall we go?' George was in his element organizing this visit, and Kenneth was treated royally, ending with a meeting with President Nicolae Ceaucescu. The President sat on one side of the magnificent room in the former royal palace, with his Inner Cabinet on his right and Kenneth, myself and George on his left. Suddenly Kenneth said 'Mr. President, why are you entering this expensive field of aero engine manufacture, when you could much more easily buy direct from us?' You could have heard a pin drop. Such questions had been asked before, and we had always received a waffling reply. But in his quiet voice the President said 'Well, we are not aiming to be a competitor of Rolls-Royce, but we would like to be a son.' What a charming answer!

It transpired that both men were keen hunters. Almost the only thing Kenneth had never hunted was a bear, and the President invited him to do just this. At Bucharest Airport the President's helicopter was waiting, and it set us down on a plateau high in the Carpathians. We stayed the night at a lovely hunting lodge, where the national head gamekeepers joined us. It was at a place called Cheia, mid-way between the vast Ploesti oilfields and the aeronautical works (and ski resort) of Brasov. Next morning the bear party set out, but I said I had a non-aggression pact with bears and instead enquired about trout-fishing. In fact we drove over mountain tracks until we reached a trout farm, where I picked out a couple of dozen beauties fresh from the icy water. That evening Kenneth trudged in, with no bear. He asked me how I had got on, and I replied 'Not too badly.' He asked how many I had caught, and I replied that it was about two dozen. 'You damned liar', said Kenneth, 'you're pulling my leg!' I said 'Nonsense, they're cleaning them in the kitchen for dinner'. My hosts did not let on, and I kept a totally straight face all through the meal. Later he discovered where they had really come from, and he got his own back next day by bagging two big brown bears.

On the way back from Romania Kenneth and I toured the Yugoslav facilities. They made cars in Belgrade and their light strike and trainer jets at Mostar, but they had imported the Viper engines. Now we felt a wind of change rippling through the scene, and we learned that not only did the two countries wish to collaborate 50-50 to build a really capable tactical combat aircraft but they both wanted to share in making the Viper engine, and in the latest and most powerful version. So Rolls-Royce now had two important licensees, and after a prolonged effort the twin-jet strike fighter, called the Orao (Eagle) in Yugoslavia and the IAR-93 in Romania, became an accomplished fact. So tight was the control on the 50-50 share that two prototypes had to make their maiden flights on the same day, one in each country; that day was 31 October 1974. Production machines followed from 1981.

The Romanians also took a licence for the British Aerospace One-Eleven jetliner and its Rolls-Royce Spey engines, and both these giant programmes were carried through to very successful production. George's patient hammering away for ten years was behind it all, and I am delighted to report that in late 1983 the collaboration between the various partners could not be closer.

On one of my last trips to Bucharest I invited Vice-President Bodnaras to visit England. I had the pleasure of collecting him in our 125 bizjet. He was like a schoolboy let loose on holiday, and especially admired our pretty little villages. On a more nostalgic note, I also got Coanda to visit us, and he went back to the office in Filton House where he had worked on the Prier monoplane in 1912. He was coming to the end of his days, but before he left us he made a tape recording for me of his pioneering period in Paris and Bristol, and this is in the archives of the Royal Aeronautical Society.

Emil Bodnaras was destined to pass on soon afterwards, but before he died he told me 'You ought to visit China.' I told him that I would like to, especially as I had been appointed a professor there so many years earlier, but that their restrictions would make it impossible. A few weeks later, in early 1972, a party from the Chinese office in London (they had no ambassador at that time) came to see me. I was up to my neck in RB211 problems, and must have been a rather preoccupied host, but I was all ears when they invited me to visit China. My colleague John Oliver, who had been in Peking (now written more accurately as Beijing) helping sell the Trident airliner, said there was no need to worry as it would take more than six months to get a visa. I forgot about it, and was astonished when in April an official invitation arrived.

To me China seemed as remote as the Moon, a completely unknown quantity. I felt I must do all I could to foster goodwill and create interest in Rolls-Royce engines. So I made up a team of four, Alan Newton and John Oliver from Derby and myself and Trevor Powell from Bristol, and collected a mass of slides and films which had all been published in the lectures and technical symposia that we were in the habit of giving. We flew from London to Sri Lanka (Ceylon), spent the night at the Pegasus Hotel on the shore of the Indian Ocean (and one of the most beautiful places I have ever visited), and flew on to Canton by Pakistan International, which apart from Aeroflot and Air France was the only airline to fly to the People's Republic. We were seven hours late getting away from Colombo, and after a 5½-hour flight arrived at Canton at about 9 pm local time.

I felt quite apprehensive when I first set foot on Chinese soil. The feeling was not dispelled when we got to Customs and Immigration, for there we found fierce-looking young men and women in khaki uniforms, all with revolvers at their waists, giving each passenger a thorough going-over and opening all their baggage. My heart sank as I thought of our massive amount of engine literature, slides and films. I presented my passport, trying to look much bolder than I felt. At once the young official reached under his desk, produced a slip of paper, read it, and waved our whole party through, baggage and all!

We had missed our connecting flight to Beijing, which at that time was a single flight each day departing at 1 pm, so we were sent on to Shanghai in an Ilyushin 18 turboprop. We arrived at about midnight and were given tickets for our first Chinese meal at the airport hotel close by. We paid no money, and in China tips are not expected. Next day we flew on to Beijing, where we arrived at about 4 pm. We were met by a top-level delegation from the Machinery Import Corporation, which later became the Technical Import Corporation, and by Derek March, Commercial Counsellor at our embassy.

While our baggage and passports were being processed we were taken to a big, airy lounge and served with cups of tea. After polite exchanges about our health and journey the head man said, 'You are our guests. Now what is your programme?' I replied, 'We have come to tell you about Rolls-Royce engines and technology, and we wish to know whether we can be of service to the development of aviation in China'. This was received with approval, and, it being Thursday evening, it was agreed we should begin lecturing at 9 am on the following Monday. Without more ado we were taken to the Minh Su Hotel, where we had splendid accommodation. I had a magnificent suite, furnished in Victorian style, with every comfort — except air-conditioning, and this did not matter as the weather was like a good British summer.

I was informed that the Romanian Ambassador would like me to call upon him, and it was nice to get such a message in this seemingly alien land. There were almost no cars; everyone, in their millions, rode bicycles. The only cars were large and rather ugly black limousines copied from a Russian design and used by top officials. Two were placed at our disposal, and it was important to remember that No. 1 was mine and No. 2 for my colleagues. If I got into the wrong car there were angry words between the drivers. We passed the weekend in peace, merely calling on our Ambassador, Sir John Addis, and visiting the Forbidden City, the Winter Palace of the old emperors. This vast building is situated on the Chang'An Avenue, which runs straight across the city with six traffic lanes between wide tree-lined borders. In front of the palace is the vast Tian'An-men Square, where we also found the colossal Great Hall of the People. Today Mao's mausoleum has been added, but in 1972 he was very much alive and it seemed the entire population was carrying his Little Red Book and wearing a Mao badge.

I was surprised to find Beijing a drab, dusty, grey city, almost totally devoid of colour apart from scarlet posters and banners. There were no illuminated signs and no displays in any shop windows. For the ordinary population there seemed to be nothing to buy except for food and a few essential household items. Foreigners, however, could go to a big shop called The Friendship Shop and purchase groceries and typical Chinese items made of silk and jade. I used to dictate into a tape recorder on my balcony after dark, and apart from Chang'An Avenue the entire vast city looked pitch-black, with just one or two tiny lights. Apart from the occasional tram it seemed that by 8 pm the entire city was asleep.

On our second evening, Friday, we were invited to a banquet by Mr Sué Chen, the manager of the Machinery Import Corporation. For such an occasion one of the best Chinese restaurants, far beyond the reach of the ordinary people, was taken over completely. We assembled at 7 pm and, after a preliminary cup of tea and social chat, we were led into the dining room. This was set out in what I learned was the usual style, with two big round tables each laid for ten places. It was my first experience of true Beijing cuisine, and I looked apprehensively at the array of at least ten laden dishes on my table, most completely unrecognisable to me. I sat next to our host, who signalled the start of the meal by serving into my bowl various helpings. It was also the first time that I saw chopsticks being used by experts, and, apologizing for my lack of expertise, I struggled along with mine. On my right was Mr Chen's interpreter, so we were able to keep a lively conversation going. The Chinese clearly attach great importance to small-talk, and take great trouble to put their guests at ease.

After we had sampled the hors d'oeuvres, they were swept away and another eight or nine dishes appeared and so on for *nine courses,* finishing with very thin soup. We had chicken, duck, prawns, small pancakes stuffed with savoury and sweet fillings, and a complete fish beautifully decorated. The whole meal was a great experience of new dishes and new flavours, and it made me wonder if, in the past, the Chinese had been so hungry that they had learned how to convert every eatable thing into deliciously palatable food.

We drank lager beer and fizzy orange, and I also made the acquaintance of mautai, the fiery, colourless spirit distilled from sorghum. It was used for the numerous toasts, and fortunately was served in tiny liqueur glasses. There were many speeches of welcome, to each of which we replied, after each of which there would be a great clinking of glasses and shouts of 'Cambai' (bottoms up). About 9 pm we finished, and returned in our limousines through the dark and silent city.

Two armed soldiers guarded our hotel, but nowhere did we see any evidence of an oppressive regime. In daytime it seemed that half the population of China was pedalling bicycles, at any time liable to change direction without warning. There were thus many spills, each of which would collect a crowd of onlookers until the affair had been sorted out by a smartly dressed traffic (ie bicycle traffic) policeman. Apart from the police and armed forces it seemed that everyone was wearing a loose white shirt, baggy blue trousers and blue canvas slippers. To a European the only way to tell the women from the men was by their hair, the young girls having pigtails and the older ladies a short bob. It was not until several visits later that I saw a female leg! In the hotel, each floor had a retinue of young men who did all the chores. Only the lift was operated by girls, and the first Chinese words I learned were 'Wu law': fifth floor.

This, then, was our introduction to the Orient, and we soon settled down to their polite and civilised way of life. Our ambassador told us that the treatment we were getting showed that our visit was regarded as very important.

On Monday morning we were taken to Er Li Co, the headquarters of the Machinery Corporation, and conducted to a large room packed with our audience, who all stood as we entered. Having been introduced to the senior people, we went to the places reserved for us at a central table, while the audience sat in serried rows. I had no idea who was who, because everyone was dressed like everyone else and I might have been talking to a tea boy or a general. There were a number of ladies present, one of whom acted as interpreter. She did a magnificent job, translating technical matter all day without rest. I discovered her name, Chou Hi Ping, means Chou calm sea, and that is what she became to us. At the final banquet at the end of this visit I caused her embarrassment by leading her into the centre of the room while our party all applauded her.

On this first working morning we set up our projector, and I opened proceedings by repeating the Wilbur Wright Memorial Lecture which I had lately given to the Royal Aeronautical Society. It was soon clear that many in the audience understood English, because they would stop the interpreter and argue in Chinese, at which she would turn to me and ask 'Did you mean so-and-so?' Our teacups were kept filled, and after a brief break at 10.30 we began a question and answer session. It was soon clear that some in the audience had been briefed to cover some particular topic, such as manufacturing, or turbine performance. At 11.30 we returned to our hotel for lunch. Then at 2.30 Alan Newton lectured on VTOL developments, and with more questions that kept us busy until 5.30.

I had arranged that I would concentrate on the overall scene, Alan Newton on VTOL and the Spey, Trevor Powell on the Olympus 593 and Viper and John Oliver on the Dart, keeping to civil engines only. Naturally, during the questions military applications arose. I had decreed that we would answer all questions to the best of our ability in a general way, and if we had to illustrate on the blackboard we would rub it out immediately. I have long experience of explaining technical things in a simple way, but it was impossible to tell how far the audience followed everything. They seemed delighted, and I think their 'need to know' would have over-ridden their great politeness and made them pursue a difficult point further.

Anyway, on the Wednesday we were bidden to rest, and at 8 am we were collected by our hosts and set off with picnic lunches on an official tour of the Ming tombs and Great Wall at Bada Ling some 60 miles away. We set off along the road to Ulan Bator, beside the railway which, hundreds of miles to the north beyond Inner Mongolia, connects with the trans-Siberian line. At first the countryside was flat, and highly cultivated. Everything was done by hand, and most fields seemed to contain 20 to 30 peasants all hoeing in unison. This gave some answer to my question: where were the thousand million Chinese? The answer was that they were spread like ants over the vast countryside, growing food. Gradually the terrain became hilly and then positively mountainous, and suddenly, as we reached the 4,000-foot level, there was the Great Wall ahead, crossing our road and stretching as far as the eye could see towards both horizons, undulating up and down across the mountains into the furthest distance.

It was a thrilling sight. On the Beijing side the wall was about 30 feet high, but on the north side the drop from the top was even greater. The wall had been repaired locally, and along the top was a track wide enough for a car (though of course there was none), punctuated at intervals by blockhouses. I believe the wall is the only man-made thing visible to the naked eye from a low-orbit spacecraft, and it stretches almost 2,200 miles along the main route, with branches and spurs bringing the total up to almost 4,000 miles. One could not help marvelling at the unbelievable toil needed to build such a wall, with a thickness of about 32 feet, in order to keep at bay the barbaric Mongolian hordes which at one time were led by Genghiz Khan himself. Today peace prevails, and we ate our lunch in a visitors' room which had been reserved for us.

We then set out for the tombs of the Ming emperors (1366-1644 AD) on the route back to Beijing. In the old days the beautiful valley was forbidden territory, but today it is intensively cultivated. The visitor enters through a pagoda-like gate and then along a drive which is dead straight for a mile. I do not think I have ever seen a more impressive sight, because the entire length is bordered by giant beasts carved in solid stone. First we passed between a pair of standing elephants facing each other. Then we passed between a pair of kneeling elephants. Then came two colossal standing camels, followed by two kneeling camels. Then came lions, horses and many other animals, in each case first standing and then kneeling. Finally came two lines of emperors, each carved in perfect detail.

The only tomb so far opened was a deep underground mausoleum, with side chambers for the particular emperor's wives. It was quite dull, but the treasures found therein were fabulous. They included solid gold plates about 2 feet across, and head-dresses for the wives looking like beehives and thickly encrusted with jewels. Everything was displayed in a museum room where, to remind everyone, large wall paintings showed the cruel treatment meted out to the peasants by their avaricious rulers.

On the next day we returned to our lectures and answer sessions. By this time we were on very friendly terms with our hosts, and I began to press them for areas of interest which we might explore further. They replied, 'Patience, we will tell you. But first, on Sunday, you are going to visit our Aeronautical Institute in Beijing, and then you will travel to Shen-yang to see our engine factory'. I was amazed and delighted, especially when our embassy told us that no Western visitor had ever been able to visit either.

Accordingly, on the Sunday morning we found ourselves entering large and attractive grounds wherein were a collection of nondescript concrete buildings, again guarded by soldiers, which housed the Institute. The whole staff were assembled to greet us with applause at the entrance, led by the Vice-Director, Dr Shen Yuan. Only later did I discover (because he never mentioned it) that he had studied at Imperial College, a year or two after me, and spoke fluent English. After the usual tea ceremony we entered a large room full of engines. Most were Russian, though a few were American, but right in the doorway was a sectioned VK-1, Soviet version of the Nene, which the Chinese call the WP-5D. As related earlier, I said 'Yes, the Russians made a good copy; they even copied the mistakes!' When this was translated there were howls of merriment. I asked how they had come by their American General Electric J47, and they replied 'It fell from Heaven!'

The ice was thus broken, and we had a good tour. The facilities were large but meagre, and when at the end they asked for my comments I told them they really needed much more equipment with which to train young engineers. In particular they had no compressor, turbine or combustion test or demonstration rigs, and they were very weak on metallurgy. Moreover, there was no entrance examination; instead the students were recommended by their local Revolutionary Party, in all parts of China, mainly on the basis of their knowledge of the sayings of Mao. It would not have done to suggest that these sayings were unimportant, but they are hardly the right way to select a nation's top engineers and today the Institute has an entrance examination.

There was no doubt in my mind that the Mao system had achieved miracles. So far as I could see, 1,000 million people were fed, clothed, housed and did useful work. Certainly the older generation appreciated what had been done, though some of the young men were clearly apathetic and prone to grumble, chiefly because of the central direction of labour which is a feature of life in modern China. I can see that this might be irksome, but as soon as a society has all the basic necessities of life it is easy for its people to forget the old adage 'Count your blessings'. One has only to think how many members of Western societies take their affluence and total freedom for granted, and spend their time in vandalism and other negative activity, to see that people appreciate things only when they are taken away. In the case of most Chinese the Revolution is recent enough to have real meaning, and I have never seen a society whose members were so universally dedicated to working for the public good. It is not possible for an oppressive regime to stage-manage a false happy picture for the benefit of foreign visitors. One might do this with a small group, but not with a city!

At 8 pm on the Sunday evening we departed to visit another city, Shen-yang. A huge crowd gathered at the railway station, because this train departure was quite an event. On the way we made just one stop, late at night, in Tianjin. Previously this city was called Tien Tsien, and I climbed out on to the platform and spent a few moments wondering what would have happened to me had I gone there in 1936 as the first Professor of Aeronautics in China. The mind boggled!

At 6 am next day we arrived at Shen-yang, also known as Mukden, in what had been Manchuria; this is a city of about 3 million lying in the plain of the Liao Ho about 400 miles north-east of Beijing. It has a recorded history of over 2,000 years, and was at one time the capital of the Ching Dynasty, many of whose palaces and artefacts are carefully preserved. Today, however, it is a vast industrial complex specializing in engineering, metals and chemicals. It was a cold and wet morning, with pouring rain. We were met by the Shen-yang Chairman of the Revolutionary Party, who corresponds roughly to a mayor, and his aides, who greeted us most politely. Chinese railway stations seem all to have an entrance opening on to a giant square, and as we emerged into the rain I was amazed to see that the perimeter of the square was packed with people — men, women and children. When they saw us they broke into loud applause. I asked my host whatever was happening, and he said 'They have come to welcome their British friends'. Nothing would suffice but that I walked around the entire square, clapping my hands in return. It was most heartwarming to us all, and since that moment I have been completely captivated by the Chinese people. The rain was forgotten.

At the factory we found throbbing activity, with a payroll of about 10,000. Two fighter engines in production made up almost the total work-load, and both were literally Chinese copies of originals designed by the Soviet Tumanskii bureau. The first, and older, engine was the WP-6 (Wo-pen 6, or turbojet No. 6), which corresponded to the Russian RD-9B, a neat single-spool engine rated at about 5,700 lb dry and a little over 7,000 lb with afterburner. Two of these engines powered the J-6 (MiG-19) and JJ-6 trainer version, which were in production at the nearby aircraft factory. I was envious of the production rate, which on this engine was estimated by us at about 50 per month. The other engine was the WP-7, the Russian Tumanskii R-11. This very attractive two-spool turbojet was rated with afterburner at about 14,000 lb and was just coming into large-scale production for the J-7, the Chinese MiG-21.

I was not surprised at the general set-up of the factory, which was mainly of 1955 vintage and equipped largely with machine tools of Soviet origin. What did surprise me was the way that tools were being remodelled and adapted on the spot for special operations, and the fact that the one giant plant made almost the entire engine including many of the accessories. The factory had its own foundry for castings and forging plant for blades and discs, and it seemed to need nothing in the way of supplies except raw material! Moreover, there was little wrong with the products. At the rear were small but effective testbeds where examples of both engines, with afterburners, were on test. I was allowed to operate the throttles of both types of engine. Though I am well versed in such matters, I was unable to stall either engine nor cause any misbehaviour, though I tried my best.

Clearly the Chinese had total competence in 1950s-technology engines, but they had no way of progressing into 1960s technology except in very localized areas where they were doing research of their own. It seemed to me that the most straightforward way of catching up would be to take a licence for a Rolls-Royce engine, and I verbally made this suggestion. I am sure my hosts agreed inwardly, but their experience with the Russians made them suspicious of licensing. When in the 1958-9 period, the ideological break came with the Russians, the latter departed en masse and took with them every single document including the drawings, material specifications and manufacturing instructions. As the Russians had done in 1947, with the Nene, the Chinese simply soldiered on and after many years succeeded in getting into production with the excellent engines I saw at Shen-yang.

This was a very impressive achievement, but they still had no background of design and development experience on which to draw, nor any designers or experienced engineers. As a result, though they strove to produce perfect engines, they were helpless in the face of in-service failures. They, therefore, had to limit the life of each engine to 100 to 200 hours, and a large part of their output was devoted to making replacement engines for ones that had failed. They showed me two persistent failures they had suffered for years. One was at a particular location on the fir-tree root of the WP-7 turbine blade, which was prone to experience first a small crack and then total failure, letting the blade fly through the engine casing — no joke in a single-engine supersonic fighter. The second was the cracks which appeared in the sheet-metal combustion chambers, spreading rapidly until a large chunk would break off and smash into the turbine nozzle vanes, often passing right through the turbine and causing severe damage.

There is an immense amount of finesse in the design of a fir-tree root, and its manufacture is far from simple. I knew therefore, that we could not deal with that problem on the spot, so I took my courage in both hands and offered to send them a detailed drawing of the root of a Spey turbine blade. After all, they had plenty of Speys in commercial service in Tridents, and could have studied the root for themselves. In fact, Chinese civil and military aviation seemed to be two distinct watertight compartments, and there was no way that a solution to a military problem could have been found in a civil engine. Their eyes shone with gratitude at this offer, and a year later they showed me their new Spey-type blade root which, they said, worked much better.

The cracking of the combustion chambers was a problem I felt we could deal with there and then. Back on Frank Whittle's engine I had run into the same problem caused by the use of thick and thin sheets welded together. As the temperature varies, according to throttle position, the thin sheet heats and cools quicker than the one to which it is attached, and the unequal expansion and contraction between the two causes severe cyclic stress which soon gives rise to a crack. The solution is to make the thin sheet thicker, and to cut in it what we used to call 'keyhole slots' to allow for any slight dimensional changes. In fact the Russian chamber was a singularly bad design. The hemispherical head was a heavy casting, which actually had fins machined in it for extra cooling, though it was obvious from its colour that it was running very hot. Downstream was a thin sheet flame-tube, and the cracking naturally began at the junction between the two, which was a seam weld.

I explained all this to them, and they followed my reasoning completely. I suggested that they try making the hemispherical head from sheet of about the same gauge as the cylindrical portion, and provide it with expansion slots. Again they could have seen all this on the Nene in the Institute. A year later they had done it all. From our brief discussion and a quick pencil sketch they had redesigned the chamber and completely solved the problem, and my reputation was sky-high. I took the opportunity of pointing out that there were many, many such practical tips we could give them if a basis of co-operation could be found.

Late that night we took our leave. Back at the railway station the great square was again packed with people who had waited to see us off. In the centre was a giant statue of Mao, and in our honour it and the whole square had been festooned with a myriad of coloured lights. We returned to Beijing via Peta Hau (Pei-tai to), a lovely seaside resort. It was entirely reserved for foreigners, so even our hosts stayed outside the area. During the very hot months of July and August this resort becomes home for the diplomatic staffs in Beijing. There are many splendid European-style villas, and even a super restaurant called Kettners after the one in London. The sea was beautiful to swim in, and a great arc of steel fencing protects the little bay from sharks. Like so many places the whole resort was guarded by soldiers, but this is natural in China and their presence was never obtrusive. When we had to leave, our hosts entered the resort to take us by car on a tour of the beautiful coastline.

Back at Beijing I learned during further talks that there was keen interest in a proposal from us that they take a licence for the Spey turbofan. They did not say which type of Spey, and I did not press them because we had no clearance from our government to make any definite commitment. All four of us — and our Ambassador — felt that our visit had succeeded beyond our wildest dreams. It was now up to the Powers that Be in Whitehall to give us the go-ahead. In fact, nothing happened until Sir

Kenneth Keith arrived as Chairman in November 1972. Then, in very short order, he took up the matter of co-operation with the Chinese with Edward Heath. Soon we were cleared to propose an agreement on the civil Spey engine, which the Chinese had been using for years in the de Havilland Tridents which they had purchased.

In November 1972, at a reception at the Chinese Embassy in London given by Ambassador Sung, I again met Mr Chen from Beijing. He took me on one side and said quite bluntly that the engine in which his government was interested was the military Spey 202, with afterburner, as used in British Phantoms. I could see all sorts of political difficulties with our Allies. When I told Kenneth, he hit the roof. 'It's taken me two months to get the civil Spey agreed. I'll never manage this one, so we must go back to the Chinese and tell them to take a more flexible approach — first the civil Spey, which will keep them very busy for a few years, and then perhaps the 202 can follow along. Or we could help them adapt the civil Spey for military use, which is how we did the 202 anyway? In the meantime, you produce a proposal for the civil Spey only'.

I consulted with Denis Jackson at Derby, who masterminded most of the company's foreign licences and is a man of great drive and energy. We produced a very broad-brush 'heads of agreement' document. Kenneth said it was a 'pretty thin effort' but told me to take it to the Chinese Commercial Office in London for transmission to Beijing. This thin effort happened to be the only piece of paper recording any discussion between our two countries; it was to be several years before the Chinese put a single word on paper, and everything was done by word of mouth — and with no tape recorders! In early 1973 Mr Peng, the Chinese Commercial Counsellor in London, invited me to return to Beijing for further discussions. Taking the same team as before I arrived in the Chinese capital in March 1973. I told Kenneth that, if things went well, he might be asked to join us. We were received with the usual hospitality, and on our arrival at Er Li Co I emphasized that Sir Kenneth was a most important man who should be invited to join the discussions.

The chairman of the meeting was Madame Wei, a fierce-looking lady of ample proportions. Suddenly it dawned on me that all was not well; there was a distinctly frosty atmosphere. Then I suddenly noticed that Madame Wei was clutching an envelope from Rolls-Royce with the address heavily underscored in red. She spoke harshly: 'This letter is addressed to the Republic of China. That is not our address. We are The People's Republic of China'. It really was an imperial brick, because the Republic is Taiwan. I apologised profusely, and ate all the humble pie around. She went on, 'People who address us incorrectly are not our friends, and we do not do business with them'. I crawled on my belly, as Hs used to say, and explained that it must have been a typist's error. She replied, 'Correspondence should not be left to people who make mistakes. We are severely displeased, and we shall therefore accommodate you in the Friendship Hotel, which is reserved for common foreigners'. She arose, and the meeting was over.

My Chinese friends were somewhat embarrassed as we were packed off to the outskirts of Beijing where the huge concrete hotel, built by the Russians for their various missions in the 1950s, was being prepared for the visitors to the first British Trade Fair, due to take place in April. Nonetheless, I had a comfortable suite, and in fact we all had excellent accommodation provided one did not mind the four of us dining alone in a room that would comfortably seat a thousand. From then on, all went well as we spent our days in discussions at Er Li Co trying to soften them up on the Spey 512 instead of the Mk 202.

When Kenneth's arrival was imminent, I plucked up courage and said that the Friendship Hotel was no place to accommodate the Chairman of Rolls-Royce. I even told my hosts that, unless they were prepared to forgive us and put him in a suite at the Beijing Hotel, I should reluctantly have to advise him not to come. They appeared to ignore this puny threat until, as we were leaving a preparatory meeting on the very day of his arrival, I was informed that all our things had been transferred to the Beijing Hotel. Kenneth finally arrived, with Sir William Cook and Denis Jackson.

I did not know Jackson very well, and what I did know seemed dour and not very likeable. He was a tough and determined character, who had trained as an engineer prior to joining the Commercial Department. It was when we were thrown together on this trip that I began to realise his worth, and to discover that under his 'stonewall' exterior there resided not only logic and leadership but also a heart of gold. But that knowledge came later, when he took over the whole of the negotiations and organised a special team to answer the myriad questions put by the customer.

We briefed Kenneth on the position, and then had a formal meeting with Mr Sui Chen's office in Er Li Co. Kenneth used all his great powers of persuasion, which I do not think lost much in translation, but our hosts shook their heads. It was the Spey 202 or nothing. At last Kenneth gave up. Rising, he said, 'I am very sorry but I do not think we can do business. It has taken a great deal of effort to get our government to agree to our licensing the Spey 512, and I cannot even discuss the Mk 202 until I have had further talks back in England, about the outcome of which I am not very sanguine'. We returned to our hotel, but within the hour we were summoned to see the Minister of Foreign Affairs, who explained to us that their sole purpose was to modernize their air force for defence, and he hoped we would use our best endeavours to get the British Government to agree. Kenneth said he fully understood the position, but pointed out that many nations (by implication, not Britain) were afraid of the might of China, and he said he doubted that he could swing the government to agree to license the military engine.

In fact, that is just what he did do. As soon as we got back to England Kenneth began to lay about Whitehall with all his great energy and influence. He tackled the Minister of Aviation, Michael Heseltine, the Minister of Defence, Lord Carrington, the Foreign Minister, Sir Douglas Home, and the PM, Mr Edward Heath. In parallel, delicate negotiations were necessary with our NATO allies. Eventually we received full permission to proceed with negotiations on the Spey 202, an afterburning engine designed to fly at over Mach 2.

In the autumn of 1973 I was back at Er Li Co, this time with a different team specializing in the Spey 202. Day after day we toiled through every detail of the engine, though we still had no formal understanding of any kind, only the spoken words that they were interested in having a proposal. Suddenly I was summoned to the office of the Minister of Foreign Trade, Li Chang, a most cultured man of the Old School. He was another Bodnaras in that he thrilled me by talking about his country's history, though the difference was that Li Chang talked only of ancient history. He produced a small slip of paper and read out that his government had decided to acquire the licence for the Spey 202, and that I could now take that as a firm decision. Wildly excited, I asked him if he wanted to know how much this would cost, because I was empowered to quote the figures we had in mind. I was dumbfounded when Li Chang said no, that was no longer the way they did things!

The first task, he said, would be to define precisely what they were going to get, and his experts would be attending to that. I then asked if it would be in order for me to inform our Ambassador, and send a cable to our Chairman, giving him the great news. He said, 'Certainly, although that again is not the way we do things in China'. But he was certainly not put out, because the next thing he said was, 'I wish to invite you to become the first Honorary Professor at the Aeronautical Institute'. He had discussed this with Sir John Addis, who had signified Her Majesty's government's agreement. I was quite overcome by this unique distinction. I reminded Li Chang of the appointment to the first professorship of aeronautics in China in 1936, and he told me he was aware of this.

I went back to the hotel walking on air, and we decided to have a celebration dinner. Long ago we had named the head waiter Gregory, because his horizontal quiff above his forehead looked like Gregory Peck. I said, 'Go and see Gregory and tell him we want plain roast duck served whole, without sauces and spices.' It was the custom to produce the most fabulous roast duck, but then to cover it with fancy sauces and spices. After displaying it to the admiring guests they would take it away and chop it up with axes into small pieces, bones and all. This time we asked Gregory to leave it intact, and not only did he do so but he started us off with a large bowl of caviare (which is plentiful and cheap, but not eaten by the Chinese) and then produced Chinese champagne. We had never sampled the latter, and Gregory proceeded to unwire the cork. Shortly afterwards there was a loud bang and the whole contents of the bottle arose like an atom bomb, hit the ceiling high above and fell to earth we knew not where. This set us off on a memorable and highly successful celebration.

Soon the day of my initiation arrived, timed for 4 pm at the Institute. Sir John Addis said he was coming, and where was the Institute? I could not tell him, and he had to follow the official car! We were greeted by the entire academic staff and conducted to the main reception room where Shen Yuan made a nice little speech in Chinese. I replied as best I could. Then, standing formally under a large picture of Mao, I was presented with a red silk certificate conferring on me the title of Honorary Professor. It was over very quickly, and then Shen Yuan invited us to a party in the adjoining room. I expected drinks and nick nacks, but not a bit of it! The Chin Sao Hotel staff had moved in, and there were the round tables seating ten apiece, each absolutely groaning under ham, pork, chickens, ducks, prawns and fish, European style, all exquisitely decorated and each plate set with knives and forks!

It was an occasion I shall never forget. The Institute has made enormous advances in the ten years since that time, and the honour bestowed on me by my Chinese friends is one I prize above all the other academic awards that have come my way. When Kenneth commissioned my portrait which hangs in the foyer of our London office he had the Chinese characters from my certificate copied into the background, and this is now read with delight by the company's many Chinese visitors.

Denis Jackson toiled with the utmost care for two further years until the licence agreement was signed on 13 December 1975. Then the transfer of extremely complicated modern technology began in earnest, and Rolls-Royce played a central role in the conversion of another big engine factory, at Xian, from the Nene to the Spey 202. Xian is situated on the south bank of the Wei Ho river, a little over 600 miles south-west of Beijing, and somewhere in its 3,000-year recorded history (the estimate is 200BC) an incredible array of life-size terra-cotta figures of soldiers and horses — each beautifully and individually sculptured, and no two alike — were placed in serried ranks in the tomb of the first Quing Dynasty emperor. They were only recently discovered, and their number is estimated at 6,000. Xian was the capital of the Tang Dynasty, between AD 618-907, and I was allowed to bathe in the Emperor's fabulous sunken marble bath, about 12 feet square, at the nearby Hua Quing hot springs. Sadly, I was alone, which I felt the emperor would not have been.

Xian eventually was tooled up to make the Spey 202. In 1979 the first Chinese-built engine was successfully tested, and in May 1980 it was brought to Derby and successfully put through a 150-hour type test. With the achievement of Spey manufacture at Xian my mission to that great country was complete. Unquestionably, we built a bridge between East and West, and my great friend Vice-Premier Wang Chen often told me, 'The ball is at your feet. All you have to do is kick it through the goal'. Changed priorities in China have slowed down the planned expansion of aviation, but they still remain by far the largest market for a vast range of all kinds of equipment, and we neglect them at our peril. I had the pleasure of welcoming Mao's successor, Chairman Hua Quo Feng, on his only visit to a British factory: Rolls-Royce, Derby.

During the period 1972/79 I paid many visits to China, and from the many Chinese engineers and high officials that I met I have received nothing but generous hospitality, respect and warm friendship. I hold them all in great affection, and have been very happy to make my contribution to the progress of aeronautics in that Great Nation.

Of course, it is the great name Rolls-Royce that opens the doors in aeronautical circles all over the world, and to have the experience of travelling under their patronage is a privilege that can never be forgotten.

Chapter 14
Farewell to Nightingale Road

In 1978 I made my last nostalgic trip down Nightingale Road, Derby. It seemed not to have changed much in the forty years since I walked along it to start my new career in aero engines with Rolls-Royce. Gone was my smart commissionaire at the main entrance, as I turned in at the familiar gate and entered the old Engineering Block.

I suppose I expected to see therein the ghosts of Elliott, Ellor, Barrington, Rubbra, Lovesey and Horace Percival Smith, walking along the corridors or in their old offices. I wanted to try to conjure up the memory of those anxious, frightening but exciting days of 1940, when the fate of Great Britain and its Empire stood in the gravest danger. And above all I wanted to remember the great camaraderie and team spirit that existed throughout the factory as we all laboured long hours, seven days a week, responding to the call of the Royal Air Force for more, more and more Merlin engines for Spitfires and Hurricanes.

But it was not to be. The internal geometry of the place had been completely changed. Gone were the large drawing offices where the aero engines and the motor cars were designed, and gone were the peripheral offices that had housed the great men of my early days. I could not even find the exact spot where my first little office had been, and sadly I turned back and left the building, my feelings numbed and flat.

Yet this was the most famous factory in the world, where the great reputation for Rolls-Royce excellence had been established, and where the aura of the magic of the name had been nurtured. It had been the nerve centre, from which the instructions emanated to the hundreds of subcontracting firms all over the country that poured in the parts to make the Merlin programme possible.

But in 1978 there was a strange quietness. Gone was the roar of Merlins, which in 1940 sang twenty-four hours a day as they were subjected to their final test before being dispatched to the Battle of Britain. It now seemed unbelievable that here, at Nightingale Road, was made every engine that fought for that historic victory, long before the great factories at Crewe, Glasgow and Manchester, and Packard at Detroit, were built. These hallowed buildings, which for fifty years had housed the pride of Rolls-Royce, were now nothing but a manufacturing centre doing the bidding of the huge new headquarters a mile away on Sinfin Moor.

But there was one ghost that nothing could lay for me: the memory of Hs sitting at the centre of this now forlorn factory, directing, co-ordinating and inspiring everyone to greater efforts, never relaxing his relentless pressure and encouraging words.

I did not have the heart to climb up to his old office, but I did go into the main hall to see the stained-glass window, and to read again the moving words: "This window commemorates the pilots of the Royal Air Force who in the Battle of Britain turned the work of our hands into the salvation of our country".

Glossary

afterburning See reheat.

axial compressor A compressor having the form of a drum, carrying many small radial blades (see stage) and rotating about the central axis, there being a row of fixed blades (called stators or vanes) between each two rows of moving blades. The compressed fluid enters at one end and flows parallel to the axis of rotation.

boost pressure Excess pressure, over and above that of a datum (usually that of the local atmosphere), resulting from the air or mixture in a piston-engine induction manifold being compressed by a supercharger.

boundary layer The layer of fluid (such as air) in contact with, or close to, a solid surface such as an engine inlet wall or an aircraft wing. Because air is viscous the layers of air slide over each other until at the surface the molecules of the fluid are at rest (measured relative to the surface).

bypass ratio In a turbofan engine the BPR is the numerical ratio of the cold mass flow to the hot mass flow, in other words the ratio of the cool airflow discharged from the fan duct to the gas flow discharged from the core jetpipe.

centrifugal compressor A rotary compressor in the form of a disc carrying radial vanes to accelerate the compressed fluid radially outwards to leave the periphery moving at high speed (which the diffuser then partly converts into high pressure).

CG, centre of gravity The point in a solid body through which the resultant force (acceleration) of gravity acts, irrespective of orientation.

detonation Extremely rapid and violent combustion (essentially, explosion) of the mixture in a piston engine resulting from a combination of high compression ratio or supercharger boost pressure with fuel of inferior octane number.

diffuser A fixed duct, often containing curved vanes to guide the flow, through which a fluid is increased in pressure at the expense of reduced velocity. For subsonic flow the duct has to expand from inlet to outlet.

drag Loosely, air resistance; in cruising flight the total aircraft drag is balanced by the total engine thrust.

Fir-tree root Turbine rotor blades are often held in the disc by a root-shaped like a fir-tree, each branch of which diffuses the stress into the disc.

HP High pressure; in a two-spool jet engine the HP spool is much smaller than the LP spool, and may have to be made of heat-resistant material.

lift/drag ratio Ratio of the lift, which always must be sufficient to balance the aircraft weight, to the total aerodynamic drag.

LP Low pressure; in a turbofan the LP spool is often the same thing as the fan.

M Mach number.

Mach number Ratio of actual speed to the local speed of sound, expressed as a decimal fraction (note: the local speed of sound varies as the square root of the fluid's absolute temperature).

mass flow In any clearly bounded fluid flow, such as that through a jet engine, the total mass of fluid passing in unit time (in Imperial measures, expressed in lb/s, pounds per second).

octane number Also called octane value, octane rating or PN (performance number), a standard numerical scale for expressing the resistance of a hydrocarbon fuel to detonation in a piston engine, ranging from 0 through 100 (pure iso-octane) up to about 150.

pressure ratio Ratio of the pressure at the delivery of a compressor to that at its inlet. The p.r. can be measured across a single axial stage, or a complete spool or the entire multi-spool system of an engine. Equivalent to the compression ratio of a piston engine.

ram compression The increase in pressure of the fluid entering an inlet duct to an aircraft engine brought about solely from the velocity of the aircraft relative to the air. The effect becomes overwhelmingly important at high supersonic speeds.

RCVs Reaction control valves, needed for the control of a jet-lift aeroplane at forward speeds so low that conventional control surfaces are ineffective.

reheat Injection and combustion of additional fuel downstream of the turbine(s) of a turbojet engine, giving greatly increased thrust (especially for supersonic flight) at the cost of extremely high fuel consumption. In North America called afterburning. It calls for a specially designed jetpipe and a nozzle of variable profile and area.

spool One complete axial compressor rotor, usually comprising a number of stages.

SST Supersonic transport.

stage Any one complete row of blades, all in the same transverse plane, forming part of a compressor spool. A centrifugal rotor forms a stage by itself, so the Merlin 60-series, with two superchargers in series, became a two-stage engine.

supercharger Any pump for increasing the density of mixture supplied to a piston engine, especially at high altitude where, without a supercharger, the density and thus the power would fall dramatically.

two-spool Gas turbine having two compressor spools in series, an LP spool feeding an HP spool.

turbofan A turbojet whose upstream axial compressor blades are much larger than necessary to supercharge the core engine, the outer parts of the blades behaving as propeller blades to discharge air past the core engine to give thrust. In HBPR (high bypass ratio) turbofans the fan generates much more thrust than the small hot core jet.

turbojet The simplest gas turbine, comprising a compressor, combustion chamber, turbine (driving the compressor) and a jetpipe giving propulsive thrust.

zero stage An extra axial stage added at the front of an existing compressor, not only increasing the pressure ratio but also increasing the mass flow and hence the thrust and efficiency of an engine.

Appendix I
The engines

Merlin

Vee-12 liquid-cooled piston engine, cylinders 5.4in bore by 6in stroke, capacity 1,649 cu in (27 litres). Designed by A. G. Elliott and others at West Wittering immediately prior to the death in 1933 of Sir Henry Royce. Early marks weighed 1,375 lb and were rated at 1,030 hp at 16,250 ft. After introduction of the improved supercharger the rated power (Mk 46, for example) went up to 1,415 hp at 14,000 ft, the weight being 1,385 lb. The first two-stage engine, the Mk 60, was rated at 1,125 hp at 29,000 ft, and weighed 1,550 lb. Late in the war many marks gave 2,030 hp for take-off, and 1,890 hp at 13,750 ft.

Welland

First British production turbojet; this was an original Whittle design at Power Jets, designated W.2B/23 after it had been inherited via the Rover Car Company in January 1943. Single double-sided impeller, ten reverse-flow combustion chambers and single-stage turbine. Flown in tail of Wellington in November 1942, at 1,250 lb thrust, and in E.28/39 research aircraft at 1,400 lb, in March 1943. Still at 1,400 lb rating, flown in F.9/40 Meteor on 12 June 1943. Passed 100-hour type test in April 1943, and put into limited production as Welland I at Barnoldswick in October 1943. Delivered to RAF from May 1944 at 1,600 lb, with 180 hours between overhauls, for a dry weight of 850 lb.

Derwent I to IV

Similar to Welland but with straight-through combustion chambers and greatly refined engineering design. Derived from Rover (Power Jets) W.2B/26 with Rolls-Royce designation B.37. Derwent I design started 1 April 1943, first run 29 June 1943, 100-hour type test at 2,000 lb completed 18 October 1943. Put into full-scale production at Newcastle-under-Lyme mid-1944 for

Meteor III, with 500 Derwent I engines delivered during the war. Derwent II introduced Whittle's W.2/700 impeller casing and gave 2,200 lb; first run 28 June 1944 at 2,200 lb. Derwent III was research engine for boundary-layer suction trials with Meteor. Derwent IV was rated at 2,400 lb and first tested on 22 February 1945, being flown in Wellington on 6 June 1945.

Clyde

This extremely advanced two-shaft turboprop, the RB.39, was designed from December 1943. It had a single-stage HP turbine driving a centrifugal compressor and an independent LP turbine driving the nine-stage axial compressor and reduction gear for contra-rotating propellers. The first runs in 1945 were at 2,560 shp, and using 11 engines the power was increased by 1947 to no less than 4,543 ehp (4,200 shp + 830 lb jet thrust) with water/methanol injection. The Clyde was a superb engine, and the first turboprop in the world to pass full military and civil type tests, but Lord Hives refused a production order (for Wyvern aircraft) because he doubted the potential market would be worthwhile.

Nene

The first totally new Rolls-Royce turbojet, designed wholly at Barnoldswick. First studies, designated RB.40, were for 4,200 lb, superseded by the B.41 rated at 5,000 lb. Similar in general layout to Derwent but only nine chambers, and disproportionate increase in airflow. Design started 1 May 1944, first run 27 October 1944, 100-hour type test at 4,000 lb on 10 January 1945, first flown (Lockheed P-80) on 21 July 1945 and type tested at 5,000 lb on 20 November 1945.

Derwent V

Totally new Derwent, designed as a photographic scale of the Nene. Design started 1 January 1945, first run 7 June 1945 and 100-hour type test completed five days later on 12 June; second type test completed on 14 July, and first flown (Meteor) on 5 August 1945. Rated at 3,500 lb, for weight of 975 lb.

Trent

This experimental turboprop, the RB.50, was basically an early Derwent fitted with a spur reduction gear to an offset shaft driving a small five-blade propeller. Rated at 1,230 ehp, this engine was first run on 20 June 1944 and became the first turboprop in the world to fly (in a Meteor) on 20 September 1945.

Avon

After the paper studies AJ.25 and AJ.50 (axial jet, 2,500 lb and 5,000 lb thrust), the AJ.65 was launched in 1945 and type tested at 6,000 lb in mid-1947. This engine, with single-stage turbine, weighed 2,400 lb, but the production RA.3 with a two-stage turbine was 125 lb lighter and was rated at 6,500 lb. Subsequently the Avon was developed in very many versions rated at up to more than 17,000 lb with reheat.

Proteus

This complex turboprop was designed from 1944 as a highly economical engine to power the Brabazon 2 and Princess. The original form had a 12-stage axial compressor and single HP centrifugal stage, eight slim reverse-direction combustion chambers, a two-stage compressor turbine and an independent single-stage LP turbine driving the propeller gearbox. First run in February 1947, and the massive Coupled Proteus for the two aircraft applications followed on the test bed in November 1949. Details of the difference between the target and achieved powers and weights are given in the text. In the completely redesigned Proteus 3 (700 series) the size and weight were greatly reduced, and the compressor and power turbines both had two stages, all except the final stage having shrouded blades. The redesigned engine was eventually put into service at 4,445 ehp, for a weight of 2,900 lb and with cruise sfc of 0.48 lb/h/ehp.

Orion

The BE.25 Orion was a completely new turboprop, which would have been an outstanding engine had the prospects justified its production. It had a 7-stage LP compressor, 5-stage HP compressor, cannular combustor, single-stage HP turbine, and three-stage LP turbine driving the LP compressor and propeller. Weight was 3,240 lb and rating a constant 5,150 ehp from sea level up to 15,000 ft (thus, potential sea level power was over 9,000 shp).

Olympus

Few engines of any kind have been developed to the degree shown by this superb two-spool turbojet. Design began as the BE.10 in 1946 and the first run took place on 13 June 1950. This original BOl.1 version weighed 3,520 lb and was rated at 9,750 lb with sfc of 0.766 lb/h/lb. From this engine was developed the Mk 101 which went into production for the Vulcan B.1 bomber in 1955 at a rating of 11,000 lb. The Mk 102 of 1956 had a zero-stage, giving seven LP stages upstream of an unchanged 8-stage HP spool, and was rated at 12,000 lb for a weight of 3,700 lb. The Mk 104 of 1957 was uprated to 13,000 lb without change in size or weight. The largely redesigned 200-series had greatly increased airflow (approximately from 200 to 300 lb/s) and achieved higher pressure ratio despite using a 5-stage LP spool and 7-stage HP. The Mk 201 was rated at 16,000 lb and went into production at 17,000 lb for the Vulcan B.2. The 300-series engines introduced a zero-stage giving further increases in airflow and pressure ratio, and for many years the standard Vulcan engine has been the Mk 301 rated at 20,000 lb. From this engine was derived the Mk 320 (BOl.22R) for the TSR.2. These engines had fully modulated reheat and were cleared to fly for over an hour at Mach 2 and also for over an hour at full throttle at supersonic speed at sea level, ratings being 19,600 lb dry and 30,160 with full reheat. Finally, from this engine the Olympus 593 for the Concorde was developed, with SNECMA jetpipe (incorporating limited reheat) and noise-suppressor/reverser nozzle. The complete power plant weighed 7,465 lb and could easily give well over 40,000 lb (and often did), but the certificated rating is 37,700 lb.

Orpheus

One of the simplest of all modern turbojets, the BE.26 Orpheus was produced in large numbers with 7-stage compressor, cannular combustor and single-stage turbine at ratings from 4,230 to 5,000 lb, and in advanced forms with ratings of 5,760 lb or 6,810 lb dry and 7,900 lb with simplified reheat. Standard production engines typically weighed 810 lb.

Pegasus

After passing through metamorphoses the BE.53/2 Pegasus ran in August 1959 with a two-stage overhung fan (Olympus), 7-stage HP compressor (Orpheus), cannular combustor (Orpheus), single-stage HP turbine (Orpheus) and two-stage LP turbine. Thrust was 9,000 lb, obtained through two 'cold' front nozzles and two 'hot' rear nozzles, all vectored in unison to give lift or thrust. The Pegasus 2 of 1960 obtained over 11,000 lb using the higher-airflow Orpheus 6 HP spool. The Pegasus 3 of 1961 was rated at 13,500 lb using an 8-stage HP spool and HP turbine with two stages of improved blading. In 1962 the Pegasus 5 gave 15,000 lb using a new 3-stage fan, annular combustor and aircooled HP turbine blades. In 1965 the Pegasus 6 was rated at 19,000 lb using a titanium fan, new combustor with water injection, revised fuel system, two-vane nozzles and aircooled stage-2 HP turbine blades. Increased temperature in 1969 enabled the Pegasus 10 to give 20,500 lb, and the production engine for the Harrier in 1969 was the Pegasus 11 rated at 21,500 lb with increased airflow and various minor improvements. Since then many small improvements have combined thrusts up to 23,200 lb with extended life with reduced costs. PCB (plenum-chamber burning) will boost thrust for later supersonic V/STOL aircraft.

BS.100

This larger vectored-thrust turbofan was developed for the supersonic P.1154 for the RAF and Royal Navy, until cancelled in 1965. It was an excellent engine, the final standard being the BS.100/8 rated at 19,200 lb dry maximum cruise (sfc 0.615) and with PCB at 35,600 lb (sfc 1.16).

RB211

As finally certificated the original RB211-22B is flat-rated at 42,000 lb up to ambient temperature of 28.9°C, for an engine weight of 9,195 lb. The RB211-524 series typically weigh 9,850 lb and have ratings from 50,000 to 55,000 lb, with outstanding sfc and performance retention (according to airline customers no competitor engine can equal the -524 family in these respects).

Appendix II
Merlin Power and Jet Thrust

When, in August 1940, I persuaded Hs (E. W. Hives, Chief of Rolls-Royce, Derby) to come to Lutterworth to see the Whittle engine running, it was producing between 800 and 1,000 lb of thrust.

Neither Hs nor myself were very impressed by this for we were unable to visualise the comparison with 'the driving force of 1,000 horse' of the Merlin piston engine, which sounded so much more. I resolved to do the comparison, which involved only a simple calculation, but which was destined to have a dramatic effect upon the development of the jet engine.

Thrust is a force which can be exerted on either a stationary or moving aircraft. In the latter case thrust horse power is produced. Thus 1 lb of thrust exerted on an aircraft moving at 33,000 ft/min, which is the same thing as 375 mph, is equivalent to 1 thrust horse power.

Hence, when Hs first saw the jet engine, its 800 lb of thrust would have become 800 thrust horse power if flying at 375 mph in, say, the Spitfire.

Now, the Merlin developed 1,000 brake horse power with which it rotated the propeller. Before this can be converted into thrust hp, it must be multiplied by the propeller efficiency, which in those days was a little less than 80%

Thus 1,000 brake horse power gave, at the most, 800 thrust horse power when flying.

The two engines were, therefore, broadly equal when flying at 375 mph, a fact which staggered both Hs and myself, and caused him to resolve to acquire Whittle's jet engine at the appropriate opportunity, which in fact came about, as related earlier, in the autumn of 1942 when Rolls-Royce took over the engine's future from the Rover Company.

It is interesting to note that at the speed of the Concorde, which is 3.6 times 375 mph (1,350 mph), 1lb of thrust is 3.6 thrust horse power, and, thus, at 50,000 ft when the Concorde is cruising at Mach 2.05 and requiring a thrust of 10,000 lb from each engine, the power produced per engine is 36,000 hp, giving a total aircraft power of 144,000 thrust horse power from the four Olympus 593 engines, which is more power than that required for the aircraft carrier HMS *Illustrious,* which has four Olympus marine engines giving nearly 30,000 brake horse power apiece.

In a span of 30 years, from 1940 to 1970, the power of jets made the gigantic steps from 1,000 to 36,000 thrust horse power, and still the end is not in sight.

Not quite as dramatic, but of greater significance is the reduction in specific fuel consumption in the same period.

The Merlin used 500 lb of fuel per hour to produce 800 thrust horse power, giving a specific consumption of 500 divided by 800 or 0.625 lb of fuel per hour per thrust horse power. This is equivalent to an overall thermal efficiency of 22% (including the propeller).

The Olympus 593 at Mach 2.0 uses 1.20 lb of fuel per hour for every 1 lb of thrust or 3.60 thrust horse power. This gives a specific consumption of 1.20 divided by 3.60 or 0.333 lb of fuel per hour per thrust horse power. This is equivalent to an overall thermal efficiency of 42%, double that of the Merlin, and one of the highest figures ever achieved. For example, few, if any, of our most up to date and complex electricity generating stations achieve 40%

Appendix III
The Propulsive Efficiency of a Jet Engine

Propulsive efficiency is defined as that proportion of the power produced by the engine which appears as thrust horse power on the aircraft.

In the case of a variable pitch propeller, whose pitch can be continuously adjusted during flight to the optimum angle, the efficiency can be maintained at about 80% for all forward speeds of the aircraft until at high speeds in excess of 400 mph, when the Mach number at the propeller tip approaches and exceeds unity, the efficiency begins to fall dramatically.

The thrust produced by a jet engine is given according to Newton's law:

$$T = M (V_j - V_a)$$

where M is the mass flow of air through the engine, and V_j and V_a are the jet and aircraft velocities respectively.

The thrust horse power (thp) is obtained by multiplying the thrust by the aircraft speed, giving:

$$thp = M (V_j - V_a) \times V_a.$$

The horse power that the engine produces is the rate of increase of the kinetic energy of the air as it passes through the engine. Thus, jet horse power (jhp) is:

$$jhp = \tfrac{1}{2} M (V_j^2 - V_a^2)$$

By definition, therefore, the propulsive efficiency η_p is:

$$\eta_p = \frac{M (V_j - V_a) V_a}{\tfrac{1}{2} M (V_j^2 - V_a^2)}$$

$$= \frac{2 V_a}{V_j + V_a} = \frac{2}{1 + \dfrac{V_j}{V_a}}$$

This formula shows that the lower the ratio of Vj to Va, the higher the propulsive efficiency, which is highly desirable. On the other hand, if we reduce the jet velocity to achieve this, the lower the thrust per unit of mass flow, and, consequently, the mass flow must be increased to compensate and restore the thrust.

This is the principle of the High By Pass Ratio or modern fan engine, where the jet velocity is reduced and the mass flow increased by a factor of four or five to restore the thrust.

Typical figures:

(a) For a straight jet engine such as the Olympus in a subsonic aircraft such as the Boeing 707:

$$Vj = 2,000 \text{ ft/sec}$$
$$Va = 850 \text{ ft/sec (580 mph)}$$
$$\text{where } \eta p = \frac{2 \times 850}{2,000 + 850} = \frac{1,700}{2,850} = 60\%$$

(b) In a fan engine, such as the RB211 in the Boeing 747, the jet velocity can be reduced to 1,500 ft/sec.

$$\text{Thus=} \eta p = \frac{2 \times 850}{850 + 1,500} = \frac{1,700}{2,350} = 72\%$$

and this would result in the specific fuel consumption being reduced in the ratio 60:72 i.e. by 20%

(c) For the Concorde, cruising at Mach 2.0 with Olympus 593:

$$Vj = 3,000 \text{ ft/sec}$$
$$Va = 2,000 \text{ ft/sec}$$

$$\text{Hence } \eta p = \frac{2 \times 2,000}{2,000 + 3,000} = \frac{4,000}{5,000} = 80\%$$

which shows the alternative way of increasing ηp, not by reducing the jet velocity but by increasing the aircraft speed.

Appendix IV
Supercharging the Merlin Engine

The supercharger has two main functions, the first to increase the power at sea level by 'boosting' the induction pipe pressure, and the second to maintain this power as the aircraft climbs to higher altitudes where the air is less dense. For the latter, the throttle must be gradually opened during the climb (done automatically on the Merlin, where a constant induction pipe or boost pressure was maintained) until an altitude is reached where the throttle is fully opened (the full-throttle altitude), and thereafter the power falls roughly proportional to the falling air density.

In 1938, the power at altitude was calculated from empirical formulae developed at the RAE, which were suspected of being inaccurate, and to over-estimate the power at altitude, particularly in regard to the full-throttle height.

With my colleagues A. Yarker, H. Reed, G. L. Wilde and W. O. Challier, I started in 1938 to develop new and more accurate methods of power assessment to account for the discrepancy between the predicted aircraft performance, mainly of the Spitfire and Hurricane, and the inferior performance actually measured.

There was also a second important reason for this work, namely, a correct understanding of how the combination of engine and supercharger worked, so that more power could be obtained from the engine, by developing more efficient superchargers and correctly matching their capacity to the engine requirements.

Let us consider a typical cylinder as illustrated diagramatically in Fig 1, and start from the condition at the end of the exhaust stroke, when the piston is at top dead centre, the exhaust valve is about to close and the inlet valve to open. The residual exhaust gases in the clearance volume S, have a pressure Pe, which, with open exhaust pipes, is equal to the outside ambient air pressure.

The exhaust valve now closes and the inlet valve opens, and a new charge rushes in from the induction pipe at boost pressure Pc, compressing the residual exhaust gas to a volume Pe/Pc.

At the end of the suction stroke, the cylinder is charged with air/fuel mixture (93% air and 7% petrol by weight) at the boost pressure Pc and charge temperature Tc. Since the Merlin had a compression ratio of 6:1, meaning that the total volume of the cylinder was six times the clearance volume S, the total volume of charge inhaled was

$$6S - \frac{PeS}{Pc}$$

and since the density of the charge is proportional to Pc/Tc, then weight of charge inhaled per stroke is

$$\propto \frac{Pc}{Tc}\left(6S - \frac{Pe\,S}{Pc}\right)$$
or
$$= \frac{6S}{Tc}\left(Pc - \frac{Pe}{6}\right)$$

If the engine is rotating at N rpm, and with the dimensions of the Merlin cylinders (6 in stroke, 5.4 in diameter, 12 cylinders), we arrive at the following equation for the charge consumpton per minute

$$Wc = 0.422\frac{N}{Tc}\left(Pc - \frac{Pe}{6}\right)$$

In this equation, it is convenient to measure Pc and Pe in inches. Hg, and Tc the charge temperature in °K. On the test bed, Pe would be equal to atmospheric pressure, namely 30 in Hg.

Hence, on the test bed,

$$Wc = 0.422\frac{N}{Tc}\left(Pc - 5\right)$$

It is easy to verify this equation by running the engine on the test bed at constant rpm (and hence constant Tc) and varying values of Pc. The charge consumption is linear with boost pressure at both 3,000 and 2,200 rpm, and is zero when the boost pressure equals 5 in Hg. Many similar tests were done, all of which verified the above equation.

We now need to know the absolute value of the charge temperature Tc. On the Merlin engine the air is first sucked through a carburettor where the fuel is sprayed, and the evaporation of the fuel has a cooling effect equivalent to -25°C. This mixture then passes through the supercharger where it is compressed, with a corresponding temperature rise ΔT, given by

$$\Delta T = 0.9 \left(\frac{U}{100}\right)^2$$

where U is the impeller tip speed in ft/sec. Thus, the temperature Tci of the charge as delivered into the induction pipe is:

$$Tci = Ta - 25 + 0.9 \left(\frac{U}{100}\right)^2$$

where Ta is the temperature of the air entering the carburettor.

Now, in passing from the induction pipe into the cylinder, the charge moves through the hot cylinder head and through the very hot inlet valve, and a certain amount of extra temperature is thereby picked up, with more added by the residual gases.

To determine the actual temperature in the cylinder, we must again have recourse to experiment, and run an engine on the test bed where we can measure the weight of charge, the rpm, the boost pressure and the back pressure, and thus determine the effective charge temperature Tc from the formula:

$$Wc = 0.422 \frac{N}{Tc} \left(Pc - \frac{Pe}{6} \right)$$

The results of these experiments are given in Fig 2 where the charge consumption in the cylinder, calculated from the above equation, is plotted against the boost temperature in the induction pipe. The shaded area shows the amount of temperature picked up by the charge in its passage through the cylinder head and inlet valves. A good approximation to the charge temperature in the cylinder is given by:

$$Tc = Tci + 0.25 (440 - Tci)$$

which fits almost exactly the experimental result shown at the top of the shaded area.

We have now reached a point where for any given air temperature at inlet to the carburettor (i.e. at any altitude or climatic condition), and for a given tip speed on the supercharger (which depends upon the gear ratio driving the supercharger and the rpm of the engine) we can calculate the induction pipe temperature from the formula:

$$Tci = Ta - 25 + 0.9 \left(\frac{U}{100} \right)^2$$

Having determined in this way the induction pipe temperature, we can refer to Fig 2, and obtain the charge temperature, Tc, in the cylinder.

Knowing the boost pressure and the back pressure and the rpm of the engine, we can now calculate the weight of charge which the engine will absorb under any flight conditions.

So far, so good, but we now have to face the problem of how we move from knowing the charge consumption to calculating the brake hp of the engine.

We must return to the test bed for more information concerning the relationship between the consumption of charge and the power output of the engine.

We make the initial assumption, which we shall check later, that the gross hp developed in the cylinder, referred to as the indicated hp (ihp) is proportional to the charge flow.

We also note that the gross hp is equal to the brake hp of the propeller plus the power required to drive the supercharger plus the frictional losses in the engine. Thus,

$$ihp = bhp + \text{supercharger hp} + \text{losses.}$$

The power required to drive the supercharger is well known to be

$$\text{supercharger hp} = \frac{Wc \; \Delta T}{95}$$

(allowing for the efficiency of the supercharger gear drive) where ΔT is the temperature rise in the supercharger due to compression. At a given rpm the indicated hp is proportional to the weight of charge, as is the supercharger hp, and both are proportional to (Pc - 5) at sea level.

Hence, if we plot the power of the engine measured on the test bed at a given rpm by varying the boost pressure and extrapolate the curves to a boost pressure of 5 in Hg, where the ihp and the supercharger hp are both zero, we shall obtain the hp which represents the frictional losses, and these losses will be proportional to N^2, where N is the rpm of the engine. An example of this is shown in Fig 3 where it will be seen that at 3,000 rpm and for two different supercharger gear ratios, the frictional hp is 210 when Pc = 5, i.e. when the charge weight is zero, and, hence, the ihp and the supercharger hp are also zero.

Returning now to the equation ihp = bhp + supercharger hp + losses, for the Merlin engine this can be written:

$$\text{ihp} = \text{bhp} + \frac{\text{Wc}\,\Delta\,\text{T}}{95} + 210\left(\frac{\text{N}}{3,000}\right)^2$$

By running the engine on the test bed we can measure the weight of charge consumed, the bhp produced, and calculate the supercharger power and the frictional losses. As a consequence, we now know the ihp per lb of charge, and the results of many tests are condensed into the unique curve shown in Fig 4, where it is seen that, for every lb/min of charge consumed, the engine produces 10.5 ihp. This particular value applies over a wide range of engine speeds from 2,200 to 3,150 rpm, and over a wide range of charge consumptions and varying supercharger gear ratios.

The problem of determining the power, therefore, at any flight condition is now solved. We can determine the charge consumption as previously described, and, hence, the ihp by multiplying the consumption by 10.5. Knowing the supercharger tip speed we can calculate the power absorbed by the supercharger, and knowing the rpm, we can get the frictional losses. By subtracting the supercharger power and frictional losses from the ihp, we obtain the bhp on the propeller.

In Fig 5, a comparison is shown between the above method of calculating the hp, and the power as actually determined in a Hurricane II, No. P3269, calculated from the aircraft speed and drag, and the agreement now is quite remarkable.

I have dealt with the problem of determining the hp of the Merlin engine in flight in some detail, because so far as I am aware, this is the first time that the results of these experiments have been published, and although at the time it was "all in a day's work", looking back, I and my colleagues can now see its importance, since the formulae described above were used to design the two-stage Merlin supercharger with its after-cooler, and to calculate the power that such an arrangement would give.

By examining the formula for the charge consumption, namely:

$$Wc = 0.422 \frac{N}{Tc} \left(Pc - \frac{Pe}{6} \right) \text{lb/min}$$

we note that the engine charge consumption (and, hence, its power) can be increased either by increasing the boost pressure, Pc, or reducing the charge temperature, Tc, or, better still, by doing both.

These features were behind the conception of the two-stage after-cooled supercharger fitted to the Merlin 61 engine. To raise the boost pressure, Pc, particularly at altitude, we fitted an extra supercharger which literally supercharged the supercharger, and, at the same time, in order to reduce the charge temperature, Tc, we fitted a water-cooled intercooler to cool the charge.

Fig 6 shows the increases in power obtained from the Merlin engine by the various stages of this work. It shows the power produced by the original Merlin III, as fitted to the Hurricane I at the beginning of the war, and the power of the Merlin XX which was subsequently fitted to the Hurricane II.

Thus, the power of the Merlin III engine at 20,000 ft was increased from 860 hp to 1,060 hp for the Merlin XX. If we look now at the power of the Merlin 61, which was fitted with the two-stage blower plus intercooler, we note that the power of the engine was increased at 30,000 ft from 510 hp to 1,060 hp by this series of supercharger developments.

The Merlin 61 was never, unfortunately, fitted to the Hurricane. These engines were reserved for Spitfires, Mosquitoes and Mustangs (and a few Lancaster Pathfinder bombers). However, we can see the effect of fitting the Merlin XX to the Hurricane by looking at Fig 7, and note that at 20,900 ft its speed increased from 300 mph (more was claimed at the time!) to 330 mph.

The Hurricane's role thus became that of a bomber killer at about 20,000 ft, and later, a ground attack aircraft, and many different marks were made, yielding an extremely versatile aircraft. Even tank-busting cannon were fitted.

The Spitfire, on the other hand, was paramount at high altitudes as a fighter-to-fighter aircraft, and the effect on its performance of the engine development is shown in Fig 8, where about 10,000 ft was added to its fighting altitude, and something like 70 mph to its top speed. These gains came at a time in the war when the odd extra thousand feet and extra speed meant the difference between death to the enemy fighter or death to the Spitfire.

I have talked of the development of the supercharger, and the increase in power which this gave to the Merlin engine. This was made possible only by the design and development work on the engine itself which fitted the jigsaw of carburettors, the two centrifugal compressors, intercoolers, coolant circulating pumps, and so on, together in order that the engine could still be installed in existing aircraft, and the numerous modifications which had to be designed and tested in order to make the carcase of the engine mechanically reliable at the greatly increased powers which were being used. At this time the Chief Designer at Rolls-Royce was A. A. Rubbra, and the Chief Experimental Engineer (who was my immediate boss) was A. C. Lovesey.

It was a great education and privilege to work under these two men, and I like to think that it was their expertise and guidance which made possible the translation of Hooker the Applied Mathematician, to Hooker the Engineer.

Needless to say, there were many others who made great contributions to this programme of Merlin development, and we all worked under the constant encouragement and drive of Hs.

To illustrate the use of the preceding equations let us calculate the bhp of the Merlin in a Hurricane aircraft. The data we are given is as follows:-

rpm	3,020
Altitude	21,000 ft
Pc Boost Pressure	48 in Hg
Pe Back Pressure	20 in Hg
Aircraft Speed	330 mph

All the above were measured in the aircraft during flight, and we require to calculate the engine bhp.

From the standard altitude tables, we know that the ambient air temperature at 21,000 ft will be 246°K. To this must be added the temperature rise of the air entering the carburettor due to the forward speed of 330 mph. This is given by the simple formula

$$\Delta T = \left(\frac{V}{100}\right)^2$$

$$= \left(\frac{330}{100}\right)^2$$

$$= 11°C$$

Thus the temperature of the air entering the carburettor is

$$246° + 11° = 257°K$$

From this must be subtracted 25°C due to the evaporation of the fuel, and thus, the air entering the supercharger is at a temperature of

$$257° - 25° = 232°K$$

The engine has the high gear ratio drive to the supercharger engaged (9.29:1), and since the diameter of the impeller is 10.25 in, the tip speed U is

$$\frac{10.25\,\pi}{12} \times \frac{3,020}{60} \times 9.29 \text{ ft/sec}$$

$$= 1,255 \text{ ft/sec}$$

The temperature rise through the supercharger is given by

$$\Delta T = 0.9\left(\frac{U}{100}\right)^2 = 0.9\,(12.55)^2 = 142°C$$

Thus the temperature Tci of the charge in the induction pipe is

$$Tci = 232 + 142 = 374°K$$

The final charge temperature Tc, which includes the heat picked up from the valves and ports is

$$Tc = Tci + 0.25 (440 - 374)$$
$$= 374 + 16.5$$
$$= 390°K$$

Returning to the equation for the charge consumption, viz:

$$Wc = 0.422 \frac{N}{Tc} \left(Pc - \frac{Pe}{6} \right)$$

$$Wc = 0.422 \times \frac{3,020}{390} (48 - 3.67)$$
$$= 145 \text{ lb/min}$$

Hence the ihp at 10.5 hp per lb/min

$$= 10.5 \times 145 = 1,523 \text{ hp}$$

From this must be subtracted the frictional horsepower and the power to drive the supercharger.

The frictional power is 210 hp and the power to drive the supercharger is

$$\frac{Wc \, \Delta T}{95} = \frac{145 \times 142}{95}$$
$$= 217 \text{ hp}$$

Thus the bhp equals

ihp - supercharger hp - friction hp

$$= 1,523 - 217 - 210 = 1,096 \text{ bhp}$$

This figure agrees remarkably with the bhp calculated from the aircraft drag, as shown in Fig 5.

MERLIN ENGINE 6 : 1 COMPRESSION RATIO
WEIGHT OF CHARGE CONSUMED

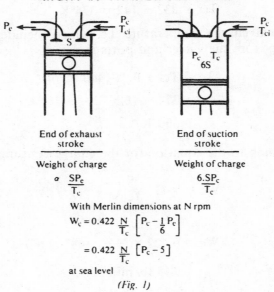

End of exhaust stroke

End of suction stroke

Weight of charge

$$\alpha \ \frac{SP_c}{T_c}$$

Weight of charge

$$\frac{6.SP_c}{T_c}$$

With Merlin dimensions at N rpm

$$W_c = 0.422 \ \frac{N}{T_c} \left[P_c - \frac{1}{6} P_c \right]$$

$$= 0.422 \ \frac{N}{T_c} \left[P_c - 5 \right]$$

at sea level

(Fig. 1)

CURVE SHOWING TEMPERATURE PICKED-UP BY CHARGE
FROM HOT VALVES AND PORTS

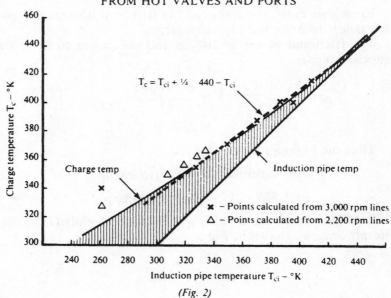

$$T_c = T_{ci} + \frac{1}{4} \left[440 - T_{ci} \right]$$

Charge temp

Induction pipe temp

✗ – Points calculated from 3,000 rpm lines
△ – Points calculated from 2,200 rpm lines

(Fig. 2)

DETERMINATION OF FRICTIONAL LOSSES

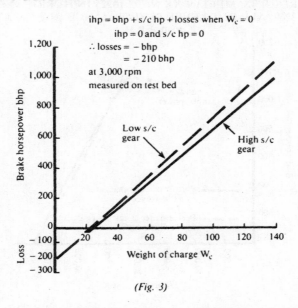

ihp = bhp + s/c hp + losses when $W_c = 0$

ihp = 0 and s/c hp = 0

$\therefore$ losses = $-$ bhp

$\qquad$ = -210 bhp

at 3,000 rpm

measured on test bed

Low s/c gear

High s/c gear

Brake horsepower bhp

Loss

Weight of charge W_c

(Fig. 3)

INDICATED H.P. GENERATED PER LB. OF CHARGE
R-R. MERLIN ENGINE

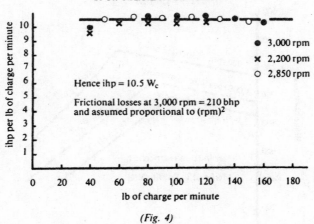

ihp per lb of charge per minute

● 3,000 rpm

✕ 2,200 rpm

○ 2,850 rpm

Hence ihp = 10.5 W_c

Frictional losses at 3,000 rpm = 210 bhp
and assumed proportional to (rpm)^2

lb of charge per minute

(Fig. 4)

ENGINE PERFORMANCE CALCULATED FROM OBSERVED
FLIGHT RESULTS. MERLIN XX No. C 10225 IN HURRICANE MARK
II No. P 3269. ALL-OUT LEVEL PERFORMANCE IN F.S. RATIO AT
3020 R.P.M.

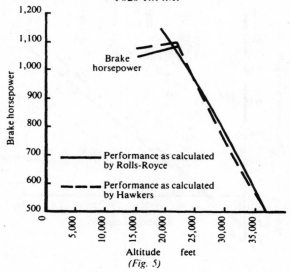

(Fig. 5)

THE INCREASE IN BHP OF MERLIN BY SUPERCHARGER
DEVELOPMENT

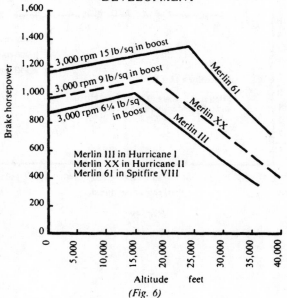

(Fig. 6)

SPEED PERFORMANCE COMPARISON
Mk.I HURRICANE MERLIN III & Mk.II HURRICANE MERLIN XX

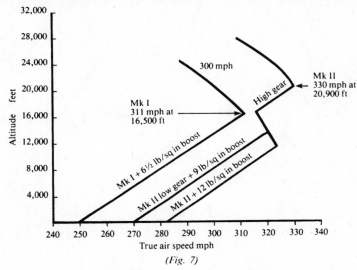

(Fig. 7)

SPITFIRE PERFORMANCE DEVELOPMENT
SPITFIRE I — 1939-40 SPITFIRE V — 1940-51 SPITFIRE IX — 1942-43

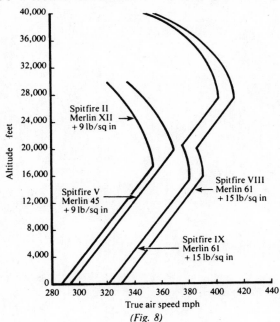

(Fig. 8)

Index